# Alachua Ambush
## Bloody Battles of the 2nd Seminole War

Christopher D. Kimball

# CONTENTS

# ACKNOWLEDGMENTS

This would not be complete without thanking the people behind the research. To Steve Abolt and his wife Cynda, who I have participated with living history for 25 years. Thanks to Earl DeBary for the many years of researching these places, and his wife Bettie who patiently put up with us. Thanks to Dr. Joe Knetsch for help and encouragement, and also his wife Linda for surviving our lengthy discussions. Thank you to Patrick Swan, who researched some faraway archives that I could not reach, and helped me immensely with editing.

Front Cover Photo: Dade Battle Reenactment, 1993.

Back Cover Photo: The Barr Trail at Levy Lake/Levy Prairie.

Both photos by Chris Kimball

# Introduction

About 25 years ago, I started a list of battles and skirmishes of the Florida Seminole Wars[1], that I have since published.[2] In the course of my research, I discovered a curious entry by Dr. Andrew Welch, 1841, "A Narrative of the Early Days and Remembrances of Oceola Nikkannochee, Prince of Econchatti, Written by his Guardian." An interesting paragraph is on page 203.

> On Wednesday, the 20th inst., while a lieutenant and two men were passing between Micanopy and a place called "Black Point," they were surprised, and fired on by a party of Indians;[3] the lieutenant and one man wounded, and one killed. Same evening, Lieut. Sanderson, in command of Micanopy, while on scout with eighteen or twenty men, discovered a fire in the woods, and ongoing to see from whence it proceeded, was surrounded by about fifty Indians; Lieut. S. and nine men, three blood-hounds and their keeper, killed upon the spot, and four men missing. On Friday, news reached Newnansville, that three men were killed between Posts No. 11 and 12. On Thursday, a

---

[1] For the record, the U.S. Army recognizes three distinct Seminole wars on one consolidated campaign streamer, which is collected over an overall "Indian Wars" category. It lists the dates as: 1817-1818 (although some contend this one began during the War of 1812 and its so-called Patriot War spinoff in Florida); 1835-1842; and 1855-1858. The Native Seminole and Miccosukee people consider it one long conflict.

[2] See bibliography, book by Kimball, *Seminole and Creek War Battles and Events*.

[3] The older term of "Indians" will be used in this text instead of Native Americans because that is the common usage from the historical documents. The language is not altered and easier to reprint the letters as such. Although some people prefer Native American or First Nation, many of the Florida Indians themselves still prefer to use Indian.

*scout discovered the trail of about 100 Indians in the 'Wolf Hammock,' six miles south of Newnansville."*

This was a battle or skirmish with a high number of casualties that no one seemed to have remembered. How had this devastating battle escaped nearly everyone?

For Florida's Second Seminole War, most people have heard about Dade's battle in 1835 or the Battle of Okeechobee in 1837. The capture of Osceola under a white flag ordered by General Jesup is the one that everyone seems to remember. Students of the war recognize the failed campaigns of overconfident Generals Scott and Gaines. After the first two years of the war, after the notable generals had departed, one hears little. But the war did continue – for five additional years!

Why has this later period of the war been covered so little? Could it be because almost every book written about the war was in the first two years? I suspect that when it became a long and drawn-out war, people had wearied of it, and popularity had waned. By 1848, when John T. Sprague published his comprehensive 500-page review, *The Origin, Progress and Conclusion of the Florida War*, a new war had captured the nation's attention – the Mexican War of 1846-1848. Sprague's book was forgotten in the shuffle.

And yet, in 1840 alone, there were more battles, skirmishes, and people killed than any time of the war.[4] Presented here are letters, Army Adjutant reports, and newspaper articles from eyewitnesses. Some have never been printed again after they first

---

[4] By "people" I mean just that. Soldiers, sailors, and Marines died. Militiamen died. Settlers and pioneers died. And, of course, the people against whom the war was waged, the Seminoles, perished as well.

appeared. My intent is to use these sources to recover stories of the forgotten, later period of the Second Seminole War.

These forgotten voices speak to us from the dead past. I have not changed or significantly edited except for punctuation or some spellings. These accounts include some harsh language that today we would not consider using. My job, though, is not to impose contemporary language norms. These words are what the people said generations ago, and it reflects their character and actions. The writing is not softened, because it would end up giving a false interpretation of what they said. For instance, clearly, the stereotype "savage", has passed from polite writing about native Americans. But, the description was common back in 1840. I present it here because that is the language used and what many local settlers believed about Seminoles. Unfortunately, the letters and writings only come from one side of the war. Oral history from the Native people is not specific to dates and events recorded in the actual letters. But, I believe enough of the picture is presented from the volume of material that we can read between the lines and see what is happening. Worthy mentions are Old Betsy or George & Joe. Enough information is given in that you can sense who they were.

I have wanted to write this book for 25 years, and years of research have made a more complete picture. The story will tell itself, and centers around a small geographical area in north central Florida, especially Fort Micanopy and Fort King. These are first-hand accounts and voices of the past, and ones that you have probably never read before.

The main actors were mostly soldiers of the U.S. Seventh Infantry Regiment because that was the regiment operating in this area. They are eventually replaced by the Second Infantry. Once I focused my lens on this specific period and location, the story rapidly became clear. In time, with newly available material, I completed this portrait of life on the Florida frontier in 1840. And maybe now it will become better known after 180 years.

If you don't have any prior experience in the Army, you may not know what an Adjutant is. The Adjutant handles all the correspondence and orders going back and forth. They act as the secretary, personnel officer, and administrative specialist. Since the only way to transmit orders at the time was by letter, then the adjutant handles all communication.

During the years when the events in this book take place, the U.S. Army Adjutant General is Roger Jones, a tough-as-nails former Marine officer. In Florida, the commanding general and the regiments serving in Florida all had officers for their adjutant. They are called Assistant Adjutant General, although many people use the shortened term of adjutant.

The Army Adjutant Corp has been in existence since 1775. I should know; I served in the Army AG Corp!

Chris Kimball

Tallahassee, Florida 2019

# Chapter 1: The Florida War

During first half of the nineteenth century, the territory and later state of Florida (along with southern parts of Georgia) served as the theater for the largest war the United States fought against any native people, tribes we call Seminole, Miccosukee, and Muscogee Creeks. (And some smaller, associated groups such as the Yuchi.) In particular, during the 1835-1842 period known as the Second Seminole War, at least half the entire eight-thousand man U.S. Army rotated into the conflict. The federal government spent approximately 40 million dollars, a figure greater than the annual federal budget at the time. The government waged war to remove these native tribes from Florida. And yet, the Seminole, Miccosukee, and Creek peoples defied removal, and their descendants remain.

The second war began in December 1835 as a response to broken treaty promises and federal demands that all Indians relocate to the western Indian Territory by the end of the year. The native warriors seized the offensive. They initiated a campaign of plantation raids in northeast Florida and then attacked a Florida militia supply train en route to Micanopy, on 18 December 1835. Ten days later, on 28 December, Seminole, Miccosukee, and Black Seminole warriors ambushed a command of regular Army soldiers under Major Francis Dade marching hurriedly from Fort Brooke (Tampa) to relieve forces at Fort King (present-day Ocala). The surprise attack wiped out the entire command. A few bloodied soldiers who survived limped back to Fort Brooke and sent a message to the United States that shocked the country.

The 1839 MacKay-Blake "Map of the Seat of War in Florida" was the most detailed map of Florida at the time, commissioned by General Zachary Taylor. [5]

---

[5] MacKay, John (Capt.), and J.E. Blake (Lt.); *Map of the Seat of War in Florida, Compiled by Order of Brevet Brig. Genl. Z[achary] Taylor*, 1839. Copy in the

With the "Dade Massacre," the country was rattled! No other Native nation had organized and conducted an attack so brilliantly coordinated against the United States.

The United States faced fighting the Seminoles/Miccosukee on multiple fronts that made it difficult to run a campaign. Fighting broke out everywhere in Florida. But where was the most contested ground? Was it the Everglades as the Seminole's last stand? The Withlacoochee River west of Ocala? Would it surprise you to find out that Micanopy was an active theater in the war? What is today Gainesville, Paynes Prairie/Alachua Prairie, or Alachua County? Did you know that one of the largest military burial grounds during the war was at Micanopy?

Although the focus of this story is the latter half of the war, a quick review will help put it in perspective. Fort Defiance[6] at the community of Micanopy was established in 1835 and abandoned in August 1836. In these nine months, several major battles and the number of sick and dying at the post made this an undesirable outpost. The post returns[7] for July 1836 have only eight personnel in the fort fit for duty, and 46 in the hospital. There was a major battle outside the gates of the fort the month before, but those listed on the July returns were casualties from sickness and not related to the skirmish. Post commander Captain Lemuel Gates dies at the fort on August 9th, and the post was abandoned. These frontier forts were not designed to last a long time, and history shows that poor health and sanitation would cause them to be abandoned. It was believed that the war would be short. After the

---

State Library of Florida, Tallahassee. By Capt. John MacKay and 1st Lt. Jacob Edmund Blake, Topographical Engineers (formerly 6th Infantry).

[6] Possibly named Defiance after Gad Humphrey's Plantation.

[7] The "Post Returns" are the monthly report of attendance at the fort that contain much valuable historical and genealogical informaton.

first few months it was proven to be a different type of war.

The fort was reactivated nine months later on April 30, 1837, as Fort Micanopy. Earlier reports and documents also refer to the fort as Micanopy in 1836 while it was officially Fort Defiance. [8]

The community of Micanopy outside the fort, founded in 1824, was Florida's most interior white settlement. Many farmers and settlers moved into the area for the fertile fields and pastures after the 1823 Treaty of Moultrie Creek with the Seminole & Miccosukee Indians. A traveler described the Micanopy settlement in 1836 as having only about a dozen homes and twenty families. This was at the beginning of the war when many residents fled further north to Newnansville or Black Creek west of St. Augustine. Other reports say that hundreds of people crowded into the surrounding posts like Fort Crum north of Paynes Prairie. An accurate number is unknown.[9]

As General Zachary Taylor became commander of forces in Florida in 1838, he divided the territory into operational areas of 20-miles square. Fort Micanopy was centrally located in Square #7, East Florida. A detailed map of this square was made by Lieut. George C. Thomas, 4th Artillery Regiment. [10] Although detailed, there are a lot of inconsistencies compared to modern maps.

---

[8] "Returns From U.S. Military Posts, 1800-1916"; M617; Records of the Adjutant General's Office, Record Group 94. (Post Returns) Fort Defiance, July 1836. "Letters Received by the Office of the Adjutant General (Main Series) 1822-1860"; Records of the Adjutant General's Office, Record Group 94; (AG) 1836 G238

[9] Newbern Spectator, 19 August 1836, 1

[10] "Returns From U.S. Military Posts, 1800-1916"; M617; Records of the Adjutant General's Office, Record Group 94. (Post Returns) Fort Micanopy. "A topographical Survey of Military Square No. 7" map, by Lieut. George C. Thomas, 4th Regt. Artillery; State of Florida Library.

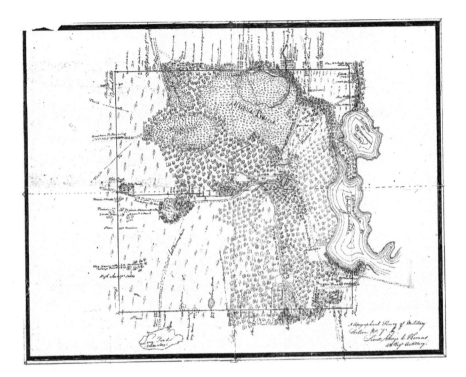

Lt. George C. Thomas, *A Topographical Survey of Military Section No. 7*. One of the most detailed section maps. It includes Forts Crane & Clarke, and Tarver's. Paynes Prairie and Fort Walker south of Kanapaha Prairie. Fort Wacahoota and Micanopy with connecting roads. There are roads down to McIntosh's plantation and Fort Drane/Clinch's plantation. It includes Moses Levy's plantation but is a little confusing compared to modern maps. What is labeled Levy's Prairie looks like Ledwith Lake. [11]

---

[11] Thomas, George C. (Lt.); *A Topographical Survey of Military Section No. 7* (2nd Seminole War); National Archives. Copy in the State Library of Florida, Tallahassee.

This map for Square Seven does not fit well with the descriptions of the battles. This could be due to the officers writing the reports that were not fully knowledgeable of the area.

Northwest from Fort Micanopy is Kanapaha Prairie. A fort at the edge of the prairie is mostly forgotten: Fort Walker, named after Captain Stephen V. Walker, who was killed at the battle of Kanapaha Prairie on June 18, 1838. Walker commanded the local militia unit, the "Spring Grove Guards," organized in January 1835.

The battle of Kanapaha Prairie occurred when 2d Dragoon soldiers discovered an encampment of Indian warriors in the thickly wooded hammock along Kanapaha Prairie. Walker was acting as a guide when he was shot and killed.

In Florida colloquialisms, a "Hammock" is a densely wooded area of bushes and hardwood trees. In south Florida it has a little different definition as a densely wooded area of hardwoods, but as a tree island slightly higher in elevation than the surrounding wet prairies and marshes. Hammocks are key terrain features where the Native warriors concealed themselves.

Fort Kanapaha was established by Capt. William Fulton, 2d Dragoons, on July 7, 1838. The post return for August mentions that the name is changed to Fort Walker, and only one death reported, reason unknown.[12] Although no other subsequent post returns, Fort Walker was maintained by the local militia. Newspapers mention slaves attacked while working outside the fort in January 1841.

---

[12] Post returns, Fort Kanapaha. Master Sgt. Thomas Kielbasa, "Seminole War battlefield visit caps Florida National Guard soil collection project"; **Florida National Guard Public Affairs Office**; https://www.dvidshub.net/news/printable/113465

# Chapter 2: The U.S. Seventh Infantry and Fort Life

In 1839, the Seventh Infantry Regiment transferred from Fort Gibson in Indian Territory (now Oklahoma) to Florida. A regiment consisted of ten companies, each with three officers and about 60 men for each company, plus the regimental staff officers. Unfortunately, the regiment was very much under-strength and in great need of soldiers. The Seventh would face great difficulty in Florida.

The Regiment was stationed in the Indian Territory (Arkansas and Oklahoma) since the early 1820s, so many officers were desirous to be in a more settled location. Florida would not offer such a respite, and the move proved difficult.

(Lt.Col. William Whistler to the Army Adjutant General)

*Fort Brooke, Florida (Tampa Bay)*
*March 30, 1839*
*I have the honor to inform you that three companies of the 7th Infantry Arrived at this post from Fort Gibson on the 23rd and six on the 27th Inst. In as much as the movement has taken more time than might reasonably be expected under ordinary circumstances, I deem it a duty that I owe to myself to inform you of the causes that produced this delay. The 7th was relieved by the 4th Infantry on the 6th and commenced its march on the 7th February. Owing to the low stage of the water in the Arkansas [River] it was necessary to march as far as Fort Smith. At that point Keel boats in use procured in which the Regiment descended the river to its mouth, not without great difficulty, however for in many instances, the boats had to be taken over the shallow bars by the men of my command. Thus twenty-one days were consumed in descending*

*the Arkansas; when in an ordinary stage of water, it could have been done in three. From New Orleans to this post we were thirteen days when the ordinary voyage is not more than five. So you perceive that the delay is to be attributed to low water in the Arkansas and headwinds at sea.* [13]

The water level of the river was not yet full of the Spring thaw. Once in the gulf, tremendous winds hindered navigation.

Leaving Fort Brooke, the Seventh arrives at Fort Micanopy in April 1839, with Major James S. McIntosh, the garrison commander. The regiment covered Alachua County and includes Fort King (Ocala) and modern counties of Marion, Levy, Gilchrist, Putnam, and Citrus. At the time, that was all Alachua County.

Capt. Gabriel J. Rains becomes the next Fort Micanopy garrison commander on 28 May 1839. A few miles to the south is the Commanding General of the Army, Alexander Macomb, negotiating with the Indians at Fort King to end the war. This would ultimately fail. Also at Fort King is the Seventh Infantry's commander in Florida, Lt. Col. William Whistler.

The overall regimental commander Col. Matthew Arbuckle remains in Indian territory out west. Arbuckle had a past history fighting the Seminoles when he was at Fort Scott, southwest Georgia, in November 1817, as he attacked and plundered the Seminole village of Fowltown on the Flint River with 300 soldiers. Chief Nea-Mathla's warriors emerged from the swamp firing back, driving off the soldiers as the First Seminole War was ignited.

---

[13] "Letters Received by the Office of the Adjutant General (Main Series) 1822-1860"; Records of the Adjutant General's Office, Record Group 94. (AG) 1839 W130. Afterwards referred to here as AG 1839 W130.

A close-up of the MacKay-Blake map for north central Florida. Although the south of the Florida peninsula is very vague, north Florida is well surveyed. [14]

---

[14] MacKay, John (Capt.), and J.E. Blake (Lt.); *Map of the Seat of War in Florida, Compiled by Order of Brevet Brig. Genl. Z[achary] Taylor*, 1839. Copy in the State Library of Florida, Tallahassee. By Capt. John MacKay and 1st Lt. Jacob Edmund Blake, Topographical Engineers (formerly 6th Infantry).

An overlook of life of the Army in 1839 is worth our detour at this point. The Adjutant papers are full of letters that paint an interesting portrait of life in Florida, not unlike the wild west.

(Lt.Col. William Whistler to Adjutant General Roger Jones.)

*June 8th, 1839*
*Fort King*
*I have also to request that Private James Edgar of "E" Co. 7th Infantry be discharged from the service of the United States because he is a murderer, having on the 30th ultimo, willfully killed Mr. Murray, an interpreter in the service of the United States at this Post. He has been turned over to the Civil Authority, but his trial will not come on until sometime in November.* [15]

Murray, the negro guide and interpreter for the Army, was well-liked. Except by Pvt. Edgar, who believed him insolent and shot him. The next day several Indian chiefs arrived for negotiations at the fort but did not speak English, and none of the soldiers spoke the Creek or Miccosukee language. The talks had to be canceled, and the Indians sent away.

Mr. Edgar was discharged from the Army to face trial for murder and sent to the local jail in Newnansville. [16] But he was soon released by the local civil authorities who did not consider killing an Indian or Black interpreter a crime. The local militia was in the same mind about killing Indians and collecting slaves, and locals didn't care about Murray's valuable service to the Army.[17]

---

[15] AG 1839 W194

[16] The county seat of Alachua County; since abandoned. It was named after Col. Daniel Newnan from Georgia who attempted to attack the Alachua Seminoles in 1812, and can be considered as starting off years of discontinuous warfare between the Florida Indians and the United States.

[17] Niles National Register, June 22, 1839

A murder mystery has occurred at Fort Micanopy:

(Captain Gabriel Rains to the Army Adjutant General)

*Fort Micanopy, Square No. 7, East Florida*
*29th September 1839*

*The report of July 29, 1839. About 11 o'clock at night, the garrison was alarmed with the cries of murder at the blacksmith shop, a hundred yards from the military enclosure. Within two minutes, a guard was formed and searched the place of Thomas Hunter who slept at the blacksmith shop, and found him dead outside his tent. Since no recent marks were found on him, it was believed that Mr. Hunter was prone to having fits of drinking and dementia, which had happened since he escaped a party of attacking Indians at Tuscawilla Pond previously. And that this evening he had, "a fit, arising from fright, from 'mania a'potee'". Later it was found that Mr. Hunter had a great amount of money that was missing, and it was believed that he was murdered by a blow from concussion to the back of the head. Money that he was supposed to have had could not be found. The surgeon tried to revive Mr. Hunter with no success. Mr. Hunter had finished his service and saved seven hundred dollars, and planned to send it to his mother when it reached a thousand. Indians are continually lurking around the post, as well as a company of Volunteers about to be mustered out of service, in addition to many regulars at the post. So there are many suspects who could have killed him.*[18]

Apparently, Capt. Rains and Dr. Sloan are the worst criminal detectives, believing this was a drinking problem until later discovering that a blow to the head killed Mr. Hunter, with a fortune of money missing. It may come as no surprise that doctors

---

[18] AG 1839 R141

did not require a board certification at the time.

Vacancies among the officer positions in the regiment have a serious impact on the Florida war effort.

(Captain Rains to the Army Adjutant General)

Fort Micanopy<br>Oct. 5, 1839.

*There is a great want of officers at the post. 2nd Lt. Shepherd is absent and has not been heard from, and 2nd Lt. Gannett is doing duty at Fort Micanopy, deprived from his command at Fort King. Lt. Shepherd left as part of his resignation.*

Rains is commanding the post with additional duties of commanding six other posts in the military square he oversees, coordinating supplies and provisions, supplying ordnance & ammunition, and providing subsistence rations to the suffering inhabitants and their protection. He is doing the job of eight officers. Since Lt. Shepherd has a drinking problem and is being drummed out of the Army, Rains was probably better off without a constantly intoxicated officer.[19]

Lt. Daniel Whiting at Fort Number Four, a few miles from the mouth of the Suwannee River, was so short of men that he could not conduct field operations.

Capt. Rains writes to the Army Adjutant General on December 6th, 1839, from Fort Micanopy, that Drummer George Hadley should not be charged with desertion because he is a minor. Hadley had deserted in New York but apprehended. He will not be put in confinement since he is a boy. Enlisting underage was a common problem in the Army, often by runaways. Age wouldn't

---

[19] AG 1839 R149

keep anyone out of the stockade, and juveniles were treated the same as adults and also thrown into prison. [20]

On December 30, 1839, Captain Rains relinquished command of Fort Micanopy to Captain Benjamin Bonneville, and his company becomes the garrison at Fort King. Besides Bonneville at Micanopy, 2d Lt. James Sanderson is commanding "I" Company as well as Acting Assistant Quartermaster and Commissary of Subsistence. Six other officers are listed as being off on other special duty and assignments, and another Second Lieutenant hasn't joined his company yet. There are four companies at Fort Micanopy, but the number of men of all four is only equal to the full strength of one company.

Many enlisted soldiers choose not to reenlist. Private Bartholomew Lynch of the 2d Dragoon Regiment writes in his journal of horrible conditions in Florida and brutal treatment of the officers upon the enlisted men. When a three-year service was up, few chose to stay, requiring many officers to go on recruiting trips up north away from their duty stations. Thus making the regiment short of both officers and enlisted men.[21] The need for more men was urgent.

(Lt.Col. Whistler to the Army Adjutant General)

*Fort Micanopy*
*22 February 1840*
*I cannot permit this opportunity to pass without calling your attention to the fact that the term of service of about two hundred*

---

[20] AG 1839 R203

[21] McGaughy, Felix P.; "The Squaw Kissing War" (Master Thesis, Florida State University, 1965). Knetsch, Joe; *Fear and Anxiety on the Florida Frontier; Articles on the Second Seminole War, 1835-1842* (Seminole War Foundation, 2008), 116.

and fifty men will expire by the 1<sup>st</sup> June which will reduce the Regiment to near one half its present number. By examining the [regimental] return you will perceive that there are but fourteen company officers serving in Florida, two of whom are detached from the regiment doing staff duty, leaving twelve with the ten companies and these occupying Seven Posts. Major Nelson and Captain Stephenson are reported under Orders to join since the 15<sup>th</sup> Oct. from neither of whom have I heard since some time previous to that date. Of other absent officers, I had the honor to address you in a former communication to which I have received no reply. [22]

Twenty-three-year-old Lt. Walter Sherwood is one of those officers on leave from his duty station to recover his health at home in Hartford, Connecticut. He has not received orders for a duty station, but in order to keep his commission due to his extended absence from the regiment, he claims to have spent his time recruiting in Connecticut and New York. The attending physician Benjamin Sherwood (apparently his brother) writes:

*Lt. W Sherwood of 7<sup>th</sup> Regiment US Infantry has been a patient of mine frequently since last March. He has been suffering from Bilious difficulties which he contracted while doing duty in a southern climate. A little exposure is sure to cause a relapse as has frequently occurred in his case. There is an enlargement of the Liver and spleen (as is always the case in protracted bilious fever) which a residence of 10 or 12 months longer in this climate will no doubt entirely restore. I am well acquainted with his constitution and health & do not hesitate in saying that a transfer to a southern climate at this time or coming summer would not only*

---

[22] AG 1840 W77

*jeopardize his health but endanger his life.* [23]

Dr. Sherwood was right about his condition; if he comes to Florida, it will kill him. But, it won't be from bilious fever.

(Capt. Stephen W. Moore, 7th Infantry)

*Fort Brooke, East Florida*
*3rd March 1840.*
*I perceive by General Order No. 64 of '39, that Lieut. Sherwood is ordered to join in May. His presence here is much needed, as of the six officers belonging to the two companies, but one is present.*[24]

Captain Benjamin L. E. Bonneville at Fort Micanopy is one of the more grandiose officers in the Army. Born in France and graduated from the Military Academy in 1815, he was in the Light Artillery, 8th Infantry, and 7th Infantry until receiving permission from General Alexander Macomb to conduct an expedition into the Oregon Territory. He departed in 1832 and was not heard from for three years, so he was presumed dead and dropped from the Army register. He reappeared in 1835 and had to petition congress to reinstate his commission. He met Washington Irving, who agreed to assist Bonneville with publishing the memoirs of his western adventures. Irving paid Bonneville $1,000 for the rights to publish, which produced the book, *The Adventures of Captain Bonneville: or Scenes, Incidents, and Adventures in the Far West.* The account Irving published seems much embellished. If you recognize Washington Irving, he is the same who wrote *The Legend of Sleepy Hollow,* using the name for the main character from a real Army officer that he once served under during the

---

[23] AG 1840 S7, S59
[24] AG 1840 M81

War of 1812, Lt.Col. Ichabod Crane. [25]

Captain Bonneville commanded at Fort Micanopy, Fort Wacasassa, and other forts in Florida. When passed up for promotion, he added his fellow 7th Regiment officers to the post returns under the column of "Absent," apparently out of spite. Writing down the regimental commander Col. Matthew Arbuckle as, "Absent on Special Duty" and Lt. Col. Whistler as "Absent on Leave," when he would have known that they were not assigned to Fort Wacasassa; especially Col. Arbuckle who was out west. [26]

Bonneville retired in 1861 but was recalled during the Civil War to serve as General in charge of recruiting in St. Louis. Finally retiring in 1866, after a total of 51 years in the army. He is most remembered for his expedition out west and opening a route for the Oregon Trail. His name is on numerous lakes, land features, cities, and buildings in Utah, Idaho, Oregon, and even a crater on the planet Mars. [27]

Fort Micanopy has strategic importance in a central location for operations in Florida. It was the center of Square Seven, East Florida (east of the Suwannee River). Many river systems and roads nearby made it central to operations. But the Seminole and Miccosukee had lived there for a century and knew the area.

---

[25] Heitman, Francis B.; *Historical Register and Dictionary of the United States Army, From its Organization, September 29, 1789, to March 2, 1903*, Volume 2, 1903 (Washington: Government Printing Office. University of Illinois Press, Urbana, 1965). Cullum, George Washington; *Biographical Register of the Officers and Graduates of the U.S. Military Academy at West Point, New York, since its establishment in 1802*; (Seeman & Peters, Saginaw, Michigan, 1920). Crane, Ichabod; *The Adventures of Captain Bonneville: or Scenes, Incidents, and Adventures in the Far West*, 1837.
[26] Post Returns, Fort Wacasassa, Sept. 1841.
[27] Wikipedia.org, "Benjamin Bonneville".

2d Lt. James Sanderson served as the 7th Infantry Regiment quartermaster in 1840. He makes a very important suggestion to establish a hospital at Fort Micanopy.

(Maj. Lorenzo Thomas, Asst. Adjutant Gen. to Lt.Col. T. Hunt)

*Fort Stansbury*
*March 5th, 1840.*

*Your communication of the 27th of February enclosing one from Lieut. Sanderson, Assistant Army Quartermaster, at Micanopy on the subject of building a hospital at the Post has been received, and I am directed by the Commanding General to say that he designs having a general hospital erected at Micanopy where the sick from the neighboring Posts can be brought and made comfortable.*

*The intention he expressed to Lt. Col. Whistler, saying at the same time, that as the Micanopy Square was a highly important one, abounding in hammocks, it would not answer to require the garrison to build the hospital, but to give such aid as may be necessary, and therefore a few persons must be employed for the purpose. You will please therefore furnish what may be necessary for the erection of a large comfortable building. It will, of course, be built of logs covered with clapboards, and floored with puncheons.*

*All quarters and other buildings at the several Posts are of course, to be built by the troops nor was part IV of Order No. 10 intended to relieve them from this necessary and proper duty, the plain meaning of that paragraph being obvious.*

*As quarters have been erected at nearly all the stations; it is scarcely requisite to prescribe the kind of buildings to be put up. They should be made airy and comfortable of logs of course, covered with clapboards, and floored with puncheons, a few nails &c being all that the Quartermasters Department need furnish for their construction. [28]*

Once the hospital was approved, there is confusion about the medical staff. A shortage of doctors and assistant surgeons requires a surgeon to visit several posts, sending them out to risk ambush by Seminole warriors. Seasonal sickness reduced a large number of soldiers from duty. Lt.Col. Whistler is under the impression that Fort Micanopy would have two surgeons but is set straight by General Taylor's adjutant.

(Maj. L. Thomas to Lt.Col. Wm. Whistler)

*Fort Fanning*
*March 23, 1840*
*The General does not see how such an impression could have originated that a second Medical Officer was to be ordered on duty at Fort Micanopy and when informed that some of the Medical officers are required to attend at two or three different Posts, which is the fact you will be satisfied that a Second Medical officer could not properly be ordered to your Post.*

*The report of Capt. Bonneville that Lt. Hanson's wagon was attacked by the Indians between Fort No. 2 and Fort Drane, resulting in the death of a teamster and a private of Company 'B' 7th Infantry has been received, and it is feared that this disaster has been caused by the neglect of Lt. Hanson to provide a suitable guard for the wagon, of which however the Commanding General is not able to judge, the particulars of the case not having been reported. [29]*

---

[28] AG 1840 T140
[29] AG 1840 T140, 12-14

(An unarmed wagon supply train makes a tempting target.)

The legal age to join the Army was 21, but you could enlist at age 18 with the parents' consent. There have always been young soldiers who enlisted and lied about their age or said that they were orphaned and had no parents to sign for them. This soldier ran away from home and enlisted, and found that the grass on the other side of the fence was not as green as he thought.

(Mr. Henry S. Deusenbury to Secretary of War Joel R. Poinsett.)

*Middlefield [New York]*
*April 28th, 1840*

*Lester Deusenbury, an adopted son of mine, aged seventeen years this 17th day of February last, is now in the United States Army in Company "I" of the 7th Regiment Stationed at Mycanopy [sic: Micanopy] in East Florida. On the 6th day of February last as I am informed by his letters that date. I took him into my family a gift from his mother as he had no other parent and called him of my name Deusenbury. He has ever since been with me until last fall or summer wither he went to work for a brother-in-law of mine in Rensselaer County near the City of Albany some time in between last. I was there and found that he had gone but could not ascertain where, until about the first of March he wrote home stating that he enlisted the 22nd day of October last, and was at the time his letter was dated (the 4th of February last) at Mycanopy. He enlisted without my knowledge or consent, and I wish to have him discharged—he has written to me desiring that I would take measures to prove his discharge immediately that he may return to his home to my family. He has no other parent or guardian to call upon but myself—you will confer a favour to order his immediate discharge—or advise such measures as will enable me to get him discharged.* [30]

It's obvious that Lester sought to run away from home but found Florida no better than New York. The irony is that Deusenbury's company is commanded by 2d Lt. James Sanderson, who also ran away from home at the age of 14 to join the Army, and was wounded at the Battle of Lundy's Lane, the deadliest battle in the War of 1812 for the United States. In 1815 he was discharged from the Army at age 15 as a sergeant who was wounded twice in the worst battles of the late war. Sanderson, now age 41, will soon be killed in Florida.

---

[30] AG 1840 D127

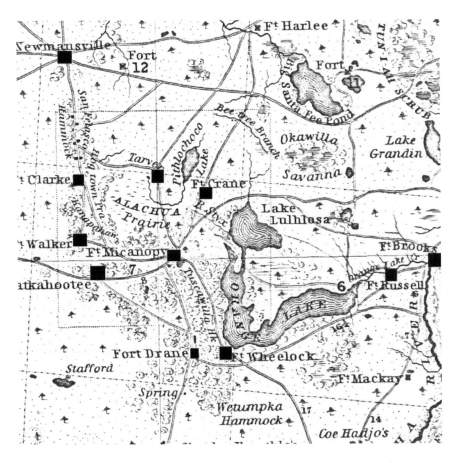

A close-up of the MacKay Blake map around Fort Micanopy. In the upper left is the town of Newnansville. Below the town on the north edge of the prairie is Fort Clarke, Tarver's plantation, and Fort Crane. Closer to the middle is Fort Walker and Fort Wacahoota, and Fort Micanopy. At the bottom is Fort Drane and Fort Wheelock. In the far right is Fort Russell and Fort Brooks. [31]

---

[31] MacKay, John (Capt.), and J.E. Blake (Lt.); *Map of the Seat of War in Florida, Compiled by Order of Brevet Brig. Genl. Z[achary] Taylor*, 1839. Copy in the State Library of Florida, Tallahassee. By Capt. John MacKay and 1st Lt. Jacob Edmund Blake, Topographical Engineers (formerly 6th Infantry).

# Chapter 3: Killing of the Circuit Rider

General Taylor's headquarters[32] communicates to Navy Lieutenant John McLaughlin about coordinated efforts in Florida. Bloodhounds have been used by both Taylor's command and McLaughlin, but have proven a failure.

(Maj. L. Thomas to Lt. McLaughlin)

*Fort Micanopy*
*March 7, 1840*

*With respect to the employment of bloodhounds, the general desires me further to say that a number were brought to the territory from Cuba by the former General R.K. Call / some of which have been tried by the regular troops, and so far they have not been found to answer any good purpose, and many doubt whether they are of the genuine species. If you design procuring any of these dogs from Cuba, care should be taken that a spurious animal be not passed upon you, for the true blood.* [33]

The failure of the bloodhounds, no matter what species, would have ramifications the next few months around Micanopy. They fail to track any of the attackers, including those who killed Rev. McRae.

The Army and Navy Chronicle report that Rev. Mr. McRae of the Methodist Episcopal Church as killed by Indians while riding

---

[32]The commanding general's headquarters are wherever the general is at the time, not confined to a particular fort.
[33] AG 1840 T140, 13

his circuit, within three miles of Micanopy. [34]

Seeking to find out about the death of Reverend McRae has proved difficult. His name is given in various sources as McRae, McRea, McCray, McCrary, or McKay. Phonetically, all sound the same. McRae and McCray are both names of families who settled in Alachua County. Unfortunately, the record of Methodist circuit riders during the war is incomplete.

Alachua County has one of the oldest Methodist missions in Florida at Newnansville. When the war broke out in 1835, it became dangerous for a lone circuit rider to be in the wilderness. His family would risk becoming targets of Indian attacks and depredations at home. [35]

Church history in "The History of Methodism in Alachua":

*One of our local Preachers, Brother McCrary, was shot from his horse and killed while returning from one of his appointments Sabbath afternoon. He was in company with a Mr. McNeil who escaped with four balls through his clothes and two in the horse.* [36]

While the Army and Navy Chronicle has a gruesome editorial:

*"...his appealing minister stabbed to the heart and horribly mutilated, his limbs writhing in agony, when gashed deep, mid the laugh of derision and shouts of triumph..."[37]*

Twelve-year-old William Daniels was riding behind. When

---

[34] Homans, Benjamin; *The Army and Navy Chronicle* (ANC), Washington, D.C., 1835-1842, Vol. 10: 269

[35] Stuart, Allan R.; *The History of Methodism in Alachua; The Alachua Methodist Church* (Alachua, Florida, 1962).

[36] Ibid

[37] ANC Vol. 11, 220

McRae was shot, the lad wheeled around, galloped past the Indians, and narrowly escaped. [38]

The Boston Post newspaper gives more details.

*The Rev. Mr. McRae, of the Methodist Episcopal Church, Mr. Archibald McNeal, [also different spellings] a citizen of this place, and a young man by the name of William Daniels, left Wacahoota for Micanopy on Tuesday the 10th, at about 9 o'clock, A.M. [The other account said Sabbath, although March 10th was a Tuesday.] And when within three miles of the latter place, at a spot known as "Suggs Old Place," near the edge of the hammock, were fired on by a party of about fifteen or twenty Indians. On the fire of the Indians, their horses darted on one side, and it is presumed that Mr. McRae's horse threw him, as he was afterwards seen by Mr. McNeal without his rider. Mr. McNeal returned to Wacahoota, and Mr. Daniels proceeded on to Micanopy. A party of about 60 men immediately repaired to the scene of the murder, and there found Mr. McRae and his horse within ten steps of each other, both dead. He was not killed by the fire of the Indians, but ran down and tomahawked in the head, and stabbed in the breast and back, robbed of his clothes, and the saddle taken from his horse. They also scalped him, and in their hurry to leave the spot, dropped the scalp, which was afterwards found by one of the scouting party. Mr. McRae was taken into Micanopy and decently interred.* [39]

Mr. McNeal returned to the spot of the bloody ambush the next day to relate his story once again to a group of spectators. He displayed two bullet holes in his coat that show how he

---

[38] Stuart, "The History of Methodism in Alachua".
[39] The Boston Post, April 11, 1840

narrowly escaped the same fate as Rev. McRae. [40]

Although details vary between sources, we learn that Reverend McRae was local and buried in the old cemetery in Micanopy. The Mississippi Free Trader newspaper indicates that Mr. Daniels was badly wounded, but other papers do not indicate that. [41]

The location of the attack is said to be halfway between Wacahoota and Fort Micanopy. Could it be the same location as the other attacks or ambushes the following months?

---

[40] The Savannah Daily Republican, Apr. 2, 1840.
[41] The Mississippi Free Trader, April 13, 1840.

# Chapter 4: "These Indians Cannot be Reached in Fair Fighting"

In September 1839, Lt.Col. William Whistler leaves Fort King on an inspection tour. On November 30th, he moves his regimental headquarters to Fort Micanopy.

Captain Gabriel J. Rains leaves Fort Micanopy and assumes command of Fort King on January 19, 1840. By March, the garrison at Fort King is Rains' "A" Company with 47 personnel. With the number of officers and soldiers on duty elsewhere, or sick in the hospital, the post strength is only 34. By March, the only officers present are Rains and Assistant Surgeon Samuel P. Moore, who treats the sick at both Fort King and Fort Russell.[42]

On April 1st, 1840, Captain Gabriel Rains reports the death of two of his soldiers, shot by Indians while herding cattle within sight of the fort.

(Capt. G.J. Rains to Lt. R.C. Asheton, Adjutant, 2d Dragoons, at Fort Heileman.)

*Fort King*
*April 1st, 1840*
*I have the misfortune to inform you that on the 24 instance, the day Colonel Twiggs' command left the bridge at the Ocklawaha, that two of my best men were fired upon and killed in sight of this post by Indians, in the absence of most of the command escorting the wagons from the river, taking up the pontoon bridge &c &c, all of which the enemy appeared to know.*

---

[42] Fort King Post Returns

The pontoon bridge on the Ocklawaha was an inflatable India rubber pontoon bridge used at the crossing at Fort Fowle, a few miles east of Fort King. This was the invention of Capt. John Lane, a Dragoon officer. Pontoon bridges have been used throughout history, but Lane's design made it simple and easy to move with only one wagon, which is considered an important innovation for the Florida war.[43] Lane killed himself in a fit of dementia at Fort Drane in 1836 while head of the Creek Indian Regiment.

Rains continues:

*One of the men, my Herdsman, was proceeding in company with another to aid him in driving up the public cattle along the road leading to the Old [Indian] agency, when they were waylaid and one shot dead. The other lived long enough to say he saw about six Indians, close to them and turned to run when they fired.*

*The enemy were immediately pursued and fired upon, flying with much precipitation and could only have missed their due and avoided the danger in the manner they did, viz, by squatting in the bushes, turning aside, suffering the soldiers to pass and then doubling on their steps at the edge of the hammock.*

*In about half an hour the horses returned from the Ocklawaha with some portion of the command, and at the head of them I searched the whole country over, but could find no trail, not even where they were in ambush, except in about two miles from this post it was seen for about three yards only, leading in the direction of the Ocklawaha.*

---

[43] United States Quarter-Master's and Ordnance Departments, "Report on India Rubber Air Pontoons, and Bridges, from the United States Quarter-Master's and Ordnance Departments" (New York, printed by Daniel Fanshaw, 1849), 3-12.

*The next day pursuit was renewed and with (12) twelve men (mounted) I passed over more than fifty-five miles of country but saw not one fresh Indian sign in this square and nowhere else, except at a pond about twenty-two miles south of this, between the Withlacoochee River and the Tampa road four or five miles from the latter, where some had been fishing.*

*I am disposed to think these Indians were routed from the Ocklawaha, and seeing the Volunteers and many of the Regular Soldiers leave this post, presumed it was nearly deserted, and from the manner in which they cleared out, had probably not anticipated so warm a reception.*

*I had fourteen Infantry and fortunately eight Dragoons / who had come with a train of wagons, to increase that force, to pursue the Indians at the moment of attack.*

*I have found no Indian sign in this square before or since except as above, though scouts have been out every day.*

*As these Indians cannot be reached in fair fighting, I have prepared and set a Bomb Shell, covered with the clothing of the murdered men, the removal of which will cause it to explode, and placed in their way. I shall pursue the same plan for a while, as a just retribution for the murder of my men and in fact for our own safety.* [44]

Rains prepared a booby trap made of an exploding shell set off when disturbed. Gabriel Rains and his younger brother George Washington Rains will become known 20 years later during the Civil War as inventors of torpedoes and land mines. Gabriel Rains

---

[44] AG 1840 T149 and T160 enclosure 5

first tested out this deadly technology here on the Indians.

Captain Rains sends a detachment of soldiers to strike against the Indians.

(Capt. Rains to Col. Twiggs)

*Fort King*
*Apr. 15, 1840*

*I have the honor to inform you that very early yesterday morning I dispatched 2nd Lieut. Scott with 15 men on a scout and to search for the ford of the Ocklawaha river S.E. from this Post.*

*Lieut. Scott reports his proceeding with five horsemen and 10 men on foot in that direction 8 miles, when he struck a fresh trail of Indians leading in the direction of the Ocklawaha. Pursuit was immediately given and their fires discovered near a small Hammock. Supposing the Indians there, he ordered the men on foot to scour it & charged round the edges, with the mounted men. On the other side he came upon two Indians, one of them a woman, was captured. The other, a warrior, endeavored to escape into the Hammock, but turned and fired, and killed Private Kelly of my company (one of the best men in it.) But though mortally wounded, Kelly fired and charged upon the Indian and wounded him more or less with his fire or bayonet over the eye. Lieut. Scott immediately fired and brought him down, and he was left dead upon the ground. Some other Indians escaped. Kelly died in about two hours after. The woman I have prisoner here with all their baggage; she seems to convey an idea that those left are her children of small size.*

*I am at a little loss what to do with the woman who might be useful if we had an Interpreter.*

*Some 15 or 20 Dragoons are much required at this Post to scour the country immediately south of the Square.* [45]

Rains also elaborates on what was found at the Indian camp.

*I have the woman here, and from her signs she had left 3 of her children about 12 years old and downward, but having no Interpreter I am at a loss to communicate, and of course if she be willing to tell, I can understand no important information.*

*Please inform me what I am to do with her, the Indians rifle, about 4 loads of powder, many balls &c &c. County[Coontie] root pounded were captured.* [Flour made from the root of the coontie plant.] *Finally, for his soldier-like efforts on this and other occasions, I have the honor to recommend that Private Henry Jackson of "A" Company 7th Infantry be appointed Sergeant in the same.* [46]

What happened here is very important to consider for the actions of the Seminole/Miccosukee warriors in the next few weeks. Soldiers came from Fort King and attacked a camp concealed in a hammock. A woman is taken prisoner, and her children are abandoned. She is taken to Fort King. The Indian warriors know that the woman has been taken back to Fort King as a prisoner (they can follow the tracks) and that there are not many soldiers there. The soldiers at Fort King had invited more trouble than they could imagine!

---

[45] AG 1840 T160 Enclosure
[46] AG 1840 T162 Enclosure

# Chapter 5: "The Indians Seemed Much Disturbed by Our Presence"

General Taylor, who traveled around Florida more than any other commanding general during the war, receives permission from the Secretary of War to step down as commander of the forces in Florida on May 1st, 1840. But before he departs, an active campaign to strike at the Seminoles is planned.

(Maj. L. Thomas to Lt. Col. Whistler, 7th Infantry.)

*Fort Fanning*
*13th April 1840*
*The Commanding General directs that you detach forty men of the 7th Infantry from Micanopy under command of an Officer to Fort Clinch on the Withlacoochee river prepared for active operations for 8 or 10 days.* [47]

(Maj. L. Thomas to Capt. B. Beall, 2d Dragoons.)

*Fort Fanning*
*13th April 1840*
*You will immediately repair to this Post with 30 Dragoons of your company prepared for active operations for a few days and report to Maj. Loomis 2d Infantry. Your post will be left in command of the senior subaltern of the company.* [48]

(Maj. L. Thomas to Maj. Twiggs, 2d Dragoons, at Fort Heileman.)

*Fort Fanning*

---

[47] AG 1840 T183, 9
[48] Ibid

*14<sup>th</sup> April 14<sup>th,</sup> 1840*

*Major Loomis has been directed to operate with a force of 200 men, South of the Withlacoochee for a few days, and a part of his command has been drawn from your district as you will see by the enclosed copies of letters to Lt. Col. Whistler and Lt. [John W.] Martin.*

*The Indian prisoner you took with you having acted with good faith, it was very well to release him from confinement. He having forfeited his life to the enemy by conducting our troops, will be careful how he puts himself in their power, and we have therefore the very best assurance of his future faithfulness.* [49]

Taylor institutes a system of communication between posts to keep a constant flow of information. This form of strategic operations will become standard in the Army. Each post will have four men sent out weekly with dispatches to the next post down the line. There will be at least one officer among the small scouting party. To avoid ambush or attack, they are encouraged to take alternate routes away from the main road. If they find parties of Indians prepared to fight, they are not to engage them but notify the post they are traveling immediately of the danger.

*The scouts are for the most part to be on foot and are to go slow and cautiously through the hammocks looking carefully for signs as well as for the enemy, avoiding all roads or trails and never going and returning the same route. When the posts to which the scouts go and return are more than 15 miles apart the parties will remain out overnight, taking care to keep a good look out and encamp without fires.*

*Should parties of the enemy be met with too numerous to be*

---

[49] Ibid

*attacked, the scouts will make their way to the nearest post, when the most efficient means will be taken by the Commanding officer of the same to destroy or drive the enemy from the country, besides communicating without a moment's delay, the necessary intelligence to the contingent posts so as to enable them to cooperate most effectively. Should the scouts be pushed they will never separate, nor will they except on the last resort all deliver their fire at the same time, by pursuing this course and taking proper advantage of the ground they can seldom fail if ever to make good their retreat.* [50]

Field operations and maneuvers continue. Capt. Theophilus Holmes, 7th Infantry, writes to Col. Twiggs' headquarters on April 22nd. He leaves Fort Russell and scouts around Okahumpkee Hammock near Lake Eustis and Lake Griffin.

(Capt. T. Holmes to Lt. R.C. Asheton.)

*Fort Russell*
*22 April 1840*

*I left this Post on the 18 inst., with the command designated in your communication of the previous day at Fort King. I met Lt. W.K. Hanson on a scout with nine men, and as he expressed a wish to accompany me on the expedition, I gave him an invitation to that effect, with my party thus increased to Thirty-five men. I proceeded southeasterly from Fort King, and after travelling ten or twelve miles, came on a large Indian trail which was followed about thirty miles to the Okeehumky hammock on or near Lake Eustis. This I penetrated about two miles, when the Indians found themselves so closely pressed, that they deserted their ponies, packs, &c and scattered through the hammock which is so thick*

---

[50] Ibid

*that no traces of them could be discovered. Having reason to believe that there were still a few Indians in my rear, I returned on my back trail until I came to the open woods, and having placed my horses in a retired place—sent a sergeant & ten men to conceal themselves about a mile back. Two warriors very soon made their appearance, one of whom was killed and the other captured.*

*Yesterday morning while passing the large Hammock that borders Lake Griffin, three Rifles were fired at the rear guard in charge of the Captured ponies—by this fire I am sorry to say that one of my horses was killed, and before I could dismount the men and secure their horses, the Indians had fled, and pursuit was vain, as the hammock was exceedingly thick.*

*To recapitulate the results of the scout is one Indian killed, one Indian & sixteen ponies captured, and a number of packs destroyed. There appeared to be no want of ammunition, a small quantity of powder & lead was found in the packs. The pouches and horns that were taken were well supplied. The prisoner is in Irons at Fort King.* [51]

With 16 horses captured along with packs of supplies and ammunition, Capt. Holmes and Lt. W.K. Hanson's operation no doubt seriously injured the Seminoles.

Near the end of April, Maj. Gustavus Loomis (2d Infantry) conducts operations in the Cove of the Withlacoochee around Tsala-Apopka Lake from April 19th to 25th. [52]

Maj. Loomis writes to Taylor, even though by the time the

---

[51] AG 1840 T160 Enclosure, T178
[52] The name is from Muscogee, Thla-thlo, or fish, and Apopka, a place for eating, meaning "Fish Eating Place."

letter reaches the headquarters, General Walker Armistead has replaced Taylor as commander of forces in Florida. Loomis might not have gotten the word, and Taylor is still in Florida responding to correspondence.

(Maj. Loomis to Gen. Taylor)

*Cedar Keys, Florida*
*Apr. 27, 1840*

*On Saturday the 18th Inst, after the arrival of the several detachments entrusted to my command, by your order No.26, dated 18 April 1840, at Fort Clinch. Consisting of 30 men of Capt. B. L. Beall's Company, 2d Dragoons, commanded by Capt. Beall & accompanied by Lieut. Saunders, and 20 mounted Militia commanded by Lieut. Sanchez of Capt. Dell's Company of Florida M[ounted] Militia & 80 men of B, E, I, & K Companies, 2d Regiment of Infantry Command by Capt's. Kingsbury & Smith, Lieut's. Patrick & [John W.] Martin, of the same Regiment, & 40 men of the 7th Regiment of Infantry, under command of Capt. Bonneville, of the same Regiment, & 30 men of the 1st Regt. Of Infantry, K Company, Commanded by Lieut. Martin of said Company & Regiment.-- I was accompanied by Asst. Surgeon Byrne. Lieut. Patrick, in addition to his duties in the time performed those of adjutant and A.C.S. & A.A. G. W. to the command.-- I made preparations for starting upon the expedition against the enemy, the primary object of which, was the destruction of his cultivated fields & to break up & destroy any parties fallen in with.*

*The Command rested on the Sabbath day the 19th. Monday Apr. 20, 1840, made an early start and proceeded on the road cut out by Col. Foster, up the Withlacoochie River. That afternoon reached Camp Scott nearly opposite to Camp Izard—distance about 18 or 20 miles.*

*The Dragoons this day came upon a fresh trail & found a camp with fires burning, & Lt. Saunders, 2d Dragoons & five men, followed the trail across the Withlacoochie River swimming it himself & men & carrying their arms & ammunitions upon a raft tied together with grape vines.*

*Tuesday, 21 April 1840. Made an early start.—We were guided by the Indian prisoner about 8 miles in a very Serpentine course, when he thought we had better leave our wagons, lest we should be discovered in our approach.-- I left the wagons & a guard by about 20 men under Lt. Martin, 2d Infantry.*

*After proceeding about 3 miles more, the Indian showed us a few dry trails on an Island, behind a large pond, which he said was Sallo-Popka. [Tsala Apopka Lake—there are various spellings.] In our approach we endeavored to keep out of sight of the place, but we found no fresh signs of the Indians. Here was a large cultivated field, growing corn, peas, beans, squash, pumpkins, melons, &c. These we destroyed.*

*Our prisoner now seemed to think he had done all he promised, or was expected of him, & sat down, not however, without expressing regret at the destruction going on.-- After searching about, we discovered several small fields which were destroyed, one of which was upon an island in the pond and approached by a canoe we found & after destroyed.* [53]

[Can one imagine how heart-wrenching this scene was? Acres of fields destroyed, and the Native guide falls to his knees, saying

---

[53] AG 1840 L88

that he has seen enough and will go no further!]

*After this the Indian guided us to an Old field, which he said had once been cultivated, but he could not tell whether it was new or not. We were informed it was about 2 miles off. We found it about 6 [o'clock], & after winding around many uncultivated islands in what I suppose to be the Cove of the Withlacoochie. We found a large old field, say from 50 to 100 acres & formerly under cultivation, but not totally.-- An Orange grove in the midst of it— all borders upon the Withlacoochie River.*

*The many signal fires or smoke rising up in various directions plainly showed we were discovered. After refreshing the command, we returned to where we left Capt. Beall with his horses. I had previously sent Lt. Sanchez to bring up the wagons to the point upon Sallo-Popka Pond, where we turned off from the Fort Cooper road which we reached a little before sundown, when we found our camp made by Lt. Patrick, who I had directed to cross, with the detachment of 'I' company 2d Infantry to cross to the Island in the canoe & destroy the field found there.*

*Wednesday, 22 April 1840. I sent Capt. Beall with the Mounted Men to destroy a field found by Capt. Kingsbury, the previous evening, who accompanied Capt. B[eall]. I moved forward toward Annuttiliga Hammock & the Homosassa. Just before leaving the Fort Clinch & Fort Dade Road. Lieut's. Saunders & Martin, who were some distant in advance of the column, discovered a mounted Indian advancing towards them apparently examining the road for trails—upon his discovering them, he fled, pursued by these officers who gave the chase by a yell & firing a pistol.-- The Indian however baffled all their activity & zeal, for he succeeded in escaping them, & Capt. Smith & John, the interpreter, allowed to go to their support.-- I did not think it worthwhile to delay my march to search for the fugitive & continued my course & encamped at the "7-mile pond" from Fort Cross.*

*I was joined by Capt. Beall & the Mounted men soon after dusk & Capt. [Julius] Kingsbury joined soon after having been detained by sickness.*

*Capt. Beall reported having discovered large fields in addition to the one he went back to destroy. Some of which he had totally destroyed & others but partially & some not touched by him. Here also the Indian said he did not know whether there were any fields in the Hammock upon the border of which we were then encamped; nor, did he know of any at the Homosassa; nor did he know whether there were any Indians there or not; but his brother had told him that they sometimes went there when hard pressed upon an island. Under all the circumstances, I deemed it best to turn back & destroy all the fields we could find in the region of the Sallo-pop-Ka [Tsala-Apopka] occupying as much time as should be necessary.* [54]

*Thursday, 23rd April 1840. This day I returned back toward Sallo-popka. [Tsala Apopka Lake].—Sent forward Capt. Beall & the Mounted men to scout. They stopped at a pond about 2 miles from the scene of our operations where I found them.*

*From this point I permitted Capt. Smith & Lieut. Patrick with about 35 men of the detachments of B & I Companies, 2d Infantry, to separate from the Command & proceed on a trail leading to the right, which would apparently bring them near our operations, which we found to be the case & Capt. S[mith] & his party found one field & destroyed it which had escaped us. I proceeded to the place pointed out by Capt. Beall with the remainder of the*

---

[54] Ibid

command—on our way, one of the wagons broke down. I however, soon had it repaired & when I came up, found the Command out, under Capt. Bonneville, destroying & hunting up fields, which were destroyed.

This morning Capt. Kingsbury was so unwell that we were obliged to carry him in wagon. I encamped near these fields upon very low ground, after having destroyed all we could find. Capt. Smith & Lt. Patrick did not join.

Friday Apr. 24, 1840.-- I started about sunrise & moved to our camp at Sallo-pop-ka.—Doctor J. Byrne is of the opinion Capt. Kingsbury should be sent through to Fort Clinch.—That he is very sick & his life might be endangered by delay.

I directed Capt. Beall to leave one Non-Commissioned Officer & 6 Privates of his Dragoons & with the remainder escort the wagon with Capt. Kingsbury to Fort Clinch. There was very little forage last night remaining. He left & before Sundown, on Friday reached Fort Clinch where he found the Steamboat Marion had arrived about 2 hours before him.

I sent out Capt. Bonneville with the detached of Capt. Beall's Dragoons, to look for Capt. Smith & his party, as I only waited for them to take up my march for Fort Clinch.—He returned in about 2 hours, having succeeded in finding him. About 11 a.m. I left our camp for Fort Clinch which I reached before 9 O'clock a.m. on Saturday 25 Apr. 1840.

I immediately crossed the Command & wagons, except B Company & a detachment of E Company 2d Infantry & the broken wagon which I put on board the boat to go to Fort Fanning.

On Wednesday the 22d, Capt. Beall reported breaking up an

Indian camp.-- Taking a rifle barrel, a musket lock & stock, the lock in pieces—destroying several villages, various articles of household furniture—hoes & axes &c. &c. One kettle, brass, was brought away by the militia.

I estimate that we have destroyed about 130 acres of corn, peas, field, beans, pumpkins, turnips, squash, melons, rice, millet, sugar cane & sweet potatoes and many seeds & corn. Though we have not killed any of the enemy, we have destroyed their means of subsistence for I feel confident that they cannot replace their lost crops this season. I hope it may be a means of bringing them to terms.

John, the Interpreter, counts the fields of 72 families having been destroyed. Many of the Officers are of the opinion that a much larger number of acres have been destroyed than I have reported.

I have no confidence in this Indian showing us anything in the Hammocks of the Homosassa or Annuttiliga.-- It is possible he may wish to do so but is not acquainted with the places & is afraid to go with the troops to look them up.[55]

[The guide John is probably afraid that the Seminole warriors will target him as a traitor because he guided the soldiers.]

Hoping my operations will meet your approval I have to report that all the officers & men placed under my command have displayed much zeal & patience & endurance of the fatigues & privation in conduct to an expedition carried on under such circumstances & at such a time of the year. [56]

---

[55] AG 1840 L88
[56] Ibid

At the same time, Loomis continues to Taylor:

*I have the honor to enclose herewith a report of the operations of the troops, placed under my command, against the enemy in or near the Cover of the Withlacoochie or Sallo-Pop-Ka.*

*You will perceive I have not been to the Homosassa.*

*Should an expedition be sent to scout the hammocks & Islands of that river, I would recommend that a force cooperated by water.—Perhaps an examination of the Islands at the Mouth by boats, might determine whether it would be advisable to send a force by land or operate down the river.—*

*If it should be thought advisable, a mounded force could leave Fort Clinch at evening & the next day visit all the fields near Sallo-pop-ka & return the next night to Fort Clinch. By this means if any fields should be replanted they might again be destroyed..*

*By this expedition many officers & men have acquired a knowledge of the country which will enable them to penetrate it again independent of an Indian guide or a negro interpreter.—*

*I believe any of the officers who accompanied me would be able to conduct a command to the same places.*

*The Indians seemed much disturbed by our presence, judging by their signal fires & I think have fled south or into the Wahoo Swamp, expecting we had come to scout these hammocks & islands as you had done those of Middle Florida & between the Suwannee & Wacasassa Rivers.*

*The Islands spoken of are sand hills, or small elevations, covered with live-oak & other timber, rising in what would otherwise be a prairie, which in wet times would be covered with water & is even now in places boggy.*

*Capt. Kingsbury is on board the steamboat Marion & is accompanied by Asst. Surg. J. Byrne. He is still quite sick, very weak. Has congestive fever.* [57]

Capt. Kingsbury will live another 16 years. A week after his death, his son Henry Kingsbury will graduate from West Point but will later be killed at the battle of Antietam in 1862.

This expedition was in the area known as the Cove of the Withlacoochee, well believed to be the stronghold of the Seminole / Miccosukees. But here in the fifth year of the war, the Army finally penetrates the area of the Cove. This was not done earlier in the war.

---

[57] Ibid

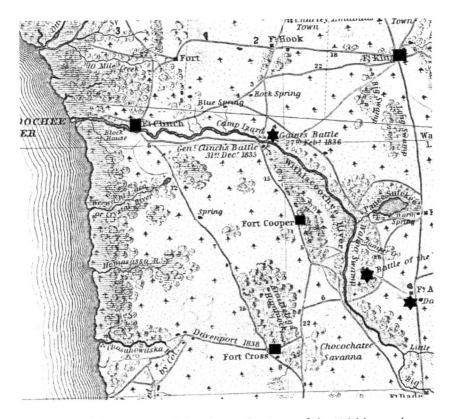

A close-up of the MacKay Blake shows the Cove of the Withlacoochee, between Fort Cooper on the west and the Withlacoochee River on the east. Lake Tsala-Apopka is this area of intermittent wet prairies and ponds that makes up the Cove. Fort King is in the upper right. Southwest of Fort King or to the far left is Fort Clinch near the mouth of the Withlacoochee River, and east of that is Camp Izard or Gaines Battle. Further south on the river or upriver from Gaines Battle, are the two battlefields of the Wahoo Swamp and Dade's Battlefield. In the lower center is Fort Cross. [58]

---

[58] MacKay, John (Capt.), and J.E. Blake (Lt.); *Map of the Seat of War in Florida, Compiled by Order of Brevet Brig. Genl. Z[achary] Taylor*, 1839. By Capt. John MacKay and 1st Lt. Jacob Edmund Blake, Topographical Engineers (formerly 6th Infantry). National Archives, copy in the State Library of Florida.

Once again, Fort Micanopy requires a physician. Dr. McDougall is ordered to St. Augustine to testify at a court-martial as a physician's opinion in the inquiry of the death of a dragoon soldier by Captain Marshall Howe. Howe tortured and beat to death one of his ill soldiers who could not perform the tasks ordered. McDougall's opinion was that since the soldier was a known drunkard, it was alcohol that led to his death, despite the obvious head trauma. It doesn't leave much faith in Army physicians at the time. Apparently, McDougall went to the same school as the previous Surgeon, Dr. Sloan, who also couldn't tell the difference between head trauma and a drunk.

A civilian physician needed to be contracted for Micanopy, who was not easy to find in the territory where most of the civilian population has fled. General Taylor approves.

(Maj. L. Thomas to Col. Twiggs)

*Fort Brooke*
*April 28th, 1840*
*Seeing by a recent letter of Captain Garner, 3d Arty, Judge Advocate, that Surgeon McDougall has been summoned to attend as a witness before the General Court Martial in session at St. Augustine, the General directs that, should it be deemed necessary, a Citizen physician be employed to attend at Micanopy during the absence of Dr. McDougall--. You are further authorized to engage the services of a Citizen Physician to attend at any place where it may be necessary.* [59]

Unfortunately, Fort Micanopy is about to be in great need of a competent physician.

---

[59] Ibid

Soon after, the Richmond Enquirer newspaper reports about a surprise found at Fort Micanopy.

*Information has reached us, that in digging at Micanopy, 15 barrels of pork and 15 or 20 barrels of bread were discovered. It is supposed that this amount of provisions was buried on the evacuation and burning of that post in 1836; but a short time previous to its having been temporarily encamped on by General Call's Army, in a state of great suffering. Can it be possible that provisions were buried there, and unknown, whilst from five to six thousand men were enduring the horrors of hunger on the very spot?* [60]

When Micanopy was abandoned in August 1836, enough supplies of salt pork and hardtack biscuits were buried to feed the army. Wagons to transport supplies were hard to come by. It was easier to leave behind and bury supplies when everyone was evacuating. (The Quartermaster Department was working very hard at the same time to buy more wagons and horse saddles & tack up north to be used in the Florida war.) The officers who departed the fort were not the ones who came back, most of whom had since died. A few months later in November 1836, General/Governor Richard K. Call encamped his command at the fort site during the end of his campaign that resulted in the battle of Wahoo Swamp. The campaign was another failure, with the men starving and eating the horses while waiting for supplies from Picolata. They didn't know that they were sitting on top of provisions that could have fed them all.

---

[60] Richmond Enquirer, May 26, 1840

# Chapter 6: "An Engine of Destruction"

The 7th Infantry Regiment fights its first large battle since 1817. In the First Seminole War 23 years earlier, it was a specific campaign against the Seminoles in northwest Florida. Nothing could prepare the soldiers for a year of guerilla warfare in 1840. [61]

(Lt.Col. Whistler to Col. Twiggs at Black Creek-Fort Heileman)

*Fort Micanopy*
*April 28th, 1840*

*It is regretted that I have to report Captain Rains, 18 men on a scout this morning was attacked by Indians from fifty to seventy within a mile & a half of his Post [Fort King]. Four men killed & four wounded. Captain Rains among the wounded, believed mortal.*

*I have ordered Capt. Fitzgerald with Twenty men to report to the commanding officer of that Post, to remain until your further order on the subject. Every post in the vicinity has been informed of it.* [62]

*This new outbreak is presumed to be owing to the destruction, by Major Loomis' command of some of the crops of the savages, in the vicinity of Annuttalliga and Homosassa, 130 acres of corn, four feet high, having been destroyed by the troops, as also some sweet potatoes, partly ready for use, and a variety of other vegetables.* [63]

---

[61] Fort King Post Returns, Captain Gabriel Rains assumes command with Company A on January 19, 1840.
[62] AG 1840 T160 Enclosure, T178 Enclosure
[63] Richmond Enquirer, May 12, 1840

Loomis' campaign the week before had destroyed crops of the Seminole and Miccosukees within a day's ride of Fort King, right before harvesting.

(Lt.Col. William Whistler to Gen. Zachary Taylor)

*Fort Micanopy*
*May 1st, 1840*
*Capt. Rains being too badly wounded to make a report of his affairs with the enemy on the 28th ult., I avail myself of the information obtained by Lieut. R[ichard] C. Gatlin, Adjutant, 7th Infantry, who returned from Fort King yesterday to lay before you a detailed account of it."*

*It appears that about 10 O'clock A.M. on the 28th ult., Capt. Rains with a party of 16 men were attacked by the enemy in force in a small hammock two miles south of Fort King. The first intimation of their presence was a volley from their rifles and it was soon perceived that the party were entirely surrounded.*

*A charge was made to the piney woods to the south of the hammock, but finding the enemy in force there and the trees too small to afford a shelter to our party, the hammock was charged again, and a strong line of the enemy posted on its north side was forced. Trees were then taken and a firing in retreat commence. The ground was contested foot by foot for near half an hour, when the leader of the enemy having been killed. The firing ceased on their part and our party withdrew to the fort.*

*Our loss was a Sergeant and one man killed. Capt. Rains and two privates were dangerously and a Corporal and Private slightly wounded. The enemy's loss was four warriors killed among them. It is supposed a chief of some importance, as their firing ceased immediately after his fall. Capt. Rains estimates their numbers at* seventy, but Private Kyle, who lay concealed in the hammock until after they had left, states that he counted, as they filed off to the southwest, ninety-three warriors, fifteen squaws—bearing off the dead (4) and four Negroes. His statement may be relied upon.

To Capt. Rains great praise is due for his courage and skill in extricating his party from the very difficult situation in which they were placed. The conduct of his men is highly commendable. They fought with true courage against an overwhelming force, and prolonged the contest not for their own safety, but to protect and bring off their wounded companions. [64]

---

[64]AG 1840 W176, T179; ANC Vol. 10, 348. The Richmond Enquirer, June 2, 1840

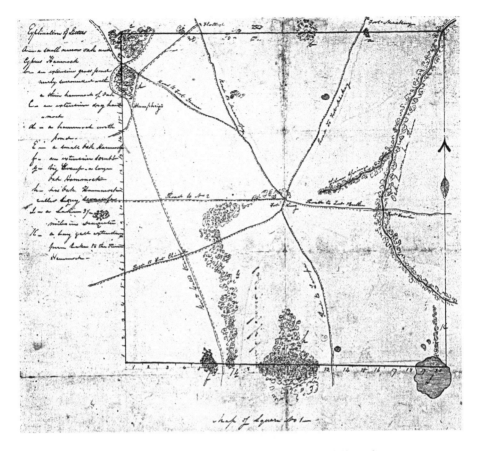

Map of Square 1 (1839?) with Fort King in the middle. The Ocklawaha River and Fort Fowle are marked, along with the Silver River that empties into the Ocklawaha. Not many natural features are on this map, but it does show the roads very well. [65]

---

[65] Map of Square No. 1. (2nd Seminole War); National Archives, 1839(?). Copy in the State Library of Florida, Tallahassee.

Finally, at the end of May, Captain Rains makes his report. Starting with events that led up to the battle, but with no mention of looting and burning nearby Indian villages and growing fields, and bringing back prisoners to Fort King.

(Capt. Rains to Col. Twiggs)

Fort King
29th May 1840.

*Owing to the state of my health, still precarious, as you are well aware, I have not been able until now of making the following report, which I have the honor to submit.*

*On the 24th of March last, two of the best men of my company were waylaid and assassin like, shot down in sight of this post.-- The murderers secure in their fleetness and with the start they had, rendered the pursuit of no avail:-- they went in a direction south about two miles where is a small Hammock and water, the latter nowhere else to be found in that direction for miles around.*

*War parties of the Indians, must pass the above for water from the south; who have sinister designs against this Post; So, at this place, I put a small box as an engine of destruction, containing a (bomb) Howitzer shell, some gunpowder, fragments of old iron &c, with a shirt of one of the above-murdered men upon the top, so fixed, that the removal of it, would explode the whole, destroy the operator, and give the alarm of the approach of the enemy to this Post."*

*A few evenings subsequent, at tattoo, the machine was set off, the military ran to the spot, but no enemy was found;-- A hard rain followed in a little time, which was calculated to obliterate every trace. Subsequently; however, I was induced from appearances to believe, it had given the enemy a premonitory caution.*

*The shell &c was removed, but in another shape, and again exploded about the same hour of the night on the 27th April. The military again rushed to the spot, but in the darkness of the night no Indians were found, while no doubt the Hammock was full.*

*I heard a hoop, as usually given by the enemy, while passing in rear of the thicket with some Dragoons under Lieut. Newton, to intercept fugitives; but the cry was thought to proceed from one of the Infantry, who were scouring the bushes under Lt. Scott, and who, as since ascertained, also heard the same some distance before them.*

*On the morning of the 28th following, with sixteen men (being all the disposable force at this post.) I proceeded to the Hammock again, which is about 100 yards wide, and 140 in length, surrounded with open Pine woods, and swept it with my men in extended order.-- The Hammock is quite full of low, thick Palmettos, which afford good hiding places, impenetrable, almost except by crawling;-- So after this diligent search we passed through to the water at the farthest ends, and found no enemy, but two cur dogs we had along, began to bark in the densest thicket at a rabbit, as one of my Command answered me upon inquiry.*

*The dogs running now to the opposite side of the ponds, about 5 or 6 yards wide, into the bushes barking furiously, again excited my suspicion; and I ordered the men to ascertain the cause and was proceeding myself to ascend the bank about 6 feet high, for the same purpose, when the men in front shouted "Indians," raised their guns and fired simultaneously with the enemy who were concealed, prostrate in the undergrowth.*

*My men rushed back past me, when finding that we were*

surrounded and <u>knowing</u> that the Indians would not show fight in such a place without having the advantage in numbers, I ordered the soldiers to "clear the Hammock, each man to take his tree and give the enemy fair fight" (other tactics would have been madness.) No sooner said than done, as I passed Sergeant Smith, my 1$^{st}$ Sergeant, and a brave soldier behind a tree, he observed, "Captain I am Killed," with the blood running from his mouth and nose; he was cool and collected, though he had received four wounds, three of which were mortal each. Another of my men had been shot dead by this first fire. On our side of about 5, and by the enemy from 20 to 30 shots. Another man of my command was also wounded here probably.

As soon as we had taken trees, firing upon the enemy, as occasion presented, assailed by innumerable shots from an unseen foe on the east side of the Hammock, a large number of painted Warriors from fifty to one hundred, rushed boldly out of the west side, at the end nearest to Fort King where we had first entered it, and began to run from tree to tree, to get upon our flanks and behind us. The same was done by the Indians on the east side, when a conspicuous warrior, who had attained our flank was shot down while passing to our rear.

After maintaining our position here unscarred by shot, which flew about us like hail, with the enemy in front, and until they had reached our flanks, both right and left and fast extending their line behind us, keeping up an incessant firing and yelling, our numbers reduced to eleven or twelve. I perceived that to storm the Hammock <u>and break through the enemy's line</u> towards Fort King or our destruction was inevitable. Having given the order, we charged through and retook the Hammock, now the center of the Indian force. Their warriors gave way before us, and we passed *fairly through them, towards the Fort, out of the thicket some 100 or 200 yards. Knowing that now we should have a rush of the foe, and their concentrated fire upon us (which sure enough immediately followed) while trying to rally my men, now reduced to 7 not wounded;-- ordering them again to take trees, so as to check the enemy's advance & fire upon us (which would have done fearful execution, could I have done it in time. To have opened a fire upon the mass expanse) while between my command and the Indians amidst a shower of balls, I was shot through the body; but this did not deter my efforts until I had stopped the retreat of my men.*

*Feeling faint from loss of blood, I informed the soldiers of my condition, when they ran to me, and Corporal Bedford by my side, fired and killed a distinguished chief on our right flank.*

*Three of the men carried me in their arms, one of these (named Taylor) being wounded through the shoulder, while by my direction three more brought up the rear as a guard. The Indians halted awhile where their chief was killed, and afterwards followed in the distance.*

*This terminated a fight of about an hour's continuance, in which we had a Sergeant and one man killed; myself, a corporal and three privates wounded.-- We killed four of the enemy—their wounded being unknown;--and all of our wounded were saved from the hands of the merciless Savage.*

*Two of my men (one badly wounded) remained hid in the Hammock, and relate that after our battle, the Indians gathered their forces, and filed off towards the southwest. That there were ninety-three Warriors, five or six negroes, and about twenty squaws, and that the latter carried away four dead men. From other circumstances, I think this enumeration correct.*

*Some of the Indians afterwards came in view of this Fort but were scattered by a few shells from a 5½ inch Howitzer; 2nd Lieut. Scott being in command.*

*The Indians as afterwards appeared had laid an ambush for our destruction in the Hammock, which was discomposed by our move in an opposite direction, to fight them, instead of retreating immediately as they expected towards Fort King.* [66]

An extremely brutal fight for Company A, 7th Infantry. Captain Rains used classic infantry tactics and bayonet charges to break through the line and retreat to Fort King with the wounded men. Quick thinking and well-trained soldiers prevented them from getting completely wiped out, though outnumbered five to one.

Many believed that Capt. Rains was mortally wounded and would not recover. But after a year and a half convalescence, he lives another 40 years.[67]

The following are the soldiers killed in action that month around Fort King: [68]

- Pvt. Charles Herring, Co. A, Mar. 24, 1840, killed at Fort King.
- Pvt. George W. Theis, Co. A, Mar. 24, 1840, killed near Fort King.

---

[66] AG 1840 A130, W176 Enclosure. ANC Vol. 11, 12-13.

[67] ANC Vol. 10, 297.

[68] Sprague, John T.; *The Origin, Progress, and Conclusion of the Florida War*; 1848 (Seminole Wars Historic Foundation Reproduction, University of Tampa Press, Tampa, Florida, 2000). Brown, George M. (Ord. Sergt.); *Ponce de Leon Land and Florida War Record*, (The Record Co., St. Augustine, Fla., 1902)

- Pvt. Hugh Kelly, Co. A, Apr. 14, 1840, killed near Fort King on scout under command of Lt. Scott.
- Pvt. Frederick Mier (also given as Myer), Co. A, Apr. 28, 1840, killed near Fort King
- 1st Sergt. George H. Smith, Co. A, Apr. 28, 1840, near Fort King, killed in action with Capt. Rains.
- Pvt. Richard Grace, Co. A, May 9, 1840, died at Fort King, of wounds received with action with Capt. Rains, Apr. 28, 1840.

(Gen. Armistead to Gen. Roger Jones, Army Adjutant General in Washington)

*Fort King*
*May 30th, 1840.*

*I cannot speak too highly of Captain Rains' fight, exhibiting throughout the greatest skill, judgment, & the utmost bravery in officers and men nor can I recommend too strongly to the department the conferring a brevet on him, as a recompense for his gallantry—his sufferings, and the saving of his command from an overwhelming force. A brevet conferred in this case, would be well awarded, not so much as an inducement to officers, who on all occasions have shown the utmost alacrity to ferret out and engage the enemy, regardless of all hardships, but as exhibiting a disposition on the part of Government to reward as far as it could, the courage, skill, & conduct in an affair which notwithstanding the great disparity of numbers, was nearly brought to a successful issue.*

*I have the honor to refer the Department to Capt. Bonneville's report [out of Fort Micanopy] of today, in which it will be seen that an Indian village of 15 huts concealed and surrounded by marshes and hammocks, and distant from here only 15 miles was entirely destroyed, with a fine field of corn, and much Indian property,* valuable only however to themselves. From the appearance of the village, it has existed for some years and been a great resort for Indians going north and south, & from whence they could sally at any moment & in a few hours destroy small scouting parties, and intercept wagon trains. Capt. Bonneville's estimate of the number of Warriors is I think too small—there are many of them no doubt out in the bands which are constantly committing depredations. The whole band would no doubt have been captured, had not the growth—scrub palmetto, through which the men had to cross given a noise which heralded the approach of our troops. Capt. Bonneville deserves great credit, not only for this affair, but for the zeal and good conduct which he has exhibited on all occasions.

The troops are constantly scouting in large bodies, Lt. Col. Riley's command is now on the Withlacoochee,--Capt. Bonneville and Ker are also out with their commands in pursuit of some Indians—Lt. Col. Harney will shortly proceed south 70 or 80 miles. [69]

(Gen. Armistead via Adjutant W. Newton to Capt. G.J. Rains.)

Fort King, June 1st, 1840

Your detailed report of the facts connected with your late gallant defense against a greatly superior body of Indians near Fort King has been received, and it enables the Commanding General to express to you the high estimate, which he in common with others, has placed upon your gallant and successful resistance to an overpowering force. [70]

---

[69] AG 1840 A130
[70] AG 1840 A175, 1

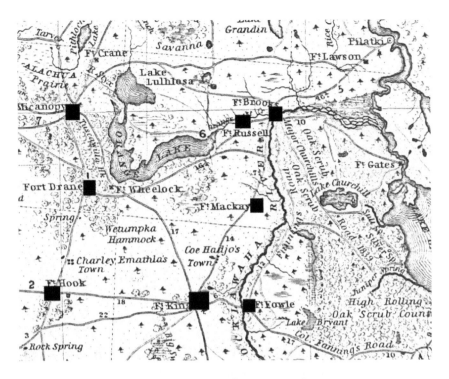

A close-up of the MacKay-Blake map for the area between Fort Micanopy and Fort King. On the west side to the left is Micanopy, Fort Drane, and Fort Hook. On the east side to the right is Fort Russell and Fort Brooks, Fort MacKay, and Fort King and Fort Fowle. [71]

---

[71] MacKay, John (Capt.), and J.E. Blake (Lt.); *Map of the Seat of War in Florida, Compiled by Order of Brevet Brig. Genl. Z[achary] Taylor*, 1839. By Capt. John MacKay and 1st Lt. Jacob Edmund Blake, Topographical Engineers (formerly 6th Infantry). National Archives. Copy in the State Library of Florida.

(Maj. Sylvester Churchill to Col. David E. Twiggs)

*Newnansville*
*April 29, 1840*

*Two men came into town last evening and reported that they with another man in company, hunting on Horseback, were fired on by Indians that afternoon about 9 miles hence, on the Fort Clarke Road. The third man came in during the night, not injured. But today about noon, two men were fired at by Indians, on the same road within four miles of this place, one killed and the other wounded dangerously, supposed mortally.* [72]

(Col. Twiggs to Gen. R. Jones, Army Adjutant General.)

*Fort Heileman*
*1st May 1840*

*Yesterday's mail from the South and West brings in no communications from either Tampa or Middle Florida. The cause of the miscarriage remains unaccounted for.*

*From Fort King, Micanopy and Newnansville the intelligence is truly distressing. Copies of letters from Colonel Whistler, Major Churchill and Lieut. Scott are for information of Headquarters herewith enclosed.*

*During my late examination of the Ocklawaha and A-ha-pop-ka country, I was led to believe a large portion of the enemy had returned north and so expressed myself in my official report to General Taylor, a copy of which I enclosed the General in chief, that such is the case can now no longer be doubted; recent and sad experience giving us daily intimations of their presence. One company of Dragoons which had served during the Winter in Middle Florida lately arrived under my command, with orders to*

---

[72] AG 1840 T160 Enclosure, T178 Enclosure

*dispose of it as I might deem expedient. Since then it has been constantly and usefully employed on the Ocklawaha and this day marched for Fort King under command of Lieut. Lawton, who has been instructed to relieve Capt. Rains should his wounds render him unable to act with that promptitude the presence of the Indians so forcibly demands.*

*The Steam Boat Gaston arrived last evening from the southern coast and brings a verbal account of an attack on the post at Key Biscayne in which there were two wounded (one Sergeant) mortally.*

*Information having reached this though unofficially that General Taylor was about to leave the Territory. I deem it a duty to give all information of a recent date, and have accordingly enclosed copies of several communications which doubtless contain the latest intelligence as regards the operations of the Army.*

*Colonel Warren's Regiment of [Florida] Militia is now being mustered out of service and the several posts, in number thirteen will shortly be rendered vacant, with but one exception— Micanopy. No one post has more than a company, and from what quarter the unprotected settlements are to receive military protection, I am at a loss to conceive.*

*An effort has been made to organize six companies of Militia to serve on foot, but from the disposition convinced by the Floridians, no reliance can be placed that the object will be accomplished.* [73]

On the Fort King Post Returns for April, since Capt. Rains is

---

[73] AG 1840 T160

recovering from wounds, 2d Lt. J. R. Scott takes command, while Assistant Surgeon Moore attends to the sick and wounded at Fort King, Fort Russell, and Fort #2 (Fort Hook). The garrison compliment is only 37, with three killed and five wounded counted on the April returns. With the number of men sick and on extra duty, there are only 19 soldiers working normal duties of the post. The battle near Fort King for Company A resulted in more casualties for a company that was already short of men. Company A departed Fort King on June 25th, and the 2d Dragoons moved in to garrison. Capt. Benjamin Beall assumes command, bringing garrison strength up to 58 troops. [74]

In 1842, the remains of some of the soldiers interned at Fort King are moved to the cemetery at St. Francis in St. Augustine. Cemetery records include: 1st Sgt. George H. Smith, died Apr. 28, 1840. Pvt. George W. Theis, died Mar. 24, 1840.[75] Although recent research now questions if any of the remains at Fort King were moved at all.

---

[74] Fort King Post Returns

[75] Ancestry.com; National Cemetery record cards, St. Augustine National Cemetery.

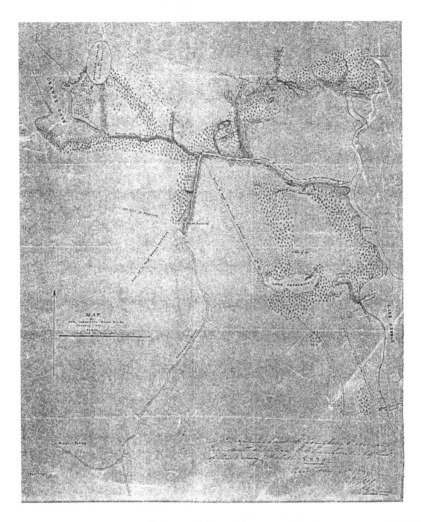

Lt. C. Tompkins, *Map of the Ocklawaha River &c &c*, January 1839. Although not much detail, it does show Fort King and Glassell Spring (Silver Springs), Paines (Paynes) Landing, to Fort Shannon in Palatka on the St. Johns River. Fort Russell is not marked. Lake Churchill in the middle is now Lake Kerr. [76]

---

[76] Tompkins, C. (Lt.); *Map of the Ocklawaha River &c &c* (2nd Seminole War); National Archives, January 1839. Drawn by [1st ]Lieut. C[hristopher Quarles] Tompkins, 3d Artillery and transmitted by Maj. S. Churchill to Adjt. Genl. Of the Army, Feb. 11, 1839. National Archives. Copy in the State Library of Florida.

## Chapter 7: Gabriel Rains After the battle

Gabriel J. Rains was born near Newbern, North Carolina in 1803, survived Florida and then the Civil War, and died in Aiken, South Carolina in 1881 at age 78. He showed great potential by graduating 13th out of a class of 37 at West Point Military Academy in 1827. Much of the next twelve years were spent at Fort Gibson in Indian Territory, now Oklahoma, with the 7th Infantry. He married Mary Jane McClellan in 1835 when he was 32 years old and she was about 14. Mary was the granddaughter of John Sevier, the first elected governor of Tennessee who was Andrew Jackson's political rival. [77]

In January 1837 at Newport, Kentucky, Lt. Gabriel Rains requested a leave of absence to take care of his wife. Her health was so fragile that Lt. Rains believes he must move her to southern climates. Assistant Surgeon Bennett says that Newport is a hotbed of consumption and recommends she be moved immediately. But moving to the southern climates was not so healthy to Gabriel Rains, as we saw. [78]

Newport, Kentucky was one of the main recruitment and Military Enlistment Processing Centers, where recruits were inspected, processed and drilled, and given their first training before shipping out to their regiment. The military facility no longer exists today, but there is a park at the site in commemoration, with a flag pole, interpretive signs, and a great

---

[77] "Appleton's Cyclopedia of American Biography, 1600-1889", 161; Ancestry.com. AG 1827 R24. Waters, W. Davis; "Deception is the Art of War: Gabriel J. Rains, Torpedo Specialist of the Confederacy", *The North Carolina Historical Review*, Vol. 66, No. 1 (January 1989), 29-60.
[78] AG 1837 R9

view of Cincinnati across the Ohio River.

While he was recovering from his wounds, the Army awarded Rains a brevet promotion to the rank of Major. (A brevet rank was a temporary increase to the next grade without the pay increase.) In the summer of 1840, he traveled to Fort Columbus, New York, which served as a hospital for soldiers returning from Florida. While there, he reviewed the Colt repeating rifle that could load five rounds instead of the single-shot, front-loading musket that soldiers had used during the previous century. He recommended that they adopt the Colt for his infantry company, but the Secretary of War declines, due to the Army conducting another board of inquiry to replace the outdated Springfield flintlock. [79]

Recovery was very slow, and Major Rains was not returned to Florida right away. He is sent to New Orleans at Fort Wood and Fort Pike. For anyone who has never been there, southeast Louisiana is no easier than Florida. The heat and humidity, and constant mosquitoes can get stifling in the summer.

Dr. John Madden reports on the physical condition of Rains from Fort Pike, May 29, 1841.

*Brevet Major G. J. Rains of the Seventh Regiment of Infantry having applied for a certificate of the State of his health. I do hereby certify that I have carefully examined this officer and find that the right Lobe of his Lung has been wounded apparently by a gunshot about a year ago, that in consequence thereof, he is in my opinion unfit for duty, where bodily Exertion, Exposure or Vocal powers are required.*

---

[79] "Letters Sent by the Secretary of War Relating to Military Affairs, 1800-1889 (Records of the Office of the Secretary of War, Record Group 107), 1840, 419.

*I further declare my belief that he will not be able to resume his duties in the field for some months to come, but is Competent for all other duties whatever.* [80]

(Bvt. Maj. Rains to Brig. Gen. Roger Jones, Adjutant General.)

Fort Pike, LA
1st June 1841

*I have the honor to report the reception of an order from Bvt. Brig. General Z. Taylor ordering me to Florida should my health be so restored as to enable me to perform Company duty. On account of the condition implied, I have the honor to forward the enclosed certificate of a Physician of my ill health which renders me at present incapable of performing Company duty in the field though adequate for any other. I am not anxious for a sick leave if I can be of any use in Florida or elsewhere.*

*My competency when last on the Recruiting service was probably equal to that of any other Officer, in the same time, and if my services would be acceptable in Newport, Kentucky, I will be glad to be so employed, should the Department think my Command here no longer necessary, as the Fort [Pike] is in the hands of an Engineer Officer (Lt. [P.G.T.] Beauregard) repairing.*

Rains closes his letter with a couple of complaints:

*P.S. This post is healthy though much troubled by mosquitoes, and any officer stationed here, should be obliged to have an eye over Fort Wood—Battre du Bien Venue and Tower du Pre'—as the two latter especially have been much injured by fishermen for the want of attention and they can all be visited in a day from this*

---

[80] AG 1840 W176, 1841 R90

*post.* [81]

[Having visited Fort Pike and nearby Fort Wood/Fort Macomb, I can personally attest to this. The mosquitoes are horrendous. Unfortunately, both forts are now closed to the public.]

In September 1841, the yellow fever epidemic in New Orleans delayed Rains' return to Florida. The mosquito-borne illness devastated all the major cities along the Gulf coast. Even Florida Governor Robert Raymond Reid succumbs a few weeks after his term of governor expires.

(Maj. Rains to Maj. L. Thomas, Asst. Adjutant General, U.S. Army, Washington.)

*Fort Pike, LA*
*30th Sept. 1841*

*The fact is mentioned lest it might be thought I was unnecessarily procrastinating my departure for Tampa Bay; while on the contrary an earlier reception would have been desirable, as the whole city of New Orleans, the most feasible point of departure, and environs are in a panic on account of the unparalleled malignity of the prevailing Epidemic (Yellow Fever) and efforts are now made to prevent the intercourse with the other places until frost.* [82]

By November, Rains was back in Florida at Fort Fanning. But, when the regiment is removed from Florida soon after, he goes with Company A to Fort Wood, Louisiana, for three years. Just where he had left.

In 1846 at the beginning of the Mexican War, he participated

---

[81] Ibid
[82] AG 1841 R175

with the defense of Fort Brown and the battle of Resaca de la Palma. He returned to Florida during the "Panic of 1849" when there was a fear for another war with the Seminoles, which quick negotiation adverted. In the 1850s he went to the Pacific Northwest.

Lt. Col. Gabriel Rains, now in the 5th Infantry, is listed in April 1861 as recruiting in Vermont. The Daily Green Mountain Freeman newspaper declares, "With the faithful loyalty of a patriot and soldier, Col. Rains declares 'that he will shed the last drop of blood in defense of the flag he has fought under,' although a southerner by birth."[83]

But he apparently soon changed his mind and resigned on 31 July 1861 and joined with the Southern States. On the post returns of Albuquerque, New Mexico, of September 1861, it lists Lt. Col. Gabriel Rains as resigning his commission, and that it was accepted by the President.

Confederate Brigadier General Rains leads a division at Wilson's Creek, and participated at the bloody battles of Shiloh and Perryville. Wounded at the Battle of Seven Pines, he was subsequently placed in charge of the conscript and torpedo bureaus at Richmond. Rains' effective use of "sub-terra shells" or land mines, changed warfare. Now soldiers could be maimed or killed without the presence of the enemy soldier. General Longstreet didn't like this new technology with no opponent to face. Union General McClellan was totally outraged when he heard about his soldiers getting blown to pieces.

Where the subterra shells should be placed and how they should be used was debated in the higher Confederate command.

---

[83] The Daily Green Mountain Freeman (Montpelier, VT) April 24, 1861

Rains argued that it was no worse than the Union artillery shelling innocent civilians during the war and important against keeping the enemy line in check to slow down their advancement. The Confederate Secretary of War George Randolph took up the issue and decided that it was very important to decide the purpose of the devices. When General Robert E. Lee became commander of the Army of Northern Virginian, he told Rains to work on protecting the waterways to Richmond and help prevent the Union from taking the city.

The torpedoes were also put in use in the waters of Charleston, Savannah, and Mobile. At the Battle of Mobile Bay in August 1864, it was a Rains designed torpedo that sank the Monitor class ironclad, *USS Tecumseh*. Admiral Farragut exclaimed at Mobile Bay, "Damn the Torpedoes!" (Although there is a question if it was really said by Farragut.) Those were Rains' submerged explosive devices that Farragut faced.

As the war continued and the Confederacy started to sustain heavy losses, the use of torpedoes and exploding mines became almost routine, and moral objections grew silent. [84]

Rains' Civil War service is only covered briefly because other articles and a biography cover that time very well. I will instead highlight the Seminole War service, which led to his unusual pension or arrangement after the Civil War.

At the end of the war, Rains moved to Augusta, then Charleston, and finally to Aiken, South Carolina. He never stopped working and improving his torpedoes and exploding devices. He

---

[84] Appleton's Cyclopedia of American Biography, 1600-1889, 161. AG 1827 R24. Waters, "Deception is the Art of War: Gabriel J. Rains, Torpedo Specialist of the Confederacy", 29-60.

argued that the development of such weapons should be unrestrained so that warfare would be abolished. Making the consequences of using weapons so terrible that nations would not want to participate in war anymore. [85]

In 1876, due to poor health, Gabriel Rains sought assistance based on his injuries received in April 1840, although his condition described is probably unrelated to his wounds. This was before pensions were given for Civil War service, so he applies due to injuries in service before 1861.  As a former Confederate General, the request for any compensation is unique. He befriends U.S. General James Allen Hardie to ask for help.

(From Rains to Gen. James A, Hardie, Washington.)

> Aiken, S. C.
> Oct. 30, 1876.

*I am still without employment, and my family destitute. Three years since my wound begat to trouble me, and I had a violent attack at Charleston, S.C. last season, pronounced Neuralgia arising therefrom by an Assistant Surgeon DeWilt U.S.A.*

*I now find myself unable almost for any bodily exertion— symptoms much like 'Angina Pectoris" and think the United States ought to support me. Please do what you can for me with the Commissioner of Pensions and the enclosed.*

*I was breveted for the actions in which I was wounded. You see I avail myself of your kind offer of friendship at Charleston.* [86]

Unfortunately, General Hardie died a few weeks later on

---

[85] Waters, "Deception is the Art of War: Gabriel J. Rains, Torpedo Specialist of the Confederacy", 29-60.
[86] AG 1840 W176 / 1876 7329 Rains pension request

December 14, 1876.

In a notarized affidavit in the State of South Carolina, County of Aiken:

*Gabriel J. Rains of the said county and town of Aiken being duly sworn doth depose and say—that on the twenty-eighth day of April A.D. 1840 was near Fort King, East Florida, when a Captain of the Seventh Regiment of Infantry U.S. Army, in the legal line of his duty commanding a detachment of Regular Soldiers in a battle with Seminole Indians, he was wounded therein, shot thro' the body, &c, which he was presented with a full Surgeon's Certificate of Disability by Asst. Surgeon Samuel P. Moore, U.S. Army, but which has unavoidably been lost rendering this document necessary to establish the claims.*

*Sworn and subscribed before me at my Office in Aiken on the fourteenth day of October A.D. 1876. In testimony whereof I have set my hand and affixed my official seal.* [87]

*Siberia Ott*
*Notary Public*

*This Army pension office claims to find no records of the battle. "Muster Roll of Co. "A" 7th Infantry for March, April 1840, reports Captain G. J. Rains, "Present, sick, Wounded in a fight with the enemy April 28, 1840".— Record of Events fail to show any engagement with Indians."* [88]

This note by the pension office is unconscionable. The battle is listed in Eaton's report/casualty reports, the Army and Navy Chronicle printed Capt. Rains' report/letter in the journal, it is

---

[87] Ibid
[88] Ibid

mentioned in the Fort King Post Returns, and other newspapers and sources of the time, besides the Army Adjutant letters. The Post Return says, "3 killed in action" and "5 wounded in action." Saying there is no record of engagement with the Indians means that the pension office was not even trying to research the case. [89]

Fort King Post Returns for May 1840 has Rains, "present but sick." Returns of December 31, 1840, "absent under orders to report to a.g.o. to Genl. Armistead," No. & date of order not given. [The order is listed on the June Post Return, Special Order, Army of the South, 26 June '40.] Jan. 1841, absent, "ordered to New Orleans by General Order 92, Adjutant General Office Nov. 18, 1840." [90]

Rains' son Sevier Rains [named after his great-grandfather General John Sevier] graduated West Point in 1876. At a time when it was rare for a southerner to be at the academy, he gained admission, no doubt to his father's reputation and connections. Sevier was a popular and promising officer but lost his life in Idaho the next year during the Nez Perce war. [91]

Pensions for former Confederates did not start until after Rains' death and were given out by state, not by the federal government. Rains' military record lists him as being under employ of the Quartermaster Department from 1877 to 1881 in Charleston. That was as close to getting a pension at the time. His technical expertise and creation of the torpedo was highly

---

[89] Eaton, Joseph Horace, Lt.Col.; "Returns of Killed and Wounded in Battles or Engagements with Indians, British, and Mexican Troops, compiled 1850-1851, documenting the period 1790-1848." (Record Group 94, Microfilm M1832).
[90] AG 1840 W176 / 1876 7329 Rains pension request
[91] Heitman, "Historical Register and Dictionary of the United States Army"

regarded and became integral in the new military doctrine. It changed warfare and Rains was still contributing to the military technical manuals on torpedoes in the 1870s.[92]

Gabriel J. Rains died at Aiken, South Carolina, August 6, 1881. His wife Mary died two years later in 1883. Both are buried at St. Thaddeus Church Cemetery in Aiken. [93]

In the 1880s, the Army developed a coast defense plan called the Endicott System. It consisted of modernized gun carriages on hydraulic lifts to defend important coastal ports. Part of this system used torpedoes or mines placed in the water and operated by electric cables as a defense against enemy ships. An advanced version of Rains' torpedoes had become standard as part of coastal defense through World War II.

---

[92] Ancestry. com; "US Civil War Soldier Records and Profiles, 1861-1865". Evans, Clement A.; "Confederate Military History: A Library of Confederate States History, Vol. IV", (Atlanta, GA., 1987 reprint, Wilmington, N.C., 1899) 339-341.
[93] Evans, "Confederate Military History, Vol. IV", 339-341.

# Chapter 8: "A Feeling of Revenge"

On February 1, 1839, Captain Hannibal Day, 2d Infantry, writes to the Army Adjutant General from Fort Fanning:

(Capt. H. Day, 2d Infy. To Brig. Gen. Roger Jones, Army Adjt. General, Washington D. C.)

> *Fort Fanning, East Florida*
> *1 February 1839*
> *I have established between this [Fort Fanning] and Micanopy two stockade works, pursuant to the Orders of Brig. General Taylor, and garrisoned them by detachments of my company, together with a small detachment of Capt. J.G. Smith's company of (mounted) Florida Militia. The one, Walkasassa [Wacasassa], seventeen miles east of this and the other, Walkahooty [Wacahoota], thirty-three miles, and eight from Micanopy. These being dependencies of Fort Fanning and being uninstructed upon the subject, no separate Returns of those Posts will probably be rendered, unless otherwise instructed. 1st Lieut. Bleach of the Florida Militia commands at "Walkahooty" and 2d Lieut. Lovell 2d Infantry at the other post.* [94]

Fort Wacahoota remains active until the end of the Second Seminole War, either as a post of regular Army troops or the Florida Militia. Only the months when it was occupied by the regulars have post returns filed.

This strange name of the fort recalls the rich history of this area. Wacahootee is from the Muscogee-Seminole word meaning

---

[94] AG 1839 D46

cattle pen or corral, with the word for cow or cattle being waca, taken from the Spanish word of Vaca. It recalls past times when Native people herded cattle in the area. The Spanish established missions nearby to raise cattle for St. Augustine. The Ocala or Timucua Indians became expert herders. Seminole chiefs raised cattle descended from the Spanish stock on Paynes Prairie and Kanapaha Prairie and became exceptionally prosperous. A famous Seminole Chief who met with naturalist William Bartram during the American Revolution was known as Cowkeeper, known to have thousands of head of cattle. Seminoles have been cattlemen as long as they have had cattle.

Brigadier General Walker Keith Armistead took command of the forces in Florida in May 1840, previously commanding the 3$^{rd}$ Artillery in Florida since 1836. The Armisteads were a Virginia family of military officers, and his brother George Armistead became famous for defending Fort McHenry in Baltimore during the War of 1812. Walker's son Lewis Armistead was at West Point Military Academy but quit before completing his instructions. Lewis was still able to get a commission with the 6$^{th}$ Infantry and served as his father's aide in Florida. Lewis Armistead, known as Lew, is better known as a Confederate general who was killed at Pickett's Charge during the third day of the Battle of Gettysburg in 1863.

The previous two years of the war under General Taylor still had no end, so Armistead changed tactics. He had the Army operate year-round, including an unrelenting summer campaign to keep the Seminoles constantly on the run. Not with a wasteful thousand man army that exhausted supplies, but large 100-man sorties to always remain on the move.

The Richmond Enquirer reports:

*General Armistead has ordered a concentration of 900 men at Fort King, on the 25th of this month. They will be composed of footmen and horsemen, and operate in divisions of 100 each, independent of each other, in the enemy's country. The season for gathering grain is near at hand as well as assemblages for their Green Corn Dance, when preparation for war and a relation of their enterprises strengthen them to renewed effort in their aggressions on the whites. Should these scouts, now charged with the duty of hunting for the enemy, come upon them, we may hope for results differing at least from those which have been had for the last twelve months. If the enemy shall have dispersed into small parties, a great and valuable gain will be effected in the destruction of his planting grounds, and he will learn with trembling that, though he has sown in quiet, he shall not reap in security. General Armistead has taken hold of affairs in Florida with a vigorous hand.* [95]

On May 5th, Gen. Armistead orders the two Seminole / Miccosukee prisoners at Fort King (including the woman captured on April 15th) moved to Fort Heileman at Black Creek.[96]

On May 19th, 1840, the army suffered one of the worst ambushes of the war, only a few miles from Micanopy.

Dr. Andrew Welch includes the account in his book about his native ward, Oceola Nikkannochee, which he had clipped from a local newspaper in East Florida.

*On Wednesday, the 20th inst., while a lieutenant and two men were passing between Micanopy and a place called 'Black Point,' they were surprised, and fired on by a party of Indians; the*

---

[95] Richmond Enquirer Jun. 2, 1840
[96] AG 1840 T185

*lieutenant and one man wounded, and one killed. Same evening, Lieut. Sanderson, in command of Micanopy, while on scout with eighteen or twenty men, discovered a fire in the woods, and on going to see from whence it proceeded, was surrounded by about fifty Indians; Lieut. S. and nine men, three blood-hounds and their keeper, killed upon the spot, and four men missing. On Friday, news reached Newnansville, that three men were killed between Posts No. 11 and 12. On Thursday, a scout discovered the trail of about 100 Indians in the 'Wolf Hammock,' six miles south of Newnansville. – East Florida Advocate.* [97]

(Lt.Col. William Whistler, to Gen. R. Jones, Washington.)

*Fort Micanopy, East Florida*
*20 May 1840*
*It becomes my painful duty to announce to you the decease of 2nd Lieut. James Sanderson 7th Infantry, who was Killed in action with the enemy eight miles from this Post on the 19th Inst.—His gallantry and daring courage in the field and his energy in the performance of his military duties renders his death a subject of deep regret to his brother officers.* [98]

The news is copied in several newspapers:

*It is reported that Lieut. Martin, of the 2d Infantry, with three men, were fired upon by Indians between Micanopy and 'Wakerhootee'. Lieut. Martin received three balls; one of his men and all of his horses were killed; the other two men are missing. Lieut. Sanderson and seventeen men went in pursuit. They fell in*

---

[97] Welch, Andrew; *"A Narrative of the Early Days and Remembrances of Oceola Nikkannochee, Prince of Econchatti, Written by his Guardian"* (Facsimile Reproductions of the 1841 edition, and the pamphlets of 1837 and 1847, 203; the University Presses of Florida, Gainesville, 1977) 203.
[98] AG 1840 S182

*with the Indians and himself and five of his men were killed. They were found on the field; three of his men are missing, supposed to be dead in the hammock. Lt. Sanderson had his fingers cut off and was stuck in his mouth. Col. Riley, with about 150 men, who were on their way to Fort King, had gone in pursuit.* [99]

The place where Lt. Martin was ambushed is known afterward as Martin's Point. Some of the newspapers identified the location as "Black Point." What could be considered the first official battle of the war happened at "Black Point" on December 18, 1835, when a supply train escorted by Florida Militia soldiers were ambushed. Col. John Warren's report of the Battle of Black Point identifies the location as Kanapaha Prairie, directly northwest of the area believed to be Martin's Point. Kanapaha Prairie was not the same place as the lower road that Martin would have traveled going between Fort Micanopy and Fort Wachahoota. [100] [101] [102]

Despite using the descriptions of these battles and trying to pinpoint them on Lt. George Thomas' map of Square 7, there is no place on the map labeled Black Point, and there are several places where it could have been.

What we know from these newspaper accounts, is that Lieut. Martin, 2d Infantry, left Micanopy to join his company at Fort "Waka-hoo-tee" when he was met en route by three men from his post. About four miles from Micanopy, when they were fired

---

[99] The Mississippi Free Trader, Jun. 10, 1840. The Times-Picayune, Jun. 6, 1840. Richmond Enquirer Jun. 2, 1840. The American Citizen, Jun. 20, 1840.
[100] Richmond Enquirer Jun. 5, 1840. Southern Banner, June 26, 1840.
[101] "Jacksonville and the Seminole War, 1835-1836, Part II"; *Florida Historical Quarterly*, Vol. III, Num. 4 (April 1925), 15-16.
[102] Boyd, Mark; 1951, "The Seminole War: Its Background and Onset"; Florida Historical Quarterly, Vol. XXX, Num. 1 (July 1951), 57.

upon by about forty Indians.

Lieut. Martin was wounded in three places and his horse disabled. He dismounted, saw that one man was dead, and the other two being pursued by Indians. Martin made it back to the garrison at Micanopy. Lieut. Sanderson takes 18 men in pursuit, following the trail of the attackers.

Lt. Sanderson entered a hammock and found a steer killed and dressed. He continued his advance when 35 or 40 concealed Indians fired in ambush. Three soldiers were killed at once, and a couple wounded. Sanderson was forced back and overwhelmed by the warriors. He was killed, with two other men and the Spanish dog keeper. The rest of the command was "scattered and confused." One man was never found and presumed dead. Sanderson's fingers were cut off and stuck in his mouth. [103]

*Lieut. Sanderson died cheering his gallant little band to sustain the well-earned fame of the "7th Infantry", but his feeble voice was lost amid the deafening yells of the savage triumph from all parts of the hammock. He was a gallant officer, and in his last moments nobly sustained the character of the 7th Regiment of Infantry.*

*Col. Riley's command arrived at Micanopy and went in pursuit. The bodies were found at the scene of the action, and brought back to the garrison, and there consigned to their final resting places.*

*Lt. Martin will recover.* [104]

Eaton's Casualty list identifies the location as Levy Prairie /

---

[103] The Mississippi Free Trader, Jun. 10, 1840. The Times-Picayune, Jun. 6, 1840. Richmond Enquirer Jun. 2, 1840. The American Citizen, Jun. 20, 1840.
[104] Weekly Arkansas Gazette, July 1, 1840.

Levy Lake. The accuracy of Eaton's list should be good since the information was compiled ten years after the battle when there were still witnesses alive who could verify the details. But as we shall see, not all accounts agree with the reports filed. [105]

This was a disaster that shocked the garrison from the loss of a good officer and several men who were ambushed and mutilated. Lt. Sanderson ran right into the trap. He died fighting and became a martyr for the regiment. The attackers got away leaving no trail, and pursuit revealed nothing.

The casualty roster has the following deaths for the 2d Infantry: [106]

- Sergt. Philo C. Griggs, Co. K, May 19, 1840. Died between Micanopy and Wacahoota. Killed or taken prisoner by Indians.
- Privt. Calvin Hotchkiss, Co. K, May 19, 1840. Died between Micanopy and Wacahoota. Killed or taken prisoner by Indians.
- Privt. Patrick Jeffers, Co. K, May 19, 1840. Died between Micanopy and Wacahoota. Killed or taken prisoner by Indians.

The casualties in the 7th Infantry: [107]

- 2d Lieut. James S. Sanderson, Co. C, May 19, 1840. Killed by Indians near Micanopy.
- Pvt. Owen Cowley, Co., F, Died Jan. 5, 1841 at Micanopy of wounds received near Micanopy May 19, 1840.

---

[105] Eaton, J. H., Lt.Col.; "Returns of Killed and Wounded in Battles or Engagements with Indians, British, and Mexican Troops, compiled 1850-1851.
[106] Sprague, *The Origin, Progress, and Conclusion of the Florida War*. Brown, *Ponce de Leon Land and Florida War Record*.
[107] Ibid

- Pvt. William Foss, Co. H, May 19, 1840, killed near Micanopy.
- Pvt. Patrick Keefe, Co. I, May 19, 1840, killed near Micanopy.
- Pvt. Abraham Maxwell, Co. I, May 19, 1840, died near Micanopy.
- Principal Musician Patrick O'Riley, May 19, 1840, killed near Micanopy by the side of Lt. Sanderson.
- Musician Samuel Okey, Co. I, May 19, 1840, killed near Micanopy.

(Col. D.E. Twiggs to Brig. Gen. Armistead)

*Fort King, East Florida*
*22 May 1840*

*I arrived here yesterday at one P.M. and was then informed that an attack two days previous has been made on a party of 2nd Infantry under command of Lt. [John W.] Martin near Micanopy which nearly proved fatal to him. Colonel Whistler as he informs me by the letter, I yesterday enclosed you, immediately sent Lieut. [James S.] Sanderson and a detachment 7th Infantry to the scene of action, when the Indians appeared in full force, numbering at least sixty.—*

*Colonel Whistler's letter being written in a hurry, no detailed report has as yet reached me, but from the information already received, Lieut. Sanderson, One principal Musician and four Privates have been killed, & three wounded.-- Anxious to intercept the Indians should they attempt a retreat in the direction of the Withlacoochee as the most probable course they would take.*

*I immediately directed Capt. Ker, Lt. Hunter and 71 Dragoons from Ft. H[eileman]. Troops to proceed in the direction of Wacahoota and cooperate with Lt. Col. Riley's command of 2nd*

Infantry, and Capt. Beall's troops of Dragoons.-- Captain Bonneville with Lieut. Judd, fifty Artillery [soldiers], Lieut. Scott and 67 Seventh Infantry [soldiers], I directed to shape his course as circumstances most demanded, and if at the end of four days he did not come up with the enemy, to return to this post.

Lieut. W. K. Hanson 7th Infantry and two details from the 2nd & 7th Infantry received instructions to proceed in the direction of [Fort] No.2, when in case of the presence of the Indians in that quarter, a force would be available to obstruct their progress.-- Lt. Asheton and 60 Dragoons are now awaiting the arrival of the guide and Interpreter to proceed South towards the O-kee-hump-ky where there is every reason to believe a large party of the enemy are concealed in going down the east side of Withlacoochee can be examined and the country lying between it and the Pannee-sufekee. The number of troops now here are so limited from the large drafts made of the details, it will be necessary to await intelligence from the Officers now out before any further movements can be put in operation.

Bvt. Major Wilcox and Lieut. Wessells left this morning with orders to report to Colonel Whistler and aid in following if the trails which the large force recently engaged with Lt. Sanderson would lead us to conclude must be in the vicinity of Micanopy. 108

Lt. Col. Bennett Riley reports the horrible details. This was a well-planned ambush by the Miccosukees, later found to be led by Halleck Tustenuggee. Lt.Col. Riley finds lost soldiers who are traumatized, and reaches the field two days after the battle.

(Lt. Col. B. Riley, 2d Infy., to Col. D.E. Twiggs, Commanding

---

108 AG 1840 T199

Eastern District.)

12 June 1840.

*I received an order from Lt Col Whistler at Micanopy, at half-past 10 o'clock p.m. to proceed immediately to succor Lt. Sanderson & party of 17 men of the 7th Infantry, who were reported by a man that had escaped from the party & had just come in to that post, as having had an engagement with a large body of Indians. Leaving about 25 men of the command who were unable to march from sickness & previous fatigue at that place, I put the remainder in motion without delay, being joined by Lt. [Richard] Gatlin & 23 men of the 7th & proceeded as near as I could judge in the proper direction. About 5 miles from Micanopy, I came upon a man who had escaped from Lt Sanderson's party, from whom I could learn nothing whatever. Continuing my route to Fort Walker (12 miles from Micanopy) where I arrived at quarter before 4 o'clock a.m. on the 20th, I found that Lt. Sanderson & party had been there late the day before. Having no other alternative, I remained there until daylight & then took Lt. Sanderson's trail from that place, which led me after a march of 2 or 3 hours to the north point of Levy's Prairie (8 miles from Micanopy) where I found the bodies of Lt Sanderson & 5 of his party lying dead upon the ground—one of his party came out of the Hammock to the command as soon as it entered the Prairie, & by sounding a bugle after reaching the point where the action took place, another made his appearance.* [109]

[If we look at this report compared to the Section 7 map by Lt. Thomas, these directions and distances from Fort Walker on Kanapaha Prairie, put this battle far away from Levy Lake/Levy Prairie. Closer to Hogtown Prairie or on the north side of Alachua

---

[109] AG 1840 A124

Prairie. Perhaps Riley confused the names of the different prairies?]

*Having examined the spot & found that the Indians (from 80 to 100 strong) had escaped in the direction of the Wacasassa, I concluded to collect the dead bodies & return to Micanopy for further orders; my command having marched 50 miles in 30 consecutive hours & being without provisions. The remainder of Lt. Sanderson's party escaped with the exception of one man.*

*On the 21st Instant, in consequence of a report that the Indians were in numbers around Wacahootee, I was ordered by Col. W[histler] to repair to that spot. Receiving the order late in the day, I reached Wacahootee that evening, scouted in its vicinity on the 22nd Inst & discovered the signs of but 5 Indians—whom I could not trail any distance.*

*Capt. Beall having reported to me with his company of Dragoons on the evening of the 21st, I dispatched him early on the morning of the 22nd in pursuit of a large party of Indians, who fired upon & killed an express rider the day before, near Fort Wacasassa--& hearing that Capt. Ker would report at Wacahootee on the 22nd, I left an order there for him to pursue Capt. Beall's trail & join his command.*

*Finding no further signs of Indians during my scout, I returned to Micanopy for provisions when Lt Col Whistler left me at liberty to proceed to this place in obedience to my original order from your Head Quarters.* [110]

(2d Lt. Asheton, Adjutant, 2d Dragoons, to Col. D. E. Twiggs at

---

[110] Ibid

Fort King.)

*Fort King*
*27th May 1840*
*Agreeably to written orders from the Commanding General*
*and your verbal instruction, I left this on the evening of the 22nd. I*
*was with sixty Dragoons and proceeded on a Southwest course to*
*the Ouithlacoochee* [Withlacoochee River—the often used French
spelling] *which I reached early the second day.*

*During this course I was particular in looking out for fresh trails*
*leading from the late scene of action where Lt. Sanderson was*
*killed and feel confident up to the time of my reaching the river, no*
*body of Indians had gone South. The river running from the*
*Pannee Sufkee was there crossed and a circuit of the Lake shore*
*and Hammock to its Northeastern point made without seeing*
*more than a single fresh trial, and that but a few yards on the*
*road--the Indian it would appear was hunting.*

*My third days' march was directed towards Pi-lak-li-ka-ha*
*which I left a little to the South and taking a northeastern course*
*entered the Hammocks of the O-Kee-hump-Kee four miles west of*
*the northern end of Lake Eustis. The extensive fields in this*
*hammock I found uncultivated and no appearance whatever of*
*having been visited by the Indians for months. The trail having in*
*many places been closed by this summer's growth.*

*During my fourth days' march I visited a hammock on the*
*Southwestern shore of Lake Eustis where more than five acres*
*were found under corn & vines. It appears my approach was*
*discovered as some of the corn had but just been hoed. Two hoes*
*were lying on the ground and fresh tracks of one man & woman*
*seen through it. A fresh mark where a canoe had pushed off was*

seen on the shore, and Billy the Indian Guide informed me that there was an Island at some distance which he was persuaded must be the retreat of the Indians round that country. Pursuant to a standing order, the corn was cut down and the vines pulled up. I reached the Northern end of Lake A-ha-pop-Ka at 8 O'clock p.m. and encamped. Having first dismounted two parties, one of whom crossed the Ocklawaha about half a mile below the usual trail in hopes of cutting off any party who might have encamped. Unfortunately, I was unsuccessful in finding any, as I had expected.

I returned to this post on the fifth day, having passed the eastern shore of Lakes Eustis, Griffin and Ware, crossing the Ocklawaha about 20 miles from this post.

During the entire route, I could perceive but two decided signs of the Indians; the first on the edges of a large prairie where "Tom" the Indian Prisoner, informed me the women had a small field. I had then marched five hours without water, and to effect anything, Billy said it would be necessary to halt my party and wait till dark.

Then half past 2 p.m. when I should march on foot and surround the camp, no water being than ten miles, and a snake suddenly springing up. I was aware my approach had been discovered and that further progress in that direction where so much injury would result to the horses without the most distant chance of success. The second evidence of Indians, a trail of two horses crossing the Ock-la-wa-ha near A-ha-pop-Ka; it was followed about twelve miles until night set in on the 25. On the morning of the 26, the trail was again taken up and followed for five miles where it was found leading in an Easterly course. The party having more than twelve hours start, and having exceeded

*by one day and time for which I had drawn supplies, the distance
to this post being thirty miles, I was reluctantly compelled to give
up any further pursuit.* [111]

Major Wilcox with 170 Infantry soldiers makes an eight miles'
radius to the west and north of Fort Micanopy in five days, only
finding signs of one trail but no warriors. At the slow pace he was
scouting, he was in no danger of capturing any. [112]

(Brig. Gen. W. Armistead to Gen. R. Jones, Washington.)

*Fort King*
*May 28th, 1840.*

*The movements of the Indians in such large bodies shows a
concentration of force simultaneous with my own and
independent of it. It was most fortunate for the settlement that
the troops were at the same time moving to Fort King, as I am
confident that the intentions of the enemy were to destroy the
settlers in the neighborhood of Newnansville. Happily, Col. Twiggs
Commanding the Eastern district had but just arrived when the
news of the affair at Micanopy reached him, he immediately
dispatched Lt. Col. Riley—Major Wilcox—Capt. Beall & Ker in
different directions in pursuit of the enemy. The reports of these
officers show that every effort was made to overtake them but
without success, owing no doubt to the breaking up of the Indians
in small parties from five to fifteen.* [113]

*The affair on the Picolata road was no doubt headed by
Wildcat, who in revenge for the discovery of his retreat at the
Wekiva has long meditated an act so similar to all his*

---

[111] Ibid
[112] Ibid
[113] Ibid

85

*depredations on that road.*

*The Indians, no doubt in all these plans, have been actuated by a feeling of revenge for the destruction of their fields which they have been permitted to plant in all directions South of Fort King. Their planting showed their belief in their perfect security, & when this was invaded—their concentration before and since the attack upon Capt. Rains carried with it the means of effecting everything they wished. By movements now they must disband, as I have, and am, now constantly sending out large bodies of men, to penetrate their fastnesses, which will soon recall them to the protection of their wives and children.* [114]

Four days after Lt. Sanderson was killed, Miccosukee warriors under Coacoochee/Wildcat attacked a theatrical troupe in two wagons on the Picolata Road, west of St. Augustine. Reported in the Richmond Enquirer, June 2, 1840.

*Sunday forenoon, between 9 and 10 o'clock, Mr. Forbes' Theatrical Company, with some others, were on their way from Picolata to St. Augustine, and when within 5 or 6 miles of the latter place, (the party occupying two wagons,) the wagon in the rear was attacked by a party of Indians, and Mr. C. Vose killed. Two others are missing, supposed to be a part of Mr. Forbes' company. Mr. Forbes it seems, was in the front wagon with the ladies of the party, who escaped, and reached St. Augustine in safety. It is supposed that the Indians conceived the wagons to be a military escort. We congratulate the estimable Mr. Forbes on his escape. Mr. Vose was formerly of Jersey City, (N.J.) and for the two or three years of Brunswick, Glynn County [Georgia].* [115]

---

[114] Ibid
[115] Richmond Enquirer Jun. 2, 1840

(Maj. S. Churchill to Gen. W.K. Armistead at Fort King.)

*Picolata*
*May 23, 1840.*

*This morning at about 10 and 11 O'clock, as a small carriage & wagon, with citizens, were going, hence to St. Augustine, they were attacked, by about 15 Indians, a mile this side of the 6-mile post (Fort Baker) and three men killed. And soon after a wagon, coming from St. Augustine was attacked a mile beyond this post, probably by the same Indians, and two men, citizens killed. I had come from St. Augustine this morning, with an escort of three men, met my van mess with a small escort about midway on the road, and neither of us saw any Indians or signs. A report was made here at half-past 12 of the attack this side, and Lieut. Ord, who was here, started off with four men mounted; and I learn he met a party from St. Augustine on arriving at the spot.*

*A negro man escaped from the wagon on the other side of the post, and ran back to town, gave the alarm, and 75 or 100 people came out directly. And I learn by a person who came here since, that two parties of 15 men each, went north of the road and other parties south in pursuit. Expresses were sent from St. Augustine to all the posts south. Here I have but nine men, and there are less at each post on the St. Augustine Road, excepting Fort Seale. Not enough at either to examine the country for more than 2 or 3 miles around the posts.*

*Should any militia be mustered into service west of the St. Johns, will it not be advisable for them to come to Black Creek for this purpose?—As there, they can be armed at once, and supplied with provisions &c, to proceed to any place where they may be wanted.* [116]

Earlier in the month, General Armistead issued orders to raise 500 militia soldiers on the west side of the St. Johns River. No one answered the call to duty. The majority of the residents in that area had all fled to either St. Augustine, Black Creek, or Newnansville.

Wildcat or Coacoochee, the famous Miccosukee warrior who raided along the St. Johns River and east coast the past five years, found a treasure trove of costumes in the actor's luggage. They would wear them in glorious array at a talk the following March at Fort Cummings with General Armistead. [117]

After the attack on the Picolata road, Coacoochee and his warriors surrounded nearby Fort Searle, wearing the costumes, dancing around and trying to entice the soldiers to come out of the fort—most likely into an ambush. The garrison having such a small number present, wisely stayed inside.

Coacoochee decided to have a victory party at the Jenckes plantation, one of the wealthiest around. Mr. Edwin T. Jenckes and his son barricade themselves in the plantation house, while Wildcat and his warriors enjoy a tremendous feast cooked by the plantation slaves.

(Lt. Col. William Gates, 3d Artillery, to Col. D.E. Twiggs and Brig. Gen. W.K. Armistead.)

*St. Augustine*
*May 28, 1840*

---

[116] AG 1840 A124

[117] Sprague, *The Origin, Progress, and Conclusion of the Florida War*, 259. Mahon, *History of the Second Seminole War, 1835-1842*, 286. AG 1841 A66.

*I have the honor of informing you that on the morning of the 26 Inst. at 6 O'clock, a negro man came to me from the plantation of Mr. Jenckes, situated at the head of the North River, 25 miles by land and 21 by water from this place, and informed me that his masters house was surrounded by Indians, where upon I called for Volunteers, and obtained 20 citizens, and taking 7 mounted regulars, we proceeded on the road. We had not gone more than 12 miles before we saw many tracks leading onward. These we followed up to the very house of Mr. Jenckes at which we arrived at 10 O'clock.*

*We found that Mr. Jenckes had entrenched himself and manfully stood ready for defense with his overseer and his son. We learned from the Blacks that Wild Cat had arrived there at 8 O'clock on the night before, that he had collected all the Blacks, made the Cooks get supper for him and his party, and that he remained there until 6 o'clock the next morning. He did not approach the dwelling so as to allow Mr. Jenckes to get a shot at him or his warriors. After obliging the Indians to bring forward their Blankets &c, and eating plentifully of the Fowls and Hominy, they all decamped, taking only a few of the negroes with them. While the party were at supper, the Cooks said they counted 30 warriors. They said they did not wish to hurt the Blacks. They only wanted the White man and plunder, 'That they saw the mailman but they did not hurt him. They had killed 2 before and got nothing but a bundle of papers.' They would not fire the House as they wanted the [gun]powder that was in it.*

*They said they had got much plunder on the Picolata road where they killed the four men there, on the 23 inst. [The actor troupe.] Wild Cat while at supper had on the Turban of "Othello" taken from the Player's trunks that were in the wagons which they*

89

captured. He said that he would not take 100 Head of cattle for the dress of Othello; black velvet richly trimmed. Thus, we see they were bold and much at their ease having been round us for 2 or 3 days before examining all our positions, and learning our force as far as practicable.

After learning all we could as to their intended route from Mr. Jenckes, I mustered 29 Persons and followed on the trail for 20 miles south—for 15 miles the trail was large and plain consisting of two horses & one mule and many warriors; after that distance we lost the foot tracks. Although we had the very best trailers with us—but we kept on after the Horse tracks—believing that we should find all together further on—we however failed. Our course was taken as far as the 12-Mile Swamp up to which we went and there we could go no further with our Horses. The Guides and others were there dismounted, and the trail followed for nearly 2 miles, when all of the trailing partly returned to their horses. They reported that it was too difficult and dangerous for the Horses to pass into—and they declared themselves too much exhausted to proceed any further that day; it being Eleven O'clock P.M.

The rain had set in 4 hours before and still continued so that every man was discouraged from further pursuit. When I ordered my adjutant to lead a party of 7 men back to the city at which we arrived on the 12 hour of our scout having gone over 55 miles, as assured by our guides. On the next morning I was resolved to go out again. Lt. Ridgely and myself with our double-barrel guns proceeded alone, for we could not obtain a man fit for duty. My little force raised at Fort Peyton & Hanson being still out consisting of 7 men. We went to the Six Mile Station on the Picolata road and there obtained 6 men. With these we went on to examine where it was said 10 or more Tracks were seen in the road at 5 O'clock on *the night before, leading south but the rain had effaced every trace made therein, on that night.*

*I am not sure but am much inclined to believe that as the Indians had their packs loaded with plunder of 18 trunks of Theatrical Dresses &c blankets &c., that they are satisfied for the present, and that they have gone south. Lt. [William] Hardee was active in search of the enemy on the 24th with 8 or 10 Dragoons— when the second alarm was given. He was brought into town yesterday on a sick bed—but his men have returned to their post. The order for the raising of a Company of Mounted men for the defense of this city will be complied with as promptly as possible and a report sent to you accordingly.* [118]

The warriors easily escaped while exhausting their pursuers. The soldiers in the surrounding posts were already undermanned and worn out from an unproductive pursuit into the swamp. Lt. Hardee's post of Fort Fulton at Hewitt's mill, south of town, was abandoned at the end of June. Fort Peyton would also be abandoned a week later.[119]

Captain Ben Bonneville, 7th Infantry, writes of his scout from Fort Micanopy to the Ocklawaha River, where they find plunder from Capt. Rains and Lt. Sanderson. The soldiers fail to surprise the village, but capture one girl and torch the village the next morning.

(Capt. B. Bonneville to Lieut. R. Asheton, Adjutant, 2d Dragoons.)

*Fort King*
*May 30th, 1840*

---

[118] AG 1840 A132
[119] Post Returns, Fort Fulton, Fort Peyton, St. Augustine.

*I have the honor to report that on the 27th Instant, I left this Post with a Detachment of the 7th Infantry consisting of Captains Hawkins & Holmes and Lieutenants W.K. Hanson & Scott and 155 Non-commissioned Officers & Privates, and proceeding to the West and South reached at dusk on the 28th the Bend upon the Ocklawaha in which my guide informed me was located the Band of the Little Potato Seminole Chief.* [This makes no sense because the Ocklawaha river is east of Fort Micanopy and Fort King, not west.] *Approaching cautiously on that evening with the desire of surrounding them so as to seize the whole band we got to within 3 or 400 yards from their fires before we were discovered. We failed in the complete surprise. We however captured one female child. It being dark, we lay down in the Indian camp all night. Next morning, I sent 100 men to cut down the corn fields while the balance of the command was engaged in burning huts, sheds, and every species of property that was to be found. here we recognized several articles of clothing, guns, knives &c taken from Captain Rains & Lieut. Sanderson's command. Captains Hawkins & Holmes upon returning from the fields, believe there were from 160 to 200 acres of corn, melons, pumpkins &c, which they completely destroyed. The village from what I saw myself might contain from 16 to 20 warriors with their families. I then returned to this Post.* [120]

Captain Benjamin Beall of the 2d Dragoons follows Indian trails on May 30th around Orange Lake. Due to the softness of the ground, the men are forced to dismount and follow on foot. The trail diminishes, and the constant rain erased anything left to track, but appears to go towards the Ocklawaha River.[121]

---

[120] AG 1840 A133. Richmond Enquirer Jun. 19, 1840.
[121] AG 1840 A130 Enclosure

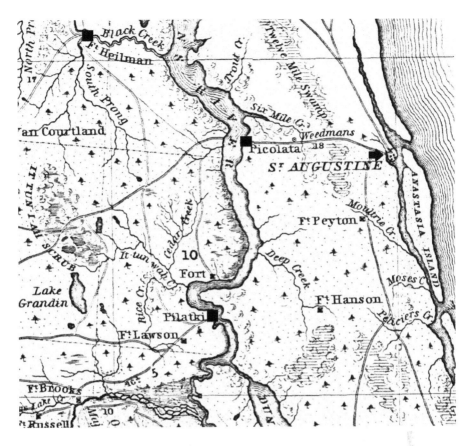

A close-up of the MacKay Blake map around the St. Johns River. In the upper left is Fort Heileman at Black Creek, also known as Garey's Ferry. Below on the St. Johns is Picolata, and road that heads east from there to St. Augustine. Further south on the river is Pilatki or Palatka, the home of the Quartermaster Depot. [122]

[122] MacKay, John (Capt.), and J.E. Blake (Lt.); *Map of the Seat of War in Florida, Compiled by Order of Brevet Brig. Genl. Z[achary] Taylor*, 1839. By Capt. John MacKay and 1st Lt. Jacob Edmund Blake, Topographical Engineers (formerly 6th Infantry). National Archives. Copy in the State Library of Florida.

# Chapter 9: Lieutenants Martin and Sanderson

Lt. John W. Martin receives unfavorable news about his request for leave of absence to spend time recovering from his wounds sustained on May 19th. He is lucky to be alive; Lt. Sanderson rode out to catch his attackers and was brutally dismembered by the same Miccosukee warriors. It is unknown if the attackers recognized Martin from his participation in taking their horses and burning their fields the month before. Most likely not, that he just presented a good target for an ambush.

(From Gen. Armistead's Asst. Adjutant W. Irving Newton to Lt. J. W. Martin, 2d Infantry, at Fort Micanopy.)

*Fort King*
*June 10th, 1840*
*Your communication of the 4th inst. accompanied by a Surgeons Certificate of ill health has been received. I am directed to inform you that the scarcity of Officers in Florida, will not permit the granting of your request at this time. Though you may be incapable of doing duty in the field, the General hopes that your health will soon permit you to perform some light duty at your post.* [123]

Finally, Lt. Martin is granted leave and departs in July to go up north. Because he left in haste to get his ride and transport his baggage, he carries with him several hundred dollars owed to his soldiers at Fort Russell. Lt. Martin has a bank in Washington send a check to Lt. Alburtis, commanding Fort Russell since his absence. He is unable to write a check from a Baltimore bank because,

---

[123] AG 1840 A175, 13

*"Baltimore money is at a considerable discount in the south."*
Several months pass before the money is returned to the soldiers,
and one had already been discharged from the army and is
working at the quartermaster depot in Palatka.[124]

Martin has an interesting but short military career where he
starts as an infantry officer who receives his commission outside
of the military academy, to a dragoon officer in the Mexican War.

In July 1839, John W. Martin was appointed 2nd Lieutenant in
the 2d Infantry Regiment, receiving notice from the Secretary of
War and returned his acceptance and oath certificate to the Army
Adjutant General.[125]

Since Martin is not a West Point graduate, there is very little
information found on him. Did he have other prior military
experience or training? There is some information in Heitman's
Register:

*John W. Martin, born in Virginia and appointed from Virginia
as 2d LT, 2d Infantry, 1 July 1839; Resigned 23 Nov. 1846.
Appointed as 2d Lieut., 3d Dragoons, 21 July 1847. Breveted 1st
Lieutenant, 19 October 1847 for gallantry and meritorious conduct
in the affair at Atlixco, Mexico. Died 18 June 1848.[126]*

Martin's commission states his home state of Virginia, and
correspondence in the adjutant letters and oath is notarized in
Washington, so he is in Washington before his commission is
issued. Since he petitioned the Secretary of War for a commission
and received it, we can assume that he came from a prominent

---

[124] AG 1840 M353, R229
[125] AG 1839 M224
[126] Heitman, "Historical Register and Dictionary of the United States Army".

and politically well-connected family.

John Martin resigned from his commission in 1846. Eight months later, he volunteered and was commissioned a Second Lieutenant in the 3d Regiment of Dragoons, a regiment that was created specifically for the Mexican War and disbanded once the war was over. When General Winfield Scott took Mexico City, the dragoons were given the task hunting down any surviving resistance. An anti-guerrilla brigade commanded by General Joseph Lane is organized, where Martin is part of the dragoon squadron attached to it.[127]

Martin is commended for his action at "the Affair at Atlixco" on 18 October 1847. This was an intense, grueling, and bloody battle where the US Dragoons dismounted and hacked the Mexican soldiers with their sabers, while the Artillery opened up on the town where the Mexican force was entrenched and pounded it to rubble. The U.S. reports count the casualties for the Mexicans at 219 killed and over 300 wounded, possibly much higher. Incredibly contrasted by US casualties as one dragoon killed, two wounded, and one missing who deserted.[128]

Martin proved unpopular among the men and got into an argument with a Louisiana Cavalry officer. They met for a duel the next morning, with their dragoon sabers as the weapon of choice. Whoever drew first blood would win. Martin's hand was cut while blocking a thrust, and the contest was over with the other officer

---

[127] Brackett, Albert G.; *General Lane's Brigade in Central Mexico* (H.W. Derby & Company, Cincinnati; 1854).

[128] Brackett, *General Lane's Brigade in Central Mexico*. Smith, Isaac; *Reminiscences of a Campaign in Mexico: An Account of the Operations of the Indiana Brigade on the Line of the Rio Grande and Sierra Madre, and a Vindication of the Volunteers, Against the Aspersions of Officials and Unofficials* (Chapmans and Spann, Indianapolis, 1848).

declared the winner. Martin returned to Mexico City, and three months later died at the "National Bridge near Vera Cruz." [129]

If Martin was a forgettable character who never achieved anything noteworthy in his military career, it is contrasted by James Sanderson. Sanderson was an officer with great potential.

The 1824 enlistment record of James Sanderson shows his birth about 1799 in Boston and profession as a clothier. Grey eyes, black hair, and a dark complexion. He enlisted in the 7th Infantry Regiment, and reenlisted at Fort Gibson in 1829, 1834, and again in 1837. His fourth enlistment and previous three at Fort Gibson is extremely rare. He is promoted to the top of the enlistment ranks to Sergeant Major.

Sergeant Major James S. Sanderson so impresses his superiors that he is recommended for appointment as a commissioned officer. On October 20, 1837, a letter of recommendation was sent to Secretary of War Joel Poinsett from Fort Gibson, signed by every officer in the Seventh Infantry Regiment in the Indian Territory, where the Seventh is stationed (Arkansas and Oklahoma.) There are signatures of 15 officers, from the Regimental Commanding General Matthew Arbuckle on down. Sanderson proved to be an outstanding soldier.

The appointment recommendation from General Arbuckle:

> *Fort Gibson [Indian Territory]*
> *20th Oct. 1837*
> *As the vacancies in the Army are more numerous than the annual promotion of Cadets from the Military Academy, the subscribing Officers of the 7th Regiment of Infantry beg him most*

---

[129] Brackett, *General Lane's Brigade in Central Mexico.*

*respectfully to recommend to the President that the appointment of 2ⁿᵈ Lieutenant be conferred on Sergeant Major James S. Sanderson of the 7ᵗʰ Infantry.*

*While a boy, the subject of this recommendation served as a Sergeant at Chippeway & Bridgewater, in each of which battles he was wounded. But having joined the Army in opposition to the wishes of his Parents he was immediately afterwards discharged on their application to the then Secretary of War.*

[These are among the bloodiest battles for the Americans during the War of 1812, and he is a 15-year-old sergeant who is wounded twice!]

*Our acquaintance with the Character and conduct of Sergeant Sanderson began in 1826 when he joined our Regiment, since which time he has always filled, and has universally been considered eminently qualified from the highest and most confidential officers to which Enlisted men may aspire. His manners, education, and habits are such as to qualify him in every respect for the associations and duties consequent on the appointment to which we recommend him, and it is our sincere belief that the interest of the service will be materially benefitted by the promotion of this excellent man.* [130]

The Secretary of War responds immediately. This is when mail takes about one month to get from Fort Gibson to Washington.

[Written on the cover of the recommendation by Secretary Joel Poinsett, Nov. 25, 1837.]

*The Secretary thinks that the good of the Service may be*

---

[130] AG 1841 G46

*promoted by advancing such men as the one herein described to the rank of a Commissioned Officer, and will not therefore object to this case if the Commanding General thinks proper to recommend it.* [131]

In April 1838, James S. Sanderson accepts his appointment as 2nd Lieutenant, 7th Regiment of Infantry, and mails his Oath certificate from Fort Smith, Arkansas to the Army Adjutant General, Brig. Gen. Roger Jones. He receives his commission at Fort Coffee (eastern Oklahoma) on 1st May 1838. [132]

While in Florida in 1840, Lieut. James S. Sanderson received approval by the President of the United States for commission as an Assistance Commissary of Subsistence and returned his Acceptance letter on May 12th. Even though he is a 2d Lieutenant, he is 41 years old at a time when the retirement age was considered to be 45. Subsistence is a desirable job away from combat. All that remains are for the orders to be issued for the position from Washington. He would move to an Army depot, probably Palatka. Unfortunately, he will never enjoy that position as he will be killed by Miccosukee warriors one week later. [133]

The casualty report has this to say about him:

*For wounds received at Bridgewater* [during the War of 1812], *and subsequent zeal and efficiency in all the non-commissioned grades, he was recommended by the officers of his regiment, and appointed 2d Lieutenant on the 1st of March, 1838. With thirteen men he attacked forty or fifty Indians, and was killed at the head*

---

[131] Ibid
[132] AG 1838 S160, S170, S208
[133] AG 1840 S193

*of the party.* [134]

Sadly, nine months after Lt. Sanderson's death, his family has not claimed his possessions at Fort Micanopy.

(Lieut. R.C. Gatlin, Adjutant 7th Infantry, to Gen. R. Jones, Adjutant General, U.S. Army.)

*Fort Micanopy*
*February 1st, 1841*
*I have the honor to inform you that the effects of the late Lieut. James Sanderson are still in my possession, not having been called for by his relatives. As the regulations do not direct any other disposition, then that of retaining them for the relatives of the deceased and as there appears to be no probability of their calling for them—more than nine months having elapsed since his death—I beg to be informed what disposition I am to make of them.* [135]

Two months after Sanderson's death, the Seventh Infantry names a fort after him.

From the Fort Sanderson post returns, it says, "On the 12 July 1840 a position was assigned to Company "D", 7th Infantry, near Garey's Ferry, East Florida, order of Col. D.E. Twiggs, 2d Dragoons, commanding the Eastern District of Florida, and the post so established has been called Fort Sanderson." 33 soldiers are present for duty, commanded by 2d Lt. Charles H. Hanson, 7th Infantry.

Post returns are filed from July 1840 to January 1841. Recruits

---

[134] Sprague, *The Origin, Progress, and Conclusion of the Florida War*. Brown, *Ponce de Leon Land and Florida War Record*.
[135] AG 1841 G46

added to the regiment brought the number soldiers at the post to 72 on the last return. Over seven months, seven deaths are recorded; all listed as, "ordinary."[136]

Fort Sanderson was abandoned on 1 February 1841.

---

[136] Fort Sanderson Post Returns; FortWiki . com

# Chapter 10: "Possessed of Much Intelligence"

General Armistead is trying to end the war through generous terms offered to the Indians.

(Adjutant W. Newton to the Commanding officers at Fort Pierce, Lauderdale, and Key Biscayne, from June Correspondence of Gen. Armistead.)

*Fort King*
*June 2nd, 1840*
*The Commanding General has received information that Sam Jones and his band have not been engaged for the last five or six months in any expedition against the whites; but on the contrary, that he has attempted to restrain his people from attacking them, in consequence of which, you are directed to raise the White Flag at your Posts, and should "Sam Jones" or any messenger from him come in, he will be treated with kindness, & informed that if he (Sam Jones) will come in and make a treaty with us in good faith, he will be permitted with his relations and family to live in the country, and a tract of land be given to hunt on & cultivate.*

*If no person can be found to carry a flag to Sam Jones (and every endeavor is to be made by you to procure someone to do so)—White flags will be placed in such conspicuous situations, as will attract the attention of himself or some of his party. The flag being once raised at your Post, no hostile demonstration will be made on your part unless the Indians are found to be inimical.*

*Great care will be taken in carrying out these instruction, to guard against surprise. -- The Indians on no pretense whatever will be permitted to enter the Forts with arms, or unarmed in large numbers at any one time.* [137]

Lt. Col. William Harney writes to Col. Twiggs' headquarters, from Fort King on June 5, 1840, reprinted in newspapers and journals that are watching the war like the Richmond Enquirer and the Army and Navy Chronicle.

*I feel justified in stating that the large body of Indians who had lived in undisturbed security on the islands in the Ocklawaha for years past, till within the last ten days, have been completely routed from their strongholds. Their extensive crops being destroyed, they no longer have any inducement to remain in this section of the country.*

*From some remarks made by Captain Ker, I am led to believe many have shaped their course towards the Weekwa [Wekiva River], where I should have proceeded, had not the sudden indisposition of my guide, Indian Billy, so broken in on my arrangements as made agreeably in the orders under which I left this post on the 1st instant.* [138]

Armistead is trying to entice the Seminoles to surrender voluntarily, while field operations continue. The tactic of negotiating while the soldiers burn the Indian's crops appears very duplicitous to the Indians.

The Army has a history of betraying the white flag, and the Indians know full well what happened to Osceola. They either ignore it, or as at one case near Fort Dallas, the Indians take the white flag down and rip it into pieces. [139]

---

[137] Ibid, 2-4
[138] Richmond Enquirer, June 26, 1840. ANC Vol. 11, 13.
[139] The National Gazette (Philadelphia, PA), August 31, 1840

On May 28th, Lt. Col. Bennett Riley leaves Fort King with 261 men of the 1st and 2d Infantry, and Florida Mounted Volunteers commanded by Capt. James B. Mason. (Who Fort Mason in Eustis is most likely named after.) One warrior is captured at Panasoffkee and guides them into the Wahoo Swamp. Several acres of crops are found and destroyed, but they do not capture any other Indians.

The captured warrior makes his escape at night when the guard falls asleep. The sentinel awakes during the commotion, and disoriented, fires at the surrounding hammock, arousing the camp to mass confusion. Gunfire erupts everywhere towards nonexistent Indians, generally towards the hammock. Capt. Mason is struck by a stray jaeger rifle ball and is dead within minutes.

Reaching the Withlacoochee 20 miles from Fort Dade, Lt. Col. Riley leaves his baggage and proceeded to Chocochatti Prairie. More fields are discovered, and the Army captures three more warriors. Three other warriors are shot trying to escape, along with a woman mistaken as a man by the soldiers.

Lt. Col. Riley finds another village at Chocochatti and spends several hours destroying huts, hogs, ripened crops, but captures no other prisoners. Lt.Col. Riley proceeds to Annutteliga Hammock to the north and finds a small field and captures one woman with small children and two ponies. Riley, satisfied that he has found and destroyed all that was in the area, returns to Fort King on June 9th. [140]

Orders are given for Lt. Robert Asheton, 2d Dragoons, to set up camp on the Withlacoochee river for the reception of any

---

[140] ANC Vol. 11, 13-14.

Indians willing to meet with the general at Fort King. The Indian woman who was captured last April is sent out with gifts, and to contact her people with a message that the General is willing to conclude a treaty. The Indians will be permitted to come in with a white flag to talk, but the officers are under orders to seize any at the first sign of hostility.

The Indians have great reason to doubt the sincerely of Armistead. Soldiers burned their fields and imprisoned women and children found in hiding. Captain Rains used explosive booby traps on their warriors. They have reason to suspect talks to come in with a white flag. Ironically, Armistead tells Asheton to watch out for the Indian's treachery.

Armistead writes to Capt. Stephenson at Fort Brooke that if any Indians show up, induce them to meet with the General at Fort King, and receive gifts of clothing and provisions. [141]

Provisions are sent to Lt. Asheton in three wagons from Fort King. But no gifts for the Indians have been sent, as the general wishes them to come to Fort King and talk with him there. Micanopy and other chiefs sent out west are returned to Florida to convince their brethren to emigrate. *"Your camp must take precaution against the treachery of the Indians and have a sufficient breastwork, and no Indian allowed to enter under arms. This caution will become doubly necessary when you distribute among them the whiskey which has been sent for that purpose."* It appears that Armistead intends to force removal using all resources available. [142]

(Asst. Adjutant to Gen. Armistead, W.W.S. Bliss, to Lt.

---

[141] AG 1840 A175, 13-16, Armistead to Col. Twiggs at Fort King, June 10, 1840.
[142] Ibid, 20, June 7, 1840, Gen. Armistead to Lt. Asheton.

Washington I. Newton, 2d Dragoons A.D.C.)

*Fort King*

*June 22nd, 1840*

*The General directs that you proceed to Lt. Asheton's camp
and await the coming in of the Indians. As soon as they arrive in
any great number, escort them to Fort King where the General is
waiting to see them. They will be at liberty to come and go as they
please. The General will do all in his power to serve them.* [143]

General Armistead sends Capt. Bonneville around the Lower
Withlacoochee and Wacasassa, with the Indian prisoner "Tom" to
contact Halick Tustenuggee, carrying presents as a measure of
good faith. "If the prisoner fails to return, it will be the last time
this will be attempted."

(Brig. Gen. W.K. Armistead to Brig. Gen. R. Jones, Adjutant
General, Washington.)

*Fort King*

*June 9th, 1840*

*The woman prisoner has communicated that some of the
bands of the Withlacoochee will come in, and I will have 30 to 50
warriors assembled in camp. I intend to give Lt. Col. Riley his own
command to move freely about.* [144]

Tom escapes with little hopes entertained for his return. Lt.
Col. Riley operates on the road to Tampa, going north towards
Fort Fanning. Lt. Col. Harney operates out of Fort Mellon towards
the Wekiva River. Lt. Asheton is along the Withlacoochee to
negotiate with any Indians who show up. Col. Twiggs remains in
camp due to an injury. Lt. Col. Green west of the Suwannee has

---

[143] Ibid, 28, June 22, 1840, Gen. Armistead to Lt. Newton, from Ft. King.
[144] AG 1840 A136

not been heard from, but is said to have captured ten Indians and killed a white man among them. Maj. Churchill, 3$^{rd}$ Artillery, was detained several days at Garey's Ferry by sickness on his way to muster into service the militia intended for the defense of Middle Florida. Since there remains a need for a command east of the St. Johns River, Capt. Ringgold's Artillery Company will be sent to Florida to help fulfill that need. (The company is famous in the Mexican War as Ringgold's Flying Artillery.)

Armistead continues in his report to Gen. Jones:

*Gopher John, an honest and intelligent guide and interpreter from Tampa, believes that if two or three chiefs are brought from Arkansas, then they can induce the rest of the nation to emigrate. The Seminoles in Florida believe that those who went west were thrown overboard, and if they can see that they are not only spared, but well treated, they will be inclined to join them.* [145]

Lt.Col. Harney leaves Ft. Mellon on the 15$^{th}$ of June to examine the country bordering Lakes Jesup and Lake Harney. South of Fort Mellon is found fields of corn, peas, potatoes, which are destroyed. An Island in the middle of the lake is examined, and the detachment went further south and east and discovered a hidden camp that they attack. A wounded warrior escaped leaving a pack of articles believed plundered from the actors murdered near St. Augustine, with a quantity of gunpowder. A woman and a Negro boy are captured. The command proceeded to the shore of Lake Jesup and captured a small party of Indians, which included the mother and daughter of Coacoochee, who had a large quantity of plunder seized from persons murdered near St.

---

[145] AG 1840 A146, Fort King, June 15, 1840, Armistead to Jones/Army Adjt. Genl.

Augustine. Eight ponies are captured, and Wild Cat's property is destroyed. The captured boy provides much information. [146]

Harney learns that Wildcat/Coacoochee has gunpowder and ammunition supplied by the slaves of Col. Hanson's plantation near St. Augustine. The boy found in the camp is the only survivor of a ship that wrecked on the Canaveral coast 18 months previous; the rest of the crew were killed. The boy says that they get gunpowder from St. Augustine. [147]

Lt. Asheton waits for the meeting with the Indians, but none show up, so he breaks camp and leaves.

Armistead is giving mixed signals. He extends an olive branch for peace talks, while detachments of soldiers are scouring the countryside looking for villages to burn to the ground. But the Indians know how to play the game as well; by gathering supplies and professing to talk, while stalling on removal.

(Brig. Gen. W.K. Armistead to the Hon. J.R. Poinsett, Secretary of War.)

*Fort King*
*June 18th, 1840*
*I have the honor to enclose you a copy of a report from Lt. Asheton 2nd Dragoons, who with Lt. Judd 3rd Artillery, and Terrett 1st Infantry, was sent out on the 15th Inst. with a mixed command of about eighty men to the Withlacoochee, for the purpose of opening a negotiation with Halick Tustenuggee, an influential Chief.*

---

[146] AG 1840 A176 Enclosure, Fort King, 26 June 1840, Lt.Col. Harney to Col. Twiggs.
[147] Ibid

*The first step was to send out an Indian woman who had lately been captured, and who had asserted to me that the chief with his band, or the greater portion of them, was desirous of coming in. The messenger sent out has brought words to Lt. Asheton that they were willing to hold a talk, and a second woman who came in with the first, has returned to her people with the message that I would hear their talk.*

*It now becomes pretty certain that they will be in and may be expected here in a few days. Should they do so, it will become my first duty to use every means to keep them, and employ their influence in inducing others to hear my talk.*

*For this service it will in all probability require bribery on our part, and the greater sum, the more certain will be the chances of a faithful performance of their promises. I therefore take leave to request that fifty thousand dollars be forwarded in specie to my care and direction, with full power to use it or not, as circumstances may dictate, with an assurance on my part that this sum or a portion of it will be faithfully applied. By these means more probably will be affected than can now be foreseen, and there may result an immense saving to the Government of treasure and valuable lives of this small but devoted Army.*

The Secretary of War and the Secretary of the Treasury probably balked at the amount asked. Armistead continues:

*If I am to consult my own opinion and be thereby governed. I will insist on the Indians leaving Florida at all events, but should difference of opinion exist as to the disposition to be made of them, I shall cheerfully fulfil the pleasure of the government.-- My own views may change, as circumstances arise, but unless a radical change in them should take place, I should certainly send* the Indians out of the country.

The following extract of a communication this day received from the Governor of Florida will show to the Secretary better than any representation of mine, what disposition exists among the inhabitants for the defense of their homes.

I assure you I will do everything I can to comply with your wishes and those of the Department at Washington, though I very much fear, footmen cannot be obtained, except by draft—and it is questionable whether in the present condition of the country, that mode can be made available. [148]

(Adjutant Robert C. Asheton to Col. D.E. Twiggs, 2d Dragoons.)

In Camp on Jumper Creek
Wednesday, June 17th, 1840

In obedience to the Instruction contained in the Commanding Generals letter of the 10th Inst., turned over by you for my guidance, I left Fort King on the same evening with 20 Dragoons, 39—3rd Artillery under Lt. H.B. Judd and 21--1st Infantry under Lieut. Terrett, and arrived at this point of the Wahoo Swamp early on the morning of the 12th, when the Indian female prisoner was sent out for the purpose of visiting her people, and inducing them to come in. Up to the evening of the 15th, no intelligence was received from her, and as she had faithfully promised to return before sunset the previous evening, I had given up all hopes of again meeting her. Anxious that no further time should be lost having spent four days in actively, I determined to proceed along the Wahoo Swamp and should appearances indicate the presence of Indians to leave my wagons under a suitable guard and commence a vigorous pursuit. Having with this determination

---

[148] AG 1840 A155, Armistead to Poinsett.

*broken up camp, I proceeded ten miles yesterday morning to the bridge on the Withlacoochee where the ammunition and provisions were placed within the temporary defense erected by Colonel Riley's command and I proceeded to enter the swamp with 47 men and continued a northerly course for five or six miles, occasionally touching the river on our left and the open pine barren on the right with the most minute examination possible for such a force; no recent signs whatever were discovered nor any vestige of the hammocks having been used for the purpose of agriculture. I much regretted at the time the state of supplies did not permit of a further examination to the North. The men having marched ten miles in the morning, added to the excessive fatigue of three hours' labor in overcoming the numerous obstacles to be met with, compelled me reluctantly to shape my course for camp where we arrived after one P.M.*

*Towards the close of the afternoon the Indian woman made her appearance, bringing with her another woman who informed me that her people having some doubt as to their security had deputed her to come forward, and if she found the assertions of the prisoner strengthened by her own observation, she would tell such a story as would cause them to come and judge for themselves. She reports the party with whom she is connected as numerous that her Chief Halik Tustenuggee has powerful influence among the Indian nation, and that in the event of the adoption of fair and advantageous measures, the war will cease. This woman who resided for two years near St. Augustine, then known as Indian Betsy is possessed of much intelligence, has been made acquainted with all affairs since Florida was in possession of the British with many of whom she had been well acquainted. She further informs me that the party who lately attacked Capt. Rains were Tallahassee's under Emathla, who returned to their town* between the Withlacoochee and Suwannee immediately after, without losing any of their party. She estimates the number of warriors at two hundred. I am further informed by her that immediately on the arrival of the female prisoner at her encampment two runners were sent out; one to communicate with Ahapopka, the other with the Ocklawaha Indians; these she expects will return before tomorrow evening & from the destitute situation which—without ammunition—they have been placed by the destruction of their crops, they will without loss of time make their appearance.

At her representation I left the Withlacoochee at 3 A.M. this morning and returned to this place where I had erected temporary shelter for the men. She considers this from its position as more central and as it has brought me ten miles nearer Fort King from which the exhausted state of my supplies will require immediate renewal the command having been on three quarter allowance for the last three days.

As several days must necessarily lapse before all the Indians expected can arrive, I would most respectfully request a liberal supply of subsistence stores and a small quantity of Forage, the prairie near affording good pasture.

The quantity of Indian presents I brought out, being much limited, a further number will be indispensable to ensure any degree of success.

Jealous of the presence of a large military force, the Indians, I feel, assured will be more easily brought to terms in a position like the present. As the Commanding General has in his letter of the 15th Inst., been pleased to place much in my judgement, I would most earnestly hope that some little time may be granted for the *development of such plans as the peculiar position of affairs would justify.* [149]

In all the various accounts, we rarely get a good description of any Seminole women during the war. This is an amazing description of a woman in the historical records. The Seminole / Miccosukee are a matriarchal society, and Lt. Asheton just met a matriarch, but he shows no understanding of this. To know the British residents of St. Augustine and being "well acquainted" with them means that she is over 70 years old. The soldiers are looking for the warriors to remove from the territory, but are caught off guard when a woman meets them instead.

It is hard to determine Indian Betsy's identity since that was a common name at the time. Osceola did have a great-aunt named Betsy Durant from Peter McQueen's band. Could this be her? [150]

(Adjutant Robert C. Asheton to Asst. Adjutant General W.W.S. Bliss at Fort King.)

*In Camp on Jumper Creek*
*June 21st, 1840*
*I have for the last two days been prevented replying to your communication of the 19th which reached me yesterday. The Indian Woman Betsy who I sent out four days since has not as yet made her appearance. Yesterday the Indian female prisoner leaving her infant went out to see and converse with her people and if possible, find out what the chances of their coming in might be, she this day returned with two warriors who remained in the camp nearly two hours. They require four days to give a decisive*

[149] AG 1840 A155 Enclosure (from A139), Genl. Armistead (Asheton to Twiggs).
[150] Wickman, Patricia Riles; *Osceola's Legacy* (The University of Alabama Press, Tuscaloosa, 1991), 21.

*answer for their bands, who are now much scattered since the destruction of their crops, their ammunition expended, leaving them no resource but wild roots. Anxious to affect some advances in the Commanding Generals favor, I have given the Indians four sticks to note the time at which they are to return when I have promised to meet them here. From what I can learn from the two who this day visited me, there at present exists much dread of placing themselves in any large number in the power of the whites.* [151]

Giving a number of sticks to count the days until an important meeting is a practice among the Creek and Seminole people that has been practiced for centuries.

---

[151] AG 1840 A159 Enclosure

# Chapter 11: "Suspicion of Having Treasonable Intercourse"

The capture of Coacoochee's mother and daughter, with the Negro boy near Fort Mellon, bring rumor of slaves supplying the Indians with gunpowder. That is all the proof the citizens in St. Augustine need to justify their fears of possible slave uprisings or Indian attacks. Slaves from Col. Hanson's plantation are arrested for aiding the Indians. A grand jury is organized in St. Augustine.

(Aide to Gen. Armistead, Lt. W. I. Newton, to Col. J.M. Hanson, St. Augustine.)

*Fort King*
*July 9th, 1840*

*I am directed by him to say that your Negroes have been arrested on strong suspicion of having supplied the enemy with the [gun]powder, and giving them the information which has proved fatal to so many travelers on the Picolata road. The mother of Wild Cat and Sam the negro lately taken confirm these suspicions as to your slaves and others in St. Augustine. And it is expected by the General Commanding, that in the efforts to ferret out the persons engages in this criminal intercourse with the enemy, he will be aided by yourself and others who having slaves in the vicinity of St. Augustine, hold your property and lives at their mercy.* [152]

(Lt. W. Irving Newton, to Capt. W.W.S. Bliss, Asst. Adjt. Gen. for Gen. Armistead.)

---

[152] AG 1840 A204 pp 13

In obedience to Special Orders No. 33, Head Quarters Army of the South, I proceeded without delay to St. Augustine where I arrived on the evening of the 3rd. Having made affidavit before Judge Bronson that I suspected two slaves "George & Joe" belonging to Colonel Hanson of aiding and abetting the Indians in their war against the Whites, these Negroes were thereupon arrested by the marshal & separately confined in the jail of St. Augustine, Judge Bronson declining to give authority for their removal out of the limits of the county. Though nothing positive may be proved against these Negroes & others in St. Augustine, I have long entertained the suspicion that they were leagued with the enemy, and gave the information which has led to results so often fatal to travelers on the Picolata road. Wildcat's forbearing to attack several small parties which must have passed him and the plunder of the players' wagons almost immediately afterwards is evidence of the specific purpose of his last incursion & the information he possessed. Col. Hanson's negroes were all aware of the arrival of Forbes company at Picolata, some days before the attack, and it is generally believed that the Enemy were informed of it.

I have long suspected these Negroes of collusion with the enemy, because, 1st, many of them are Indian negroes, have relations among them, at the same time that intercourse with the Indians brings with it great profit to themselves. 2nd, because Col. Hanson's house holding out every inducement for an attack is never invaded, while the Indians passing through the hammock, in the rear of his house, make their attacks from it on the Picolata road, and go thirty miles north to commit depredations on other plantations showing themselves openly at these plantation to the

*Negroes there, while it is a little remarkable, that Colonel H's slaves who are almost constantly in the hammocks contiguous to his plantation, pretend they never see an Indian or the sign of one. In arresting these two Negroes of Col. Hanson's, I have acted upon information derived from Officers of the Army, and from facts communicated by the Interpreters & Sam, who was lately captured by Colonel Harney's Command.* [153]

(Brig. Gen. W.K. Armistead, to U.S. Judge I. H. Bronson in St. Augustine, July 15, 1840.)

*Fort King*
*July 15th, 1840*

*I have the honor to acknowledge the receipt of your communication of the 8th inst. Had it not been for severe indisposition, I would have before this, seen you in regard to Colonel Hanson's negroes, who were arrested by Lt. Newton on suspicion of having treasonable intercourse with the Indians.—It will be as well here to state what evidence can be adduced against these Negroes in order that you may arrive at a decision in regard to their continued confinement or release. The Mother of Wild Cat informed two of my interpreters that on the day of Wild Cat's last attack on the Picolata road, he was supplied with a dinner by Col. Hanson's negroes as also with some powder.* [Although it was actually the Jenckes plantation, as told earlier.] *The Negro "Sam" lately taken from Wild Cat, says that on the return of this chief from his last expedition, he exalted in his success and exhibited leather bags of powder as proof of it. The Negro Joe now with Wild Cat & who usually accompanied his Chief in his forays, was telling Sam the particulars of the last one, when he was stopped by Wild Cat, who ordered him to be silent, remarking at the same*

---

[153] AG 1840 A192 Enclosure.

time, that if all the Whites were like Col. Hanson, there would be no difficulty between the Indians and themselves. Sam further says that some months ago, Wild Cat told Philipps John, a hostile Negro, to go and see his cousin (believed to be George) near St. Augustine, & obtain powder from him. John refused to do so at the time.

This is the principal evidence against Col. Hanson's negroes. It is not as specific as could be wished, but it is enough to confirm the suspicions entertained by many citizens of St. Augustine, by officers of the Army generally, especially by those who have been stationed East of the St. Johns. These Negroes range in all the hammocks & part of country in which the Indians secret themselves when they come up, and no vigilance, even if any was exercised, could prevent them from aiding and abetting the enemy, but supplying them with [gun]powder and giving them any information sought after. [154]

(Secretary of War Joel Poinsett to General W.K. Armistead.)

July 9, 1840.

I have only time to reply to the portion of your letter to the Adjutant General of the 29th June which treats of the disclosures made by the negro found in Wild Cat's camp.-- The investigation ought to be vigorously prosecuted, and to ensure its being so, you are instructed to employ—Westcott, Esquire as Assistant Council to aid the District Attorney Mr. Douglas, in the legal proceedings against Colonel Hanson's negroes. [155]

(Brig. Gen. W.K. Armistead, to Mr. Douglas, US District

---

[154] AG1840 A204, 18-20.
[155] Letters Sent by the Sec. of War, 1841, 327.

Attorney in St. Augustine.)

> Cedar Keys
> July 27th, 1840
>
> The Secretary of War in a communication of the 9th Inst, has authorized me to employ—Westcott Esqr., as Assistant Council to aid you in the legal proceedings against Col. Hanson's negroes. You are accordingly requested to procure the assistance of Mr. Westcott should you deem it necessary. [156]

James D. Westcott, Jr., 1802-1880, was an important territorial legislator and one of the first two state senators with David Levy Yulee.[157]

(Gen. Armistead's Asst. Adjutant General W.W.S. Bliss to Lt.Col. W.S. Harney at Fort Reid.)

> Cedar Keys
> July 27th, 1840
>
> The Commanding General directs that you immediately send the Negro "Sam" and Wild Cat's mother, with a sufficient guard to St. Augustine, to be delivered to the United States marshal, or such other officer as may be indicated by Judge Bronson. Should their presence not be required by the Judge, they can return immediately to Fort Mellon. [158]

Col. Hanson complains that his slaves were arrested by Lt. Newton, a military officer, who has no authority to make civil arrests. Hanson complains that he is losing labor for the daily operations of his plantation. The general sends his reply by Lt. Newton, who made the arrests, who is serving as the general's

---

[156] AG 1840 A204, 36
[157] findagrave.com
[158] AG 1840 A204 pp 39

Aide-de-camp.

(Lt. W.I.Newton, A.D.C. to Gen. Armistead, to Mr. J.M. Hanson, Esqr., St. Augustine.)

*Cedar Keys*
*August 5th, 1840*
*General Armistead can see nothing reprehensible in the manner of the arrest of your slaves by his aide.*

*...it is notorious to all has been and is prolonged by slaves and others, who gives intelligence to the enemy and supply them with powder. The Commanding General is determined to arrest these treasonable dealings, by bringing to trial all who may be suspected of lending assistance to the enemy.* [159]

(Brig. Gen. W.K. Armistead, to Mr. T. Douglas, District Attorney, St. Augustine.)

*Cedar Keys*
*August 17th, 1840*
*In answer to your letter of the 6th inst, you are respectfully informed that Judge Bronson has been furnished with a statement of the principal evidence that can be brought against Col. Hanson's negroes, a copy of which I herewith enclose. The two interpreters John and Primus, to whom the mother of Wild Cat gave the information relative to the intercourse between Hanson's negroes and the Indians, are now here, and will be sent to St. Augustine by the first opportunity if their presence there can be useful, in regard to which I respectfully request I may be informed.* [160]

---

[159] AG 1840 A234 pp 11, 12
[160] Ibid, 29-30

After the witnesses are interviewed by the grand jury, there is not sufficient evidence to keep George and Joe imprisoned. Four months later, the finding is quietly announced in the Wetumpka Argus newspaper.

*George and Joe, two negro slaves belonging to Col. Hanson, who were committed to prison on charges of Treason, and insurrectionary intercourse with the Indians, were discharged on Monday last. The Grand Jury examined upwards of 30 witnesses, embracing officers of the Army, negroes, and captured Indians; and no bill was found against the slaves.* [161]

In November, Miccosukee warriors led by Wildcat / Coacoochee, raid Col. Hanson's plantation. All the blankets and winter clothing of the slaves are taken, and three slaves forced to leave with the Indians and their plunder. During the flight across Hanson's fields, those slaves escape and run to St. Augustine.

An Army detachment from Picolata responds by attempting to sneak up on the plantation because they believe the Indians are still there. There are none, but the plantation guard mistakes the soldiers for Indians and fires upon them, killing the sergeant and wounded Lieut. Graham. Fortunately, a visiting physician at the plantation immediately tends to the wounds.

The Indian warriors ambush another escort of soldiers, killing three and taking the head of a sergeant who they tauntingly display outside Fort Searle.

Due to the ineffectiveness of the small garrisons at the forts south of St. Augustine that don't have enough men, Fort Hanson, Peyton, and Fulton are abandoned. Now, after five years of war in

---

[161] The Wetumpka Argus, Dec. 16, 1840

Florida, St. Augustine is defenseless just like it was at the beginning of the war. [162]

The only two working plantations outside of St. Augustine are owned by Col. John M. Hanson and Mr. Edwin T. Jenckes. All others have been destroyed. Because of the attacks, the owners reside in the town and leave their slaves virtually unattended. [163]

The Richmond Enquirer reports:

*However callous may be Northern hearts, these two owner of 140 slaves feel a responsibility. They have 140 mouths to feed, and 140 persons to clothe, lodge, and protect. Were the country quiet, this would be an easier matter; but it is not easy when Seminole Indians come when they please to destroy crops, and plunder negro houses.* [164]

---

[162] The Richmond Enquirer, Nov. 13, 1840. The Pilot and Transcript, Nov. 18, 1840.
[163] Camden Journal (SC) Jan. 20, 1841
[164] The Richmond Enquirer, Jan. 9, 1841

## Chapter 12: "Fired Upon by a Party of Red Devils"

The Army does not run on hardtack and salt pork alone. It is subject to the public purse, or the Congressional budget. General Armistead tries his best to lower the cost of the war.

(Asst. Adjutant General W.W.S. Bliss, to Lt.Col. Riley, 2d Infantry at Fort King.)

> *Cedar Keys*
> *August 17th, 1840*
> *In answer to your communication of the 10th inst., enclosing a requisition for boards for Fort King. I am directed by the Commanding General to say that he does not deem it expedient to order any more lumber for that post, if more be required, it must be sawed by the troops themselves.* [165]

One big expense is the upkeep and care of horses. The infantry marches on foot, not hoof. Therefore, infantry posts should not spend hours each day tending to stables.

(Gen. Armistead's Asst. Adjutant General W.W.S. Bliss to Lt.Col. Hunt at Garey's Ferry.)

> *Fort King*
> *July 15th, 1840*
> *In answer to your communication of the 13th inst. Soliciting instruction as to the number of horses allowed each post, I am directed by the Commanding General to say, that posts of three or more companies will be allowed* <u>*ten*</u> *horses, all other posts, five*

---

[165] AG 1840 A234, 23

*horses.* [166]

The improper use of horses by infantry will factor into the worst ambush of the war at the end of the year. Lt.Col. Whistler requested an exception to the number so he could have additional horses for Fort Micanopy, but the request is denied. [167]

The county seat of Dade County in the Florida Keys is Indian Key, which was established by Jacob Houseman to salvage ships that wrecked on the reefs. It is raided by Spanish Indians led by Chakaika on August 7, 1840, who loot and burn the town. Thirteen people are killed, including Dr. Henry Perrine, a well-known horticulturist. [168]

The hot August summer sees the territory enflamed from the Florida Keys to the Okefenokee Swamp. In St. Mary's Georgia, similar to Indian Key, 11 individuals are killed, and the same number of settlements burned. Several families near Fort Moniac building a school flee to the stockade. Of the several killed, most are women and children.

The families who occupy Fort Moniac are assisted with defense by local militia Captian Aaron Jernigan. They soon abandon the fort for Capt. Jernigan's place, considered better fortified. The fort is burnt soon after. Lt. May of the 2d Dragons and Capt. Tracy of the Georgia Militia goes in pursuit of the attackers to no avail. [169]

On August 13th, a report from Newnansville tells of more

---

[166] AG 1840 A204, 22

[167] AG 1840 A234, 24

[168] AG 1840 A233; Mahon, John K., *History of the Second Seminole War*, 279-280

[169] The Evening Post, Sept. 9, 1840. the Cheraw Advertiser, Sept. 16, 1840

attacks. Mr. Samuel Smart and James Lanier, both young men, are at Fort Tarver guarding their slaves working in the field. A little before sundown, the two men stroll towards the hammock where watermelons have ripened. While eating one, they are fired upon by Indians in concealment. Mr. Smart is instantly killed. Mr. Lanier is wounded but escapes. The Indians take Mr. Smart's rifle, powder horn, and some silver change.

The next evening, two Dragoons soldiers are killed near McIntosh's plantation, about ten miles east of Micanopy by Orange Lake. To the north, Indians are seen on top of a house at Fort Crane celebrating their victory. They hold up and dance around the rifle from Mr. Smart. General panic ensues over the possibility of hundreds of Indians hiding out near the settlements. Express riders continue to be ambushed. [170]

The National Gazette reports:

*On the afternoon of Wednesday the 2d, Hilary Parsons, a young man of about 18, was shot by a party of Indians, about seven miles from Black Creek, on the Newnansville Road. Upon the first fire of the Indians, he was perforated by five balls. After shooting him, they mangled his body in a horrid manner.* [171]

A lost dragoon soldier from Fort Reid (one mile from Fort Mellon) wanders the woods for two weeks until captured by Indians. He is bound to a tree to be shot, but the Indian guns misfire. Found by an approaching company of Dragoons and untied, his mind is "destroyed," and he is a mere skeleton. The rumor is that the Indians had a mulatto and a white man with

---

[170] Ibid
[171] The National Gazette, Sept. 17, 1840

them.[172]

An unnamed surgeon recalls a close call near Orange Creek, as printed in the Cheraw Advertiser newspaper:

*Fort Russell, East Florida*
*August 29, 1840.*

*I have been the attending Surgeon for two posts, viz: Forts Russell and Holmes. At the former are four companies, and at the latter two companies, 2d Infantry, U.S. Army. The posts are distant eleven miles, and I can assure you that with two and three men as an escort, I have run no light risk in visiting them, which I have been doing every third day.*

*It was on one of my visits and within a few miles of the ambuscade, that I was met by a party of five Dragoons, two of whom had been wounded by the Indians at a spot which I would have reached in a half hour.*

*It was a fortunate circumstance for Lieut. [William] Alburtis (who accompanied me) and myself that the Dragoons passed the spot ere we could arrive at it.*

*Dr. Turner has also had a narrow escape, having been ordered from Fort Wheelock to Micanopy, where he was fortunately detained, but his escort was fired upon by a party of the red devils, and alas, two out of four killed and one wounded.* [173]

---

[172] Ibid
[173] Cheraw Advertiser, Sept. 16, 1840

# Chapter 13: "A Cool, Steady Fire of Musketry"

An ambulance is also not safe from ambush:

(Capt. B.L. Bonneville, 7th Infantry, to Bvt. Brig. Gen. R. Jones, Adjutant General, Washington.)

> *Fort Micanopy, E.F.*
> *September 1st, 1840*
>
> *Herewith I have the honor to enclose muster role for Companies E, F, and I of the 7th Infantry and post return for Fort Micanopy for August 1840. This post for a few days past is becoming very sickly...*
>
> *On the 30th ulto., I sent my ambulance for a sick man at Fort Tarver. Upon their return they were attacked at 6 pm—the escort fled—the sick man jumped out and severely wounded an Indian, that they [the Indians] had to make a litter to carry him off—two of the escort are killed, one wounded and one missing. It was very dark before the relief arrived. The sick man & all eleven of "E" Company reached the post in safety and saved the life of one of the escort.*

Bonneville further writes that the Indians burnt the wagon, and the attackers numbered about 25 and came from the west. The relief arrived in the dark and was unable to follow. [174]

From the casualty list in Sprague, we find the list of killed: Pvt. Henry Elridge, Co. I; Pvt. Patrick Fynn, Co. E; Pvt. David M. Finney,

---

[174] AG 1840 B391 and B408

Co. E (taken prisoner & killed.)[175]

The Section 7 map by Lt. Thomas shows a road that goes south from Fort Tarver across Alachua Prairie to Micanopy. Most likely, this was the route where the ambulance was attacked.

A few days later, there is a large battle near Fort Wacahoota. Fortunately for Lieut. Weightman K. Hanson, he was more prepared than his fellow officers in previous ambushes. A cool head and standard infantry tactics prevailed.

The Army and Navy Chronicle details part of it:

*Lieutenant Turner was proceeding from Fort Walker to Wakahootee, where he discovered a large body of Indians in the open woods. He wheeled his horse, as he supposed unperceived by the enemy, but no sooner had he done so, then four or five rifles were fired at him; and turning round to look from whence they came, he saw Indians in pursuit of him. He returned to the post from whence he had started, loosing cap, saddle-bags, &c. He was, however, determined to prosecute his journey, and started again on another road, where he discovered a similar body of Indians, in a like manner, apparently in council in the pine barren. He was again fired upon and pursued by several warriors, and again escaped. He took the news to Wakahootee when Lieutenant W. K. Hanson left the post with thirty-five men.*

*It is supposed that it was not the intention of the Indians to kill Lieutenant Turner. Their object was to massacre the command of Lieutenant Hanson, which must have been the case, but for the*

[175] Sprague, *The Origin, Progress, and Conclusion of the Florida War*. Brown, *Ponce de Leon Land and Florida War Record*.

*gallant conduct of its leader.* [176]

(Lt. W.K. Hanson to Capt. E.S. Hawkins, Fort Wacahoota.)

*Fort Wacahoota, E.F.*
*Sept. 6th, 1840*

*I have the honor to report that I left this post today on a scout, in command of thirty-five men of "B" & "H" Companies, 7th Infantry. When about two miles north of this post, moccasin tracks were discovered which we trailed for six hundred yards, when we suddenly received a heavy volley of Indian rifles from a hammock on our right flank. The troops returned the discharge, but finding that the enemy far outnumbered them, were compelled to retreat some hundred paces from the continuous stream of his fire. They then rallied, cheered, and stood to their work handsomely. The enemy by the superiority of his numbers soon succeeded in outflanking us, being joined in this movement by the adjacent hammocks. I withdrew the command into the open woods, the men being deployed, and steadily "firing in retreat" as if on drill. The Seminoles supposing this movement to be a complete fight, rushed yelling from the hammocks and once more attempted to beat in our flank. The troops however were now securely posted behind trees, and greeted the enemy with such a cool steady fire of musketry, that he fled precipitately and gave us up the field. Being too weak to attempt pursuit, I contented myself with maintaining my position until your arrival with reinforcements, at which time the command devolved upon you. I have to report on our side one man killed and four wounded, one mortally, a list of whom is subjoined. Loss of the enemy not ascertained. Their estimated strength was eighty men. The action lasted thirty*

---

[176] ANC Vol. 11, 250.

*minutes.* [177]

List of killed and wounded: [on Lt. Hanson's report.]

- *Private Hefferman of "H" Co., 7th Infy, killed.*
- *Sergt. Armstrong of "B" Co., 7th Infy, wounded.*
- *Sergt. Hall of "A" Co., 7th Infy, wounded.*
- *Private Eckard of "B" Co., 7th Infy, mortally wounded.*
- *Private Conley 2nd of "H" Co., 7th Infy, wounded.* [178]


(Captain S. Hawkins, to Lt. R.C. Gatlin, Adjutant, 7th Infantry.)

*Fort Wacahootie, E.F.*
*September 8th, 1840*

*I have the honor to report that an Express came in to this post between 3 and 4 O'clock P.M. on the 6th Inst., bringing information that a citizen had been fired on by a party of Indians between this post and Fort Walker, at a point about 2 miles distant from here. I ordered Lt. W. K. Hanson, 7th Infantry, with a command consisting of 35 men, commissioned Officers and Privates, to the spot. About half an hour after the departure of Lieut. H., and his command, I heard a heavy firing in the direction of Fort Walker, and immediately started with 21 men who had just returned from detached service, and marched as rapidly as possible in the direction from whence the firing proceeded to his support. After proceeding about 3 miles, we came up to Lieut. Hanson and found him in possession of the field; the enemy having fled. The whole command was here formed in Extended order, with an advanced guard, and marched to the point where the action commenced, bordering on a Hammock. A few moments before we advanced, Lieut. Col. Dancy of the Florida Volunteers, came up with 10 or 12*

---

[177] AG 1840 A261 Enclosure
[178] Ibid

*mounted men, and promptly offered his service. We saw nothing of the enemy during this advance, and entered the hammock, thinking it possible that they might give us battle there, and passed through it; however, examining it carefully, without seeing them, and finding no trail, concluded that they had scattered to meet again at some distant point, as is their custom. It being now too dark to discover any signs of them, I returned with my command to this post, bringing with me a soldier mortally wounded and the body of the men killed. Besides the soldier mortally wounded, 3 others were wounded severely, but are in a fair way of recovery. I consider it my duty to state that the wounded men suffered severely for want of surgical aid, no Medical Officer having been furnished to this post; Asst. Surgeon Moore came here with great readiness from Micanopy, and did all which skill and zeal could effect in relieving the wounded.*

*I consider that great praise is due Lieut. Hanson from his conduct during the engagement, and particularly from the skillful manner in which he prevented the enemy from turning his flanks and getting his rear. He speaks in high terms of the behavior of the men engaged. From the great extent of ground occupied by the Indians and the heavy and continuous fire kept up by them, their numbers could not be less than 80, and probably exceeded 100. I am also supported in the opinion by the extent of their encampment on the night of the action, which was yesterday discovered several miles from here, in the direction of Wacasassa. From various circumstances, I feel justified in the belief that at least 4 of the enemy were killed. From their trail, it supposed they have gone towards Fort Clinch. It affords me great pleasure to state that Lieut. [Paul D.] Geisse as well as the Non-Commissioned Officers and privates who marched with me to the support of Lieut. Hanson, displayed great zeal, and manifested the greatest anxiety to engage the enemy. It is due also to the citizens of this place to state that, a number of them accompanies me with great promptness.* [179]

The following are the soldiers who were killed in action in the area in August and September:[180]

- Pvt. Jeremiah Austin, Co. A, Aug. 13, 1840, killed near Fort Wheelock escorting Asst. Surg. Griffin to Fort Micanopy.
- Pvt. Henry Eldridge, Co. I, Aug. 30, 1840, killed near Micanopy.
- Pvt. Augustus Eckard, Co. B, Sept. 7, 1840, at Ft. Wacahoota, of wounds received the day before.
- Pvt. Patrick Flynn, Co. E, Aug. 30, 1840, killed near Micanopy.
- Pvt. David Finney, Co. E, Aug. 30, 1840, near Micanopy. Taken prisoner and killed.
- Pvt. Michael Hefferman, Co. H, Sept. 6, 1840, died at Ft. Wacahoota.
- Pvt. Thomas I. Smith, Co. C, Aug. 13, 1840, killed near Ft. Wheelock escorting Asst. Surg. Griffin to Ft. Micanopy.

The next month, Capt. Beall near Fort Fanning captures an Indian who states that in the battle with Lt. Hanson, 18 Indians were killed and many wounded; some since died. [181]

Mr. Geiger, a civilian, had his luck run out near Wacahoota the same day. (The Geiger family still lives in this area of Alachua County.) As told in the Cheraw Advertiser newspaper:

---

[179] AG 1840 A261 Enclosure. ANC, Vol. 11, 214-215
[180] Sprague, *The Origin, Progress, and Conclusion of the Florida War.* Brown, *Ponce de Leon Land and Florida War Record.*
[181] ANC Vol. 11, 268

*The body of Mr. Geiger was not found until Thursday the 10th.*
*When found, it exhibited one of the most revolting spectacles of*
*fiendish vengeance, seen since the commencement of the war. He*
*was first whipped until his back was a mass of clotted gore; his*
*legs ripped from his feet to his hips then cut with a knife entirely*
*round until his upper parts were nearly separated from the lower,*
*his heart taken out, and his head cut off. He was one of a party of*
*volunteers stationed at Fort Walker, who carried the express of Lt.*
*Hanson, informing him of Indian signs. His companions had left*
*Wacahoota but a few minutes before, and passed the*
*battleground unmolested. There were about 100 Indians.* [182]

On Sept. 8th, the express rider from Fort Holmes (between
Palatka and Fort Russell) discovered Indians in a hammock three
miles from the post. His horse became startled, and he was not
able to turn away as it galloped forward. He rode flat against the
saddle through the ambush and rifle fire. His hat shot away, but
he escapes unharmed. The horse ran about a hundred yards and
fell dead to the ground. He keeps running until he reaches Fort
Russell. The Indians pursue but stop at Orange Creek, three miles
from the scene of the action.

The rider was forced to drop the mail while running. Several
hours later, when word reached Fort Holmes, Lt. McKinstry, 2d
Infantry, takes 25 men to the scene of the incident. He continues
looking for the Indians without success until eight o'clock, and
bivouacs along the Ocklawaha River. Convinced that the Indians
are hiding in the hammock on the other side of the river, he tries
to cross the river the next morning by raft, but the raft brakes
apart and the river is too swift to attempt to cross, so he returns

---

[182] the Cheraw Advertiser, Sept. 30, 1840

to the scene of the action the day before.

The Lieutenant extends his men out in a line until they discover the remains of the mailbag that the express rider dropped. He finds that the only letters opened being addressed to the Commanding General and staff. One order from Washington to General Armistead is never found, except the envelope. This convinces McKinstry that the Indians had someone who could read and that they have gained important information on the movement of troops.[183]

Due to the continued need for a surgeon at Fort Wacahoota, the general sought a civilian doctor to fill the need. Sept. 28th, 1840, from the correspondence of Genl. Armistead for September in Tampa to Capt. Hawkins, 7th Infantry at Fort Wacahoota. *"Genl. Armistead has approved the contract of Mr. Daniels pay of one dollar a day and rations. Spec. Order No. 63 directs Asst. Surg. Crittenden to report to Capt. Hawkins."* [184]

Col. David Twiggs has a harder time procuring a civilian doctor when he is unable to get a military surgeon and seeks approval from U.S. Surgeon General Thomas Lawson to contract with a civilian doctor. Normally, Twiggs would need at least three bids, and the government would contract one of the three. But only one local doctor in the area still practices because of the war; Dr. Wood. Unfortunately, Lawson was unmoved and said that no exceptions to the rules would be allowed.

Personal bias may have factored in the decision. Twenty years earlier, Twiggs and Lawson were involved with a dispute with Col. Matthew Arbuckle at Fort Scott in the southwest corner of

---

[183] ANC Vol. 11, 268.
[184] AG 1840 A273, 32-33.

Georgia after the First Seminole War. The dispute became so violent that it involved a brawl of the participants, and Lawson ended up being hit over the head and locked up in the stockade. It didn't seem like a good idea to jail a doctor at a fort with a lot of sick men. Lawson and Twiggs later brought up charges and were able to have a court-martial organized in 1823 against Col. Arbuckle, with eight charges of "Conduct unbecoming of an officer and a gentleman," neglect, disobedience, lying, and fraud. Lawson even accused Arbuckle of promoting prostitution. The court determined the case frivolous, that the statute of limitations had passed, and found Arbuckle "Not Guilty" on all counts and dropped the case. Nothing showed up on Arbuckle's record as he commanded out west in the Indian Territory for the next thirty years. Lawson, Twiggs, and Arbuckle, all had strong personalities that didn't work well with each other. [185]

(Col. D.E. Twiggs to General R. Jones, Adjutant General, Washington.)

*Headquarters, East District*
*Fort Heileman*
*29 September 1840*
*A few days since, I addressed you on the subject of the employment of Dr. Wood at this post. The contract with Dr. Wood, and an explanation to the Surgeon General accompanied my letter. I was sick at the time & the letter was written in great haste as the steamboat was waiting. I omitted to mention that Wacahoota and Wacasassa garrisoned each by two companies of the 7th Infantry are without a Medical Officer—by an order from the Genl. Commanding the "Army of Florida," the Medical Director is directed to post the Medical Officers & they are not to be*

---

[185] The Arkansas Gazette, May 20, 1823.

removed without the sanction of the General after once assigned to a post by the Medical director. Thus, it will be seen three posts in Florida & two in Georgia, amounting in all to seven companies, were at the time of the employment of Dr. Wood, without Medical Aid, and this to, at the most sickly season, & acknowledged to be the most unhealthy portion of the United States. Where the Medical Officers are, I do not know, & ought not to be held accountable for. I do not profess to be the depository of all the military economy in this country, but I defy any of the departments to show, where I have ever profusely squandered the public money, if it can be shown that, I could have controlled the services of a single medical officer of the Army. I am willing to pay Dr. Wood, if it can be shown that I could have obtained the services of a Citizen Doctor other than Dr. Wood <u>at any price</u>. I am willing to pay Dr. Wood if it can be made appear that another Dr. could have been found to attend to the sick at this post within 100 miles of this. I think, take this case altogether, it is a most extraordinary one, and I confidently appeal to the Commanding General to shield Officers of the line from unmerited censure when in the <u>honest discharge</u> of their duty. I profess to follow the regulations and orders to the letter, and I had both before me when I made the contract with Dr. Wood. Indeed, I had all the rights before me that could apply to this case—but the disapproval of the Surgeon General. [186]

Dr. Woods treats 126 soldiers in the next ten days, paid by Colonel Twiggs. [187]

---

[186] AG 1840 T328, 13-14
[187] AG 1840 T370

# Chapter 14: "Pacific Measures"

At the beginning of October, General Armistead attempts to continue negotiations. The Indian Woman who took the message to the Indians in the Withlacoochee area brings news that Halleck Tustenuggee's people are starving. Genl. Armistead says he is not willing to meet at Fort King but only at Tampa. [188]

The Indian woman returns with a message saying that Halleck Tustenuggee will not meet at Tampa but wants to meet at Fort King on the 20th. [189]

On October 21st, Genl. Armistead rides out 20 miles from Fort Brooke to the camp of Halleck Tustenuggee and Tigertail for a conference. The chiefs are unwilling to leave Florida but will discuss the proposal and meet further at Fort King in 14 days. Halleck Tustenuggee and Tigertail are offered $5000 each to emigrate, but they decline the offer. Another option by Armistead is to give the Indians a portion of land in south Florida to settle down if they remain peaceful. [190]

This idea was tried and failed the year before when General Alexander Macomb negotiated the same thing. Many people in Florida are furious and make their opinions known. As far as they are concerned, the Indians did not deserve any land and had forfeited it all with the Treaty of Paynes Landing. Not even land where no one else lived.

Armistead asks General Leigh Read of the Florida Militia to

---

[188] AG 1840 A306, 13-14
[189] AG 1840 A287
[190] AG 1840 A295

suspend active operations during his negotiations. [191]

And of his command, Armistead instructs Lt.Col. Clarke of the 8th Infantry.

(Asst. Adjutant General W.W.S. Bliss, to Lt.Col. Newman S. Clarke, 8th Infantry.)

*Tampa*
*Oct. 27th, 1840*
*It is the direction of the Commanding General, that should you meet with Indians on your march to Fort King, they be treated with kindness unless they give evidence of hostile intentions, in which case of course, they will be regarded as enemies and dealt with accordingly.* [192]

The Secretary of War Joel Poinsett is pressured to end the war. The national election is looming, and nowhere is the war as unpopular as in Congress. Northern states argue in Congress that the war should end and has gone on long enough.

Unlike previous commanding generals in Florida who had relatively free reign to direct policies, Armistead is in constant communication with the Secretary of War Joel Poinsett for approval of everything. Most of the Secretary's term involved Indian removal and the Seminole War, but there is no indication that he ever visited Florida. In a letter to General Armistead, Poinsett writes on November 2, 1840, that he disagrees with Armistead continuing the policy that General Macomb negotiated with the Seminoles the previous year.

---

[191] AG 1840 A306, 25
[192] Ibid, 31

(Sec. of War Poinsett to Gen. Armistead.)

*Nov. 2nd, 1840*

*I did not receive your letter from Tampa dated on the 7th of October until yesterday (Sunday the 1st Instant) and hasten to reply to your suggestion to give the Indians the section of country designated in General Macomb's treaty as a measure most likely to stay this uncertain and protracted war. After mature deliberation, it appears to me that the President has no right to give any portion of the territory of Florida to the Indians. By a treaty made with them and ratified by the Senate, they ceded their lands for a valuable consideration to the Government, and this Department cannot sanction any arrangement which, in the contravention of the treaty, would retrocede any portion of that purchase. If, however, it should be found utterly impracticable to prevail upon the Indians to emigrate to the new home provided for them in the West, for an indefinite period, a truce may be made with them, confining them South of a line of posts to be established from Tampa Bay to New Smyrna, occupying as nearly as may be, the sites of the old posts which it is understood proved to be healthy when formerly occupied.*

*It is hoped that the coincidence from which you augur beneficial results will have occurred; and that the delegation of Seminole Chiefs from Arkansas, will have reached Florida about the same time that your interview with Halick Tustenuggee was to have taken place. I perceive that Fort King is fixed upon by that chief as the place of Rendezvous, and I am afraid it may embarrass your operations to have the Indians collected at a spot so far within the line designated above: for these attempts at negotiation must not be suffered to interrupt hostilities against the other bands. It is believed the probable success of our pacific policy will depend upon the vigor of your operations in the field.*

*You had better therefore, at once fix upon some point on the proposed line from Tampa to Fort Mellon inclusive for the Indians to assemble, assuring them of their safety South of it, but sending out detachments to scour the country to the North, and urging the Officers to the utmost diligence and activity in discovering and pursuing the enemy.* [193]

Having Poinsett direct the war by long distance from Washington and be in disagreement with the overall commander in Florida (General Armistead) only prolongs the war.

Joel Poinsett has a familiar plant named after him, the Poinsettia. With his passion for botany, he has flowering plants sent to him from around the world. When Dr. Leitner was killed at Jupiter Inlet during Naval Lt. Powell's skirmish in January 1838, Poinsett inquired about the doctor's botany notes to try and get them published posthumously. Poinsett has an amazing history of diplomacy and botany, but as Secretary of War, he is a hardline Jacksonian for Indian removal. [194]

As for Fort Micanopy, the post adjutant is killed in September. Lt. William B. Greene, 7th Infantry, is left explaining the problems to the unsympathetic Army Adjutant General Roger Jones.

(2d Lt. W.B. Greene, to Brevet Brig. Gen. Roger Jones, Adjutant General.)

*Fort Micanopy, E.F.*
*November 4th, 1840*
*I have the honor to acknowledge the receipt of a letter from your office, dated Oct. 14th, 1840, enclosing my September*

---

[193] Letters sent by the Sec of War 1840, Nov. 2, 51.
[194] ANC Vol 6, 108. Cunningham, Denyse; "Edward Fredrick Leitner (1812-1838) Physician Botanist", *Broward Legacy*, Vol. 27, Number 1 (2007).

*"Monthly Post Return," which was returned for correction, and completion. I am sorry to perceive that the incorrectness of the return, and the apparent careless manner in which it is made out, fully justify your remarks on the subject. But, as there are circumstances which tend to exonerate me from the charge of willful neglect, I conceive it due to myself to offer an explanation.*

*My Company Clerk was killed by the enemy a short time before this Return was made out, and I was obliged to call in requisition the services of a man totally unacquainted with the Post Papers. I was also at the time very sick, and almost unfitted for any exertion, for which reason I failed to perceive the mistakes with which the paper abounded. The excuse for the mistakes opposite the names of present and absent officers, I have only to state that I am very young in the service, and that when circumstances made it necessary for me to assume command of a Post, I found myself in a situation for which I was wholly unprepared; and the mistakes in my papers result, not from want of will, but from want of information. I ordered my clerk to make the remarks in the manner which you have disapproved and in so doing I acted to the best of my knowledge.*

*I send herewith another copy of the Monthly Return which will I hope prove correct. I perceive that Capt. Rains, and Lieut. Montgomery, are put down in the pencil remarks upon the incorrect Return as being on Recruiting Service. As I am not able to find any Order placing them on that duty, I suppose the remark was intended as an exemplification of the manner in which the Return should be made out, and I have reported them, therefore, as they have hitherto been borne on the Returns.* [195]

---

[195] AG 1840 G265

Secretary Poinsett fires off another letter to General Armistead. Just as Zachary Taylor believed the futility in the Cherokee delegation negotiating with the Seminoles two years earlier, Poinsett is skeptical of any success of the delegation of Seminoles brought from the West. Armistead will meet at Fort King by the insistence of Halleck Tustenuggee and Tigertail.

(Sec. of War Poinsett to Gen. Armistead.)

*November 10th, 1840*

*I have the honor to acknowledge the receipt of your letters of the 23d and 26th Ultimo, and am pleased to learn that the Indians remain steady in their intention to treat with you. Although in my communication of the 2d instant, I expressed an apprehension that Fort King was too far north to be desirable as a place of negotiation, I did not mean to interdict your assembling the Indians there if you judge it expedient to do so. In that event, the only change required in the instructions is, that the forces under you Command should operate North of Fort King until the negotiations are concluded.*

*With regard to the proposal to dispatch a delegation of Seminole Chiefs to the Seat of Government if you are not engaged too far in the project, I beg you will suspend it altogether. The President [Martin Van Buren] thinks that such a mission would not lend to hasten the termination of the negotiations; but on the contrary, would occasion great delay, and might hazard its entire failure.*

*The Militia you speak of, cannot be disbanded until the territory is pacified, and the peaceable intentions of the Indians positively ascertained.* [196]

General Armistead arrives at Fort King to negotiate with Halleck Tustenuggee. (There are different spellings for Halleck's name; Halick, Alick, and others.) In the morning, the general is informed by his Native negotiators that Halleck and Tigertail have departed before dawn, and the camp is empty.

(Brig. General W.K. Armistead, to the Adjutant General, Washington.)

Fort King
*Nov. 18, 1840*
*I have the honor to inform the Department of the renewal of hostilities in consequence of the departure of Halick Tustenuggee and Tiger-tail with their warriors from their encampments taking with them three Indian prisoners.*

*The troops under my command were instantly put in motion, and are now scouting from different points. The 2nd and 7th Infantry are now concentrating at Forts Micanopy & King in order to operate from these places. Two columns of the 8th [Infantry] of 150 men each are examining the country eighteen miles south. In a few days this whole Regiment in columns of 150 men will be traversing the country between the Ocklawaha river, the lakes at its head, and the Withlacoochee as far down as Tampa and below it if necessary.* [197]

(Brig. General W.K. Armistead, to Hon. J.R. Poinsett, Secretary of War, Washington.)

Fort King

---

[196] Letters sent by the Sec. of War, 1840, Nov. 10, 60.
[197] AG 1840 A315

*Nov. 15<sup>th</sup>, 1840*

*Early this morning, I was informed by the Arkansas delegation that some of the prisoners in camp had disappeared during the night. On sending out to the Indian Encampment it was discovered that all the Indians had gone.*

*Thus has ended all our well-grounded hopes of bringing the war to a close by pacific measures, confident in resources of the Country the enemy will hold out to the East and can never be induced to come in again.*

*But the day before yesterday the chiefs not only expressed a willingness but a desire to emigrate to the West. Acting up in full faith to the promises I had made to them, their conduct is only to be attributed to faithless disposition which has ever characterized them.*

*Immediately upon this withdrawal of the Indians—orders were transmitted to Commanders of Regiments to put their troops in motion, and before this communication reaches you—they will be scouting in every direction. Having left nothing unattempted with the means in my power, I shall now press the war with increased energy and hope soon to appraise the department of the capture or destruction of some of the enemy.* [198]

Finally, Fort Micanopy receives a new surgeon. And they will certainly need him. From Armistead's headquarters at Fort King to Lt. Col. Whistler at Micanopy, Nov. 22, 1840.

(From. Gen. Armistead's Asst. Adjutant Gen. W.W.S. Bliss, to Lt.Col. Whistler, 7<sup>th</sup> Infantry, Fort Micanopy.)

*Fort King*

---

[198] AG 1840 A312

*Nov. 22, 1840*

*Surgeon [Edward] Macomb, now at Tampa, will be ordered to report to you; in the meantime, an arrangement will be made to supply Micanopy with a Medical Officer.* [199]

Conflicting orders and actions can come when the mail is slow. General Armistead had ordered Coacoochee's mother and daughter sent to Palatka. This location on the St. Johns River is a good port location where they could be moved to just about anywhere in the territory. Since Armistead is trying to entice Coacoochee to surrender, he is using his mother and daughter as hostages. But Major Fauntleroy of the 2d Dragoon Regiment takes them 90 miles south to Fort Reid, not far from where they were originally captured.

(Gen. Armistead's Adjutant W.W.S. Bliss, to Major T.T. Fauntleroy, 2d Dragoons, Palatka.)

*Fort King*

*Nov. 23, 1840*

*It has been reported to the Commanding General that the Indian prisoners from St. Augustine (Wild Cat's mother & child and two women captured by Lt. Sibley) have been sent to Fort Reid, instead of being detained at Pilatka, agreeably to his instructions of the 10th inst. The General directs you to report why his orders relative to these prisoners were not complied with and further directs that upon their arrival at Pilatka, from Fort Reid, they be sent by the first opportunity to this place. The Head Quarters will move in a day or two for Tampa. Please direct accordingly.* [200]

Fauntleroy is slow to respond, and Armistead sends the

---

[199] AG 1840 A342, 28
[200] Ibid, 29

request again on December 29th.

Armistead has now reopened the campaign with vigor.

(Brig. General W.K. Armistead, to the Honorable Secretary of War.)

*Fort King*
*Nov. 24th, 1840.*
*The whole army is now & will remain in pursuit of the enemy. Every inducement is however held out to them to treat. The bands of Halick Tustenuggee & Tiger-tail are pursued by a detachment of the 2nd Infantry.*

*The 7th [Infantry] is now in the field. The Dragoons of which six companies are on the upper St. Johns are actively employed in that section. The 8th [Infantry] Regiment leaves this morning for Tampa, scouring the country on the route embracing the Wahoo and other hiding places on the Withlacoochee.*

*The 6th [Infantry] Regiment is in the country between the Hillsborough & Withlacoochee. The 1st [Infantry] Regiment is scouting along the gulf shore below Tampa with boats accompanied by a steamer and two schooners.*

*I have deemed these movements necessary as the center bands of the enemy have confined themselves to the swamps and along that coast from whence they make predatory excursions & it is there and there alone that they can be most annoyed.*

*To the north of Fort King, they make occasional inroads, but to bring them to sense of what they ought to do, their families and strongholds must be broken up.*

*The [Arkansas Seminole] delegation is in utter astonishment at the manner in which Halick Tustenuggee & his party left them, as they had given me & the party repeated assurances of their determination to emigrate. This want of faith has not deterred me from using exertions to communicate with the Seminoles, & I have dispatched three of the delegation with their consent, to hold intercourse with their relations and friends. I will continue every exertion to fulfill the requirements of the Government, by treaty or otherwise.*

*I shall leave this place in a few hours for Tampa, where my Head Quarters will be established. Please direct accordingly.* [201]

(Gen. Armistead's Adjutant W.W.S. Bliss, to Major T.T. Fauntleroy, Commanding St. Johns District, Fort Reid.)

*Tampa*
*Dec. 6th, 1840*

*If Wild Cats' mother, or any of the prisoners taken by Lt. Sibley will be within the limits of your command, it is the direction of the Commanding General that they be sent to this station without delay. Billy the Indian guide has been dispatched hither under a misapprehension of the General's instructions. He will return with as little delay as practicable to Fort Reid, where he can render useful Service.* [202]

Still holding out for the possibility that talks may resume at Fort King, Armistead sends instructions to Lt.Col. Bennett Riley, 2d Infantry, now commanding out of Fort King.

(Gen. Armistead's Adjutant W.W.S. Bliss, to Lt. Col. Riley, 2d Infantry, Fort King.)

---

[201] AG 1840 A331
[202] AG 1840 A357, 4

*Tampa*
*Dec. 8th, 1840*

The Commanding General is unfortunately absent having left last night on a visit of inspection to Boca Sarasota, purposing to be absent three days. I shall proceed to join him this afternoon to hasten his return to this post.

In the absence of the Commanding General, it is, of course, impossible to give any instructions relative to the Indians who may come in at Fort King. But as I know that the General is anxious to open a communication with the Indians, I would venture to suggest that as soon as you can ascertain that they wish to treat, every facility be afforded them for so doing.

The orders of the General have rendered it necessary for you to confine those who came in, but should it be expedient in your judgment to release them with a view to communicate with the main body. I entertain no doubt that such a course would receive the full approbation of the Commanding General.

Agreeable to your request, the Interpreter Primus and two of the delegation will immediately be dispatched to Fort King, where they will enable you to communicate with the Indians, and at all events ascertain their wishes.

Not knowing whether the General will again be willing to go to Fort King, for the purpose of meeting the Indians, I would respectfully suggest that they be urged to come to Tampa. Any pledge you may give them for their safety here will doubtless be fulfilled by the General. It would also be sanctioned by him should you issue provisions to those who may propose to come through.

You will understand Colonel, that these are mere suggestions made by me in the absence of the General, and knowing his *anxiety to adopt measures of pacification if possible. You will of course adopt such a policy as under the circumstances you may think proper.* [203]

Armistead soon returns and gives further instructions. There are still problems with crossed communications, of Indians who show up voluntarily and are imprisoned.)

(Gen. Armistead's Adjutant W.W.S. Bliss, to Lt. Col. Riley, Fort King.)

*Tampa*
*Dec. 10th, 1840*

*The Commanding General has returned from Boca Sarasota, and I hasten to communicate his instructions relative to the Indians who have come in, or who may come in, at Fort King. The General would himself proceed to Fort King, but that the arrival of an Indian family at this post and the expected arrival of a party from Pease Creek render it advisable for him to remain here.*

*If the Indians who came in at Fort King are still detained prisoners, the General directs that they are at once released, and all means used to restore and preserve their confidence. If deemed expedient, all or a part of them will be dispatched to bring in their people.*

*The General is anxious to see the Indians at this place, and you will use every inducement to bring them here, assuring them that they will be kindly treated and no effort made to coerce them into emigration. Should any circumstances arise of an extraordinary nature, the General expects that you will adopt such measures to meet them, as in the exercise of a sound discretion you may deem*

---

[203] Ibid, 11-13

*expedient.*

*The General desires that you will communicate with him as soon as possible, and when anything of importance occurs, particularly if his presence at Fort King be deemed necessary. He also directs that the Indian goods now at Fort King be forwarded as soon as possible to the Quarter Master at this station unless you should deem it for the public interest to retain a portion of them at Fort King for issue.* [204]

No doubt, the Indians no longer trust the soldiers. Having to come all the way down to Fort Brooke and told that they wouldn't be forced to emigrate does not seem realistic. Why else would the general invite them there, except to put them on the ships?

(Lt. Col. Wm. Whistler, 7th Infantry, to Capt. W.W.S. Bliss, Asst. Adjutant, Army of Florida.)

*Fort Micanopy*
*December 11th, 1840.*
*I have the honor to report the return of myself and command from an eight days' scout from this [Fort Micanopy] to [Fort] No. 3, thence to the Blue Spring [now called Rainbow Springs] and thence North to this Post. The country has been closely examined, but no recent signs of the enemy discovered, except the sign of two Indians seen near Stafford's Pond, and they have gone South. When I wrote on the 4th inst., I intended to have scouted the Wacasassa River and should have done so, had I found a Depot established at Fort Clinch, but to have undertaken it with the few days' provisions I had with me, would have been useless, besides— between thirty and forty of my men were taken with ague. At [Fort] No. 3, I met Captain Wheeler, 3rd Infantry, with a*

---

[204] Ibid, 13-14

*detachment of that Regiment, scouting the Wacasassa.*

*To keep the Indians out of my district, one half of my
command is now continually in the field scouting the country for
twenty miles around.* [205]

Some of the Seminoles have surrendered in Tampa, while
others request transportation from the Withlacoochee River.

(Gen. Armistead's Adjutant W.W.S. Bliss, to Maj. Belknap, 3d
Infantry, Commanding at Fort No. 4.)

*Tampa
Dec. 26<sup>th</sup>, 1840*

*You are respectfully informed that on the 23<sup>rd</sup> inst., the party
of Tallahassees who came in at Fort King, 16 in number, arrived at
this post. When the party left Fort King, nothing had been heard of
Echo-Emathla's nephew who however arrived here the following
day from Fort King in company with a young warrior. He reports
that the chief desires to make Fort Clinch [near the mouth of the
Withlacoochee River] a rendezvous for his people, as being a
central point suitable for that purpose. The General approves this
arrangement believing it will facilitate the collection of the
Tallahassees.*

*The General desires that you will send to any party of Indians,
which may be supposed desirous of coming in even if they be
beyond the Suwannee River.* [206]

(Gen. Armistead's Adjutant W.W.S. Bliss, to Maj. H. Wilson,
Commanding Fort Fanning.)

---

[205] AG 1840 A349 Enclosure
[206] AG 1840 A357, 29-30

*Tampa*

*Dec. 26th, 1840*

*Should there be any Indians in your neighborhood, west of the Suwannee, who are supposed anxious to come in, it is the direction of the Commanding General that you take measures to induce them to do so. If any of the Tallahassees visit you, they can be told that 16 of their people have come to Tampa from Fort King, and that Echo-Emathla their chief has come in to Major Belknap at Fort No. 4. The General directs that they be kindly treated, and invited to visit him at this place.* [207]

Despite all the overtures and peaceful efforts to bring in different bands of Indians to emigrate, two days later would be the most shocking ambush of the war near Micanopy.

---

[207] Ibid, 30

# Chapter 15: "I Did My Duty"

1st Lt. Daniel Whiting, 7th Infantry, is ordered to Micanopy on December 5th, 1840.

(From Lt. Daniel Whiting's diary.)

*While at Micanopy, our duties were of the most arduous and exacting nature. This vicinity had been the seat of the most depredations and Indian outrages of any other during the war, and at this time the murder of inhabitants and burning of settlements by small bands of Indians was an occurrence of frequent occasion. A scouting party of one or two companies was constantly in the field for four days at a time, searching the hammocks and pursuing the trails, seldom meeting with success though contributing to the safety of the settlers, who were scattered about the country in this region in considerable degree. I myself, became quite expert and skillful as an Indian hunter in discovering signs and following a trail.* [208]

News is heard of Lt. Col. William S. Harney and his detachment of 2d Dragoons that entered the Everglades, destroyed hidden villages, and hanged Chakaika, the leader of the Spanish Indians. The newspapers proclaimed: *"Glorious!—Forty Indians captured!—Ten Indians hanged!"* [209]

General Armistead continues on his news of the surrender of a few Seminole bands. Then announces word of a devastating

---

[208] Givens, Murphy (Editor), Daniel Powers Whiting; *A Soldier's Life: Memoirs of a Veteran of 30 Years of Soldiering*, Nueces Press, Corpus Christi, Texas, 2011, 49
[209] Richmond Enquirer, Jan. 9, 1841.

attack near Micanopy.

(Brig. General W.K. Armistead, to the Adjutant General, Washington.)

*Tampa*
*Jan. 4ᵗʰ, 1841*

*I have the honor to report that the Tallahassees are gradually coming in at several posts. Tiger Tail has been at Fort Annuteliga with several warriors and is now collecting his people, with a view of emigration. Echo Emathla is still at Fort No. 4, where a large number of Indians is expected. I shall leave Tampa tomorrow for Fort Armistead (Boca Sarasota) to meet the Seminoles, who were to assemble there about this time; my absence, however, will be but temporary.*

*Herewith I respectfully enclose Major Nelson's report of a recent Indian attack near Micanopy, of a peculiarly melancholy nature. It is believed to have been made by the Miccosukees, who are the most hostile of the bands.* [210]

(Major J.S. Nelson, 7ᵗʰ Infantry, to Capt. Bliss, Asst. Adjt. Gen.)

*Fort Micanopy*
*Dec. 28, 1840*

*Early this morning, 2ⁿᵈ Lieut's. Sherwood and Hopson and the Lady of Lieut. Montgomery with an escort of eleven mounted men left this Post with a view of visiting Fort Wacahoota. They had not proceeded more than four miles when they were fired upon by a large body of the Enemy. It becomes my painful duty to inform you that Lieut. Sherwood, Mrs. Montgomery and Sergeant Major Carrol and two privates of the 7ᵗʰ Infantry were killed. Their bodies fell into the hands of the Enemy, but they have been recovered*

---

[210] AG 1841 A5

*and brought into this Post for internment. I am unable at this time to give you any further particulars of this melancholy affair, not having received a report from Lieut. Hopson who is now on a scout. When his report is made it shall be forwarded.*

*All the effective force under my command is now in pursuit. Every exertion will be made to destroy the Enemy, nor will the pursuit be given up so long as a trace of him can be found.* [211]

This attack is one of the worst in the war. What is different from other skirmishes and ambushes, is that a young woman of high social status is killed. She was the wife of Lt. Alexander Montgomery. Word quickly spread of the attack to almost every newspaper in the country. It is reported in the Richmond Enquirer on January 9th and the Baltimore Pilot and Transcript on January 11, 1841. That is about a week faster than what normally takes for Florida correspondence to be in the newspapers. The accounts are sometimes contradictory, where a version of the battle has Lt. Sherwood grabbing a musket to fight off the approaching Indians, dying next to Mrs. Montgomery defending her body. In the official accounts, it is Private Burlingham who defends her. [212]

The attack *"caused indignation of officers and soldiers, created alarm and aroused the spirit of retaliation throughout the country."* [213]

Most newspapers report the following description.

*Florida—A Touching Scene. We have just read an account of the cruel murder by a party of Indians, of Mrs. Montgomery, wife*

---

[211] AG 1841 A5 Enclosure
[212] Camden Journal (SC) Jan. 20, 1841. Baltimore Pilot & Transcript, Jan. 11, 1841. Richmond Enquirer, Jan. 9, 1841. The Times Picayune, Jan. 21, 1841.
[213] Sprague, *The Origin, Progress, and Conclusion of the Florida War*, 249.

of Lieutenant Montgomery, of the Army. Contrary to instructions from the war department, and in opposition to positive orders issued by the commanding general, forbidding any escort being sent from post to post under thirty men, a wagon was dispatched from Fort Micanopy to Fort Wacahoota with only eleven mounted infantry under the command of Lieutenants Sherwood and Hopson; as the morning was fine, Mrs. Montgomery rode out with them. About an hour after their departure some of the horses returned to Fort Micanopy without their riders, and shortly after two soldiers rode up and announced that the party had been attacked. Mrs. Montgomery and Lieut. Sherwood and several soldiers killed. The garrison immediately sallied out, within three miles of the fort found the bleeding corpse of Mr. Montgomery with a soldier still breathing, lying by her, with just strength to say to her agonizing husband who threw himself on the ground beside his wife's bleeding body, "Lieutenant, I fought by your wife as long as I could." Lieutenant Sherwood was mounted, and might; it is reported, have escaped, but would not abandon his fair charge. This barbarous act it is believed was committed by a band of the cruel and bloodthirsty Miccosukees.

The frontier posts in Florida are not fit places for the residence of ladies. The same reason which renders it improper for them to be on board ships of war, might be urged against their being allowed to accompany their husbands to these posts of danger. Officers ought to be left to act free in moments of emergency, without the uneasiness of them having to protect helpless women and children.

This unfortunate lady had been only three weeks in Florida,

*and but lately married.* [214]

And chronicled in Sprague's book:

*Lieutenant Sherwood rallied his escort, determined to stand his ground; and to protect Mrs. Montgomery, persuaded her to dismount and get into the wagon; in the act of so doing she received a ball in her breast, which was fatal. A general panic ensued; the mules became entangled in the harness, and were killed on the spot. Lieutenant Hopson returned to Micanopy for reinforcement. With the few that remained, Lieutenant Sherwood fought hand to hand with the savages as they advanced from the wood. Exhausted from loss of blood, and overpowered by numbers, he fell a sacrifice to his one intrepidity and bravery, with the sergeant-major by his side.* [215]

Private Lansing Burlingham, becomes the tragic hero when he is immortalized by his selfless, chivalric act.

*Alone and mortally wounded, protected the body of Mrs. Montgomery from the merciless barbarities of the savages, who gathered around her, determined to gratify their diabolical revenge. 'Lieutenant,' said he (addressing Lt. Montgomery who had arrived); 'I fought for her as long as I could; but they were too strong for me,"—his voice here faltered—"but I did my duty." These were his last words. His ear was deaf to the repeated thanks of his officer, from a heart already overburdened with grief.* [216]

The heroic last words put in the official Army report; adding, "I did my duty." In a terrible and seemingly endless war that had dragged on for years, there were very few cases of such chivalry

---

[214] Baton Rouge Gazette, Feb. 6, 1841.
[215] Sprague, *The Origin, Progress, and Conclusion of the Florida War*, 249, 484.
[216] Ibid, 484

and heroics displayed. And probably none that would capture the attention of the newspapers such as this.[217]

Lt. Daniel Whiting writes in his journal:

*On the 28th of December, Lt. Hanson [it should be Hopson, not Hanson], who had just joined and who had left his bride at Wacahoota until he could prepare his quarters, went back after her with a wagon for baggage accompanied by an escort of 12 mounted men under command of Lt. (Walter) Sherwood.*

*This distance of ten miles was considered safe and had been undisturbed by Indians for a long time, with but one point of danger where a hammock terminated near the road along its route. This route had been considered so safe that officers had frequently ridden from one post to the other without escort. But this very spot, called Martin's Point, had formerly been the scene of repeated ambuscades and had received its name from a young officer who was shot there in passing some months before. [2d Lt. John W. Martin.] No Indian signs had been detected or reported recently, however, in its vicinity, and believing in the absence of danger, Mrs. Montgomery concluded to ride over on horseback with the party, to accompany her friend Mrs. Hanson [Hopson] in returning. Her husband, Lt. [Alexander] Montgomery, being unwell, entrusted her to care and protection of the two other officers of the escort; he stayed at home.*

*The party started in high spirits about 6 a.m. under these favorable auspices, but about 8 a.m. the quiet of the garrison was disturbed by the rush of horses and shouts of men. On hastening from my breakfast to ascertain the cause, I found horses dashing in riderless, save with one or two bareheaded and breathless*

---

[217] Ibid, 484

soldiers, while the air rang with the news that the party had been attacked by some 100 Indians at Martin's Point, about four miles distant, and Lt. Sherwood, Mrs. Montgomery, and others had been killed or wounded.

The men of the garrison were thronging onto the parade, equipped and eager, and in about three minutes, not more, the whole command, nearly 300 men, were under full speed running the whole distance to the fatal scene. We arrived on the ground in breathless anxiety and apprehension to realize a tragedy equal to our fears. There lay the bodies of Mrs. Montgomery, Lt. Sherwood, a sergeant [Sgt. Maj. Carroll] and three men, with the wreck of the wagon and carcasses of the mules, the former still warm and glowing with recent life. Nothing remained of the perpetrators of the deed to relieve the impressive silence of the spot.

The bodies were all stripped and in a state of nudity, except that of Mrs. Montgomery, who had only her outer skirts torn away. Her gloves were still on, fortunately concealing her rings which would otherwise have been taken, probably with loss of the fingers. She was neither disfigured nor mutilated, with only the livid mark on her bosom made by a fatal bullet, through which the blood was even yet slowly welling. [Lt.] Montgomery had thrown himself on one of the horses, bareheaded and coatless, and had with reckless speed preceded us to the spot. When we reached the scene, he was found prostrate and insensible with grief at the body of his wife.

Sad and mournful was the party's return to the post. Mrs. Montgomery was yet but a bride not long wedded, very youthful and engaging and whose amiability of character and artless, cheerful disposition had endeared and attracted all our social interest and regard. Her husband seemed like one demented for a long period, and there are those who detect in the absent and dreamy temper, fitful and melancholy mood that have distinguished him ere to the present time, the evidence of the enduring impression upon him of the day's calamitous events.

Except the return escort with the bodies, our whole command in different parties scattered from the fatal ground in search of the perpetrators, with untiring zeal and eager thirst for vengeance, but although some of us must have been in close vicinity and near success, our exertions were in vain, for Montgomery afterwards said some Indians were still loitering there when he arrived.

We never overtook them, though for many days the whole force of the adjacent country was in active operation for the purpose. The party I was with discovered the trail that night and next morning, the first camp of the murderers, about the smoldering embers of whose fire were found several scraps of the dress of the unfortunate lady.

Although the excitement of this catastrophe subsided after a time, the usual periodical scouting from our post was continued, it is necessary to say, with unabated activity, some expeditions proceeding far into the interior, seeking the concealed haunts of our savage foe into the recesses of their own swamps and hiding places. [218]

Whiting gives a different account from the official report. Missing is the heroic and romantic last words of Private Burlingham. Lieutenant Montgomery claims that there were still Indians when he arrived. This account seems believable,

---

[218] Givens, *A Soldier's Life: Memoirs of a Veteran of 30 Years of Soldiering*, 48-50.

considering that it is written in a diary not intended for the public.

In May 1840, Lt. James W. Anderson writes his fiancé Ellen Brown with an important observation.

*The Indians are infuriated by the loss of their crops & are now wreaking their vengeance in a most summary manner.* [219]

Anderson is keen to observe that the cause of the attacks in the recent few weeks might be a result of recent expeditions by Maj. Loomis and others that destroyed the many growing fields of the Indians.

1st Lt. James W. Anderson and Ellen Brown married in Newnansville on October 26th. [220]

Both Anderson and Montgomery had married only a few weeks apart. Young officers with newlywed brides, moving to a dangerous area with their spouses.

Mrs. Anderson stayed with her sisters in Newnansville before moving to Fort King to be with her husband. Lt. Anderson is affected deeply by the death of Mrs. Montgomery. On Jan. 5, 1841, he writes Ellen and gives an important account of the Battle of Martin's Point that had been obtained by his fellow officers. He does confirm that the attack was in the same area where Lt. Martin was shot the previous May. Anderson and Martin were

---

[219] Denham, James M.; and Huneycutt, Keith L.; 2004 *"Everything is Hubbub Here": Lt. James Willoughby Anderson's Second Seminole War, 1837-1842*. The Florida Historical Quarterly (Winter 2004) Vol. 82, No. 3, 319.
[220] ANC Vol 11, No. 24 (Dec. 10, 1840) 384.

both in the 2d Infantry Regiment.[221]

*I wrote you a few lines by the last mail including Lt. [Richard C.] Gatlin's account of the tale of Mrs. [Elizabeth] Montgomery know not why it is, unless it be that my mind reverted to you, that I have been so affected by her fate. It appears that Lt. [Nevil] Hopson was going to Wacahoota with a wagon for his wife & that Lt. [Walter] Sherwood & Mrs. Montgomery rode out with him, having the Sgt. Major & 11 mounted men with them—when they arrived near the point of [the] hammock where [John W.] Martin of our Regt. Was shot; they saw the Indians advancing & Lt. Sherwood who was ranking officer, & in whose charge Mrs. Montgomery was placed, ordered the whole party to dismount & prepare for action, directing Mrs. M. to get into the wagon. Lt. Hopson was ordered back to Micanopy to bring a reinforcement. — Bad management & showing Lt. S' want of experience. It is a most unfortunate affair—but perhaps I may have done as he did rather than risk the imputation of cowardice. I think however I should have looked to the safety of the lady by sending her back forthwith, but Lt. S. no doubt thought her safer in the wagon than in going back. I am disgusted with these butcheries, & since that affair have kept aloof from all Florida topics. Would to God that this horrible war was ended.* [222]

In a letter to Anderson from Captain Richard Gatlin, it says that one soldier was found mortally wounded near Mrs. Montgomery's body. He said, "Lieutenant, I fought for your wife

---

[221] Denham and Huneycutt; *"Everything is Hubbub Here"*. Denham, James M.; *Echoes from a Distant Frontier: the Brown Sisters' Correspondence from Antebellum Florida* (University of South Carolina Press, Columbia, SC, 2004).
[222] Denham and Huneycutt, *"Everything is Hubbub Here"*, 349-350. Denham, *Echoes from a Distant Frontier: the Brown Sisters' Correspondence from Antebellum Florida*, 144-145.

as long as I could stand. You see that I am now dying."[223]

Anderson says his true feelings when he writes:

*The Cursed Indians—I try to restrain, but it is useless. Were I in Montgomery's place, I would get to Tampa, give a great feast to all the Indians there and blow them to the Devil while they were at the table by springing a mine of powder under them. I will shake no Florida Indian by the hand again. That is a sign of friendship I will not extend to them as I cannot feel it.* [224]

The Richmond Enquirer newspaper published similar sentiments:

*..the wily Savage has perpetrated the most heart-rending atrocities. At this very moment a deputation of Tallahassees are at Tampa... God grant that we who are 'expected to die in our tracks' rather than disgrace our commissions, may yet to live to see the day when these wretches will meet their deserts.* [225]

The reaction from Washington is almost immediate. A letter sent from Florida to Washington would normally take three weeks. Secretary of War Joel Poinsett writes to Gen. Armistead in Tampa thirteen days after the incident on January 10, 1841.

*I have been informed from a source entitled to credit, that an escort of eleven mounted infantry accompanying a wagon from Fort Micanopy to Fort Wacahoota was attacked by a party of Indians and the commanding officer and several soldiers of the escort killed. The force of this escort was, contrary to my instructions and in opposition to your orders, entirely inefficient,*

---

[223] Denham and Huneycutt, *"Everything is Hubbub Here"*, 349.
[224] Ibid, 351
[225] The Richmond Enquirer, Jan. 16, 1841

and I think it proper to call your attention once more to the subject.

Officers in command of posts must be required to obey orders or be brought to a court martial if they violate them on any pretext whatever, whether, as in this case, loss of life and defeat be the consequence of such disobedience or not. Discipline in the field and in presence of the enemy must be enforced.

The circumstances attending this attack render it necessary that the department should state its views in relation to escorts. It appears that the eleven infantry soldiers were mounted.-- A circumstance calculated to ensure a disastrous defeat in the event of encountering an enemy. It is not probable that any number of infantry soldiers will be good horsemen, and when mounted, such men will be fully occupied with keeping themselves in the saddle, and taking care of their arms and accouterments. Indians invariably get the first fire, and if the soldier is not shot, he is either thrown from the startled animal's back or keeps himself on by throwing away his musket; as appears to have been the case in this and other similar cases. If a sufficient number of men should unexpectedly and providentially retain their seats and their muskets to make battle, they have to dismount exposed to the enemy's fire, and a certain number of the remaining few must be detached to hold the horses while the rest defend the baggage train. This is so obviously wrong that the department positively forbids the continuance of the practice and directs that the horses stationed at the posts to mount infantry soldiers for the purpose of escorting trains from post to post be immediately withdrawn, and orders issued that in future Infantry escorts proceed on foot, the *wagons accommodating their pace to the march of the soldier.* [226]

As in the previous year, the deaths at Fort Micanopy are so great that the regiment files a quarterly casualty report. Lt. Col. Whistler, 13 January 1841, Fort Micanopy, "Transmitting "Return of Casualties" &c. in the 7th Regt. Of Infantry & Transcript of the Registry of Deceased Soldiers for the 4th Quarter 1840." Signed by Capt. Richard Gatlin. [227]

Four are listed as "Killed in Action with the enemy" near Fort Micanopy on 28 December 1840. (Other than Lt. Sherwood.)

- Francis Carroll, Sergeant Major; "Private effects left in the hands of his wife."
- Lancing Burlingham, Private; "Due to the Quartermaster Department, 83 Cents."
- John R. Smith, Pvt. "Due Laundress, Mrs. Carroll (Sgt.Maj. Carroll's wife?) $6.00, due Sutler A.B. Moyes $40.63, 1st Pay till 9th October 1840."
- Alexander McDonald, Pvt. "Due A.B. Moyes, Sutler $17.95. Due Mrs. Cowden, Laundress $1.50" [228]

On January 16, 1841, Gen. Armistead forwards his reports to the Army Adjutant General. Maj. Nelson says that he included Lt. Hopson's report, but it is not among the Adjutant General letters. It is possibly attached to a report of the court of inquiry. [229]

(2d Lt. W. B. Greene, to Maj. J.S. Nelson, 7th Regt of Infantry.)

*Fort Wheelock, E.F.*

---

[226] "Letters Sent by the Office of the Adjutant General (Main Series) 1800-1890", 1840/1841, 132.
[227] AG 1841 W27
[228] AG 1841 W27 Enclosure
[229] AG 1841 A11

*January 1st, 1841*

At one o'clock, on the 28th day of December 1840, I left this Post with twenty-nine men of Comp. "A" 7th Infy., under command of Lieut. Scott, and twenty-three men of Comp. "F" 7th Infy, under command of Lieut. Lee, of the 8th Infy, who volunteered his services for the expedition. I scouted this day, in a westerly direction, towards Fort Wacahoota; but saw no signs.

At daylight on the 29th, having procured a guide, we left Wacahoota and proceeded to scout the hammocks north of Levi's Prairie. At about ten o'clock, while the command was in the vicinity of Lieut. Sanderson's battleground, a rifle was fired in the hammock; this was probably a signal from some of the enemy's scouts, to warn the principal party of our approach. At about eleven o'clock, we found the enemy's camp; it was situated in the edge of the hammock, and had been left about an hour before our arrival—probably immediately after the signal gun was fired. In this camp were four blazing fires, with meat roasting before them. Near the fires we found about twenty-five pounds of fresh beef, not cooked. From the circumstance of the meat being left, I should judge the camp had been left in some haste. We remained two or three hours in the hammock, and endeavoring to find the trail; but the Indians, having seen us cross the area of the prairie, scattered, leaving no perceptible signs. Stopping to find the trail in an easterly direction, we marched towards the old plantation; and at the distance of nearly two miles from the first camp, we found another containing four fires like the first. The fires at this camp were burned down but the ashes were still hot. About a mile beyond the Plantation, we fell in with the scout from Micanopy, & Capt. Holmes assumed command of my party.

On the morning of the 30th, we left Micanopy, and scouted the hammocks south of Levi's Prairie, but saw no fresh signs.

*On the morning of the 31ˢᵗ, we proceeded to scout the country between Forts Wacahoota & Wheelock, but saw nothing of interest.*

*In pursuance of Orders, I then proceeded to Ft. Wheelock, and arrived at that Post, on the second day after leaving Fort Micanopy, in time for muster.* [230]

The "Old Plantation" is probably the former settlement of Moses Levy, father of David Levy Yulee, who attempted to start a Jewish colony in the 1820s. It came to an end in 1835 when it was burned by the Seminoles.

(Capt. E.S. Hawkins, to Lt. R.S. Gatlin, Adjutant, 7ᵗʰ Infantry.)

Fort Wacahoota, E.F.
January 3ʳᵈ, 1841.

*I have the honor to report that about 12 o'clock on the 28ᵗʰ Ulto., I received information that a large party of Indians had made an attack on an Escort about 3 ½ miles from Micanopy, on the road leading from there to this post, killing Mrs. Montgomery, Lt. Sherwood, and several soldiers. In about 20 minutes after I received the information, I left with a command consisting of Capt. Lee and 65 Non-commissioned, officers & privates of companies B & H, 7ᵗʰ Infantry, provisioned for 2 days. Learning that a large command from Micanopy had arrived on the ground where the attack was made and believing it probable that the Indians would endeavor to make their escape by the upper end of Levy's Prairie, I thought it advisable to march in that distance with a view to cut off their retreat.*

*I accordingly marched from here in a course nearly due North*

---

[230] AG 1841 A11 Enclosure

leaving Fort Walker on my left and after passing through some small hammocks, entered the upper end of that prairie, and shirted the edge of the hammock bordering on it for about 3 miles, and then passing through the hammocks between Levy's and Alachua Prairie, skirted the edge of the latter for about 4 miles and encamped, without having seen any signs of Indians. The distance marched, about 12 miles.

The next morning (29th) at sunrise, I proceeded by Levy's field to Micanopy, and traversed several miles of hammock without seeing any signs of the enemy and arrived there between 10 and 11 A.M., having by report of my guide marched about 8 miles. On the morning of the 30th, I left Micanopy with my command and marched towards the Welika Pond, and when near it, turned off in a direction due south; after proceeding between 1 ½ and 2 miles, I discovered the tracks of 3 or 4 Indians, made apparently about 2 days before. I followed them from near the Micanopy Hammock where first seen, for about 2 miles towards the Wakahoota Hammock, where they scattered and became very indistinct, and finally disappeared altogether. I continued my march for 8 or 9 miles in a southwest course and encamped after passing through and carefully examining the Wakahoota Hammock, at a point about 14 miles from Micanopy, and 8 from this Post. On the 31st, my command returned to this Post passing through the Wakahoota Hammock, without discovering any signs of Indians.
231

(Capt. T.H. Holmes, to Lt. R.C. Gatlin, Adjutant, 7th Infantry.)

Fort Micanopy, E.F.
31st Dec. 1840

---

231 Ibid

*Immediately after the melancholy affair that resulted in the death of Lt. Sherwood on the 28th Inst., I proceeded by Maj. Nelson's order to the place of action. On my arrival—a soldier left on the ground informed me—that the Indians had gone in a northwest direction about half an hour before. With a command of ninety men, I immediately commenced a close and active search for them, which was kept up from about 10 o'clock in the morning until nearly night, but they had scattered, and at the distance of two hundred yards from the field of action no trace of an Indian could be seen. Having furnished myself with a guide, I resumed the scout sometime before daylight on the following morning hoping thereby to find the Indians, by their fires, which yet it was dark and having failed, I continued to search the neighboring hammocks until late in the evening when I returned to this post.* [232]

(1st Lt. R.H. Ross, to 1st Lt. R.C. Gatlin, Adjutant, 7th Infantry.)

*Fort Micanopy, E.F.*
*January 3rd, 1841*

*I have to inform you that, in obedience to instructions received from the commanding officer, I proceeded on the 30th Ulto., with companies G and K, 7th Infantry, towards the river Styx, crossing it between the Pilatki [Palatka] road and Orange Lake, thence along the hammock to the Alachua Prairie, thence through the hammock on the eastern side of this prairie near the Pithlochoco Lake and coming again into the Prairie near Fort Tarver where my party bivouacked for the night.-- From Fort Tarver I returned to this post, having closely examined the country passed over without seeing any signs of the enemy.* [233]

---

[232] Ibid
[233] Ibid

(Lt.Col. B. Riley, to Capt. W.W.S. Bliss, Asst. Adjt. General, Army of Florida.)

*Fort King, E.F.*
*January 1ˢᵗ, 1841*
*I report that a Teamster was killed by Indians on the 28ᵗʰ Ulto. At 9-mile hammock between Pilatka and Fort Holmes, under the following circumstances.*

*About ½ past 12 M. on that day, Lt. Anderson left Palatka in command of 100 recruits of the 2ⁿᵈ Infantry for Fort Holmes. About an hour after he left, the wagons destined for Fort Holmes, whose drivers had been directed by Lt. McKinstry to join Lt. A's command & leave Palatka with it, but did not do so. I started alone—sometimes afterward (perhaps an hour), I left Pilatka myself in company with Lt. McKinstry and 4 of my escort of mounted men, having 5 others on my rear with the wagon.-- I reached nine-mile hammock about ½ hour before sundown, discovered two Indians and on passing into the Hammock I found the body of one of the Teamsters lying dead in the road—the other teamsters, left his team & ran into Lt. A's command 3 or 4 miles ahead.-- The Indians when I flushed them had succeeded in taking the wagon covers & a few articles from the wagons, but the Wagons and teams remained uninjured.-- I directed Lt. A to return immediately in pursuit, giving him all the mounted men that could be raised on the spot but ere he could reach the Hammock it was dark.-- During the night, he was joined by Lt. Woodruff and 16 footmen from Fort Holmes and by Lt. Rogers and 23 dragoons from Pilatka, the latter party coming out in consequence of an express from me to the Commanding Officer of that post. As soon as it was light, the whole vicinity we scoured but without success. Lt. A reports that there were 5 or 6 warriors and that a part if not the whole of them must have crossed the Ocklawaha during the night.* [234]

Lt. Hopson's actions at the battle are questioned since he left the battle at Martin's Point to get help at Fort Micanopy. There is an inquiry to determine if he was ordered or fled in cowardice.

(From Gen. Armistead, W.W.S. Bliss, Asst. Adjt. Gen, to Maj. J.S. Nelson, 7th Infantry, Micanopy.)

*Tampa*
*January 16th, 1841*
*As it is believed that there are reports in circulation, injurious to the character of Lt. Hopson, as connected with the attack on Lieut. Sherwood's party, the Commanding General desires you to investigate the circumstances of the case and report the result confidentially to him.* [235]

(Army Adjutant General Roger Jones, to Gen. Armistead)

*February 13th, 1841*
*Lieut. Hopson's Report shows that he left the party commanded by Lieut. Sherwood after it had been attacked by Indians, without the authority of his Commanding officer, and at a time, it would seem when his presence was necessary, the party not having then been defeated or much injured.-- The case required investigation.* [236]

Lt. Hopson is eventually cleared and continues in the Army until the Mexican War when he is dismissed for drunkenness.

---

[234] Ibid
[235] AG 1841 A33, Jan. 16, 1841.
[236] "Letters Sent by the Office of the Adjutant General, 1841, 41.

# Chapter 16: Lt. Montgomery and His Family

No previous biography is written about Alexander Montgomery and his two wives other than scattered newspaper articles. The following is research you will not find anywhere else.

Alexander Montgomery was born near Pittsburgh, Pennsylvania about 1811. He was appointed to West Point from Pennsylvania and graduated as the goat, the last of the class of 1834. [237]

Lt. Alexander Montgomery's wife, Elizabeth Francis (or Fanny) Taylor, was the most eligible bachelorette in Cincinnati, the daughter of one of the city's founding businessmen and a millionaire, Griffin Taylor. She turned 19-years-old one week after her marriage. They were married at Christ Church in downtown Cincinnati on September 2, 1840. [238]

Elizabeth was born on September 9, 1821, and died December 28, 1840. She was married for less than four months. She was first buried in Micanopy, and then exhumed and reinterred at the Taylor family crypt at Spring Grove Cemetery in Cincinnati on July 18, 1849. Ironically, Spring Grove is also a Florida place name northwest of Micanopy, near where she was killed. [239] The local Florida militia unit there is known as the Spring Grove Guards.

---

[237] Cullum, Biographical Register of the Officers and Graduates of the U.S. Military Academy at West Point, New York, since its establishment in 1802.
[238] Cincinnati History Library; Christ Church Records, 1821-1996, MSS 1034 & 1052, Hamilton County, Cincinnati Library; http://library.cincymuseum.org. ANC Vol. 11, 175.
[239] ANC Vol. 11, 175. Spring Grove Cemetery, Cincinnati, Ohio. Cemetery card for Spring Grove Cemetery, SpringGrove.org.

The North Alabamian newspaper says that Elizabeth's father disapproved of the marriage because Montgomery was not a man of the higher social class. Once married, he refused to see his daughter. It is unknown if this was true. [240]

Elizabeth's father, Griffin Taylor, was born in 1797 and died December 22, 1866 at age 69. His wife Mary Smith Thomas survived until 1882. They had five daughters, but only one, Sarah Kilgour Taylor Miller, lived longer than her parents. [241]

Griffin Taylor had a successful grocery and mercantile business. He was a bank president, president of the Chamber of Commerce, and also on the board of trustees for the Spring Grove Cemetery and director from 1845 to 1852. Spring Grove Cemetery is one of the first public and secular cemeteries in the country and is a famous park and gardens today. There are many ornate and decorative mausoleums and statues in the Cemetery, but the family vault of Griffin Taylor and his family is very plain, showing how frugal a businessman he was. So plain, that I could not find any modern photos of it, and had to go there and take a photo. [242]

---

[240] North Alabamian, April 17, 1841
[241] Family trees for Griffin Taylor, Ancestry.com.
[242] Spring Grove Cemetery, cemetery card.

The tomb of Griffin Taylor and his family in Spring Grove Cemetery in Cincinnati, Ohio.

The marble door to Griffin Taylor's family tomb. His name "Griffin Taylor" is engraved across the front of the door. [243]

[243] Photos of Griffin Taylor tomb by Chris Kimball.

In October 1840, post returns showed Lt. Montgomery serving as Acting Quartermaster at Newport Barracks in Newport, Kentucky, across the Ohio River from Cincinnati. At the same time, Lt. Walter Sherwood was serving at another large recruiting center, of Fort Columbus, New York City. (Later known as Fort Jay, and now also a city park.) Both officers would soon arrive in Florida.

Lt. Alexander Montgomery received the wrath of the Army Quartermaster, Major General Thomas Jesup. On October 13, 1840, General Jesup rebuked Montgomery for using Quartermaster funds for his moving expenses and transportation. This is not the last time Montgomery runs afoul with Jesup. [244]

After Elizabeth died, Lt. Montgomery is on the post returns at Fort Pickens near Pensacola from June 1842 to May 1843. Then from June 1843 to April 1845 on the opposite side of the bay at Fort Barrancas. Both are coastal brick forts guarding the opening of Pensacola Bay and can be visited today. The lieutenant worked at Pensacola harbor under the Quartermaster Department. [245]

Almost three years to the day of his first wedding on September 1, 1843, Lt. Montgomery marries a second time. To another young bachelorette of the wealthiest man in town, at the plantation of the bride's father at Mount Vernon, Alabama. [246]

The bride Matilda E. Eastin was born in 1823 or 1825, depending on which source you check.

Matilda's father, Thomas Eastin, was reappointed by President

---

[244] "Letters Sent by the Office of the Quartermaster General (Main Series) 1818-1870", Record Group 92, 1840, Oct. 13, 102-103.

[245] Post Returns for Fort Barrancas, Fort Pickens, Pensacola Harbor.

[246] Mobile County book of Marriages, Alabama, 1843, Ancestry.com.

Van Buren in 1840 as Naval Agent of the Port in Pensacola, which is a customs agent. Since Lt. Montgomery was in a similar profession of quartermaster and subsistence, Eastin's daughter Matilda probably attracted his attention when Mr. Eastin and Montgomery crossed paths while working at the port. [247]

Thomas Eastin had connections to President Jackson. His brother had married Jackson's niece, Rachael Donalson. Thomas Eastin was Quartermaster for Jackson during the War of 1812 and the First Seminole War in Florida. Eastin's letters to Andrew Jackson are written in a very familiar and personal nature, showing that he was a close ally of Jackson. (At least considered himself as such.) Montgomery couldn't have picked a better-connected bride.

Thomas Eastin started "The Halcyon," the first Newspaper in Alabama Territory at the territorial capital of St. Stephens. He served as quartermaster for the Alabama militia and was appointed Justice of the Peace. Eastin had a mansion at Mount Vernon near the Alabama state arsenal until it burned down in 1859. [248]

Also like Jackson, Eastin was strongly Presbyterian, and his business practices reflected this when he refused to publish names of women in the newspaper unless as marriage notices or obituaries.

Eastin's wife Lucinda was the sister of future Alabama Governor John Gayle. The daughters married rich and successful husbands, except for Matilda, who married Lt. Montgomery. [249]

---

[247] Alexandria Gazette, May 18, 1840
[248] The Cahaba Gazette, Oct. 21, 1859
[249] Arkansas Democrat, Feb. 16, 1892.

The Post Returns of Fort Barrancas in August 1843 show Lt. Montgomery was taking a week off for personal leave for his marriage and honeymoon. At the same time on leave was Assistant Surgeon Samuel P. Moore, who was a fellow officer with Montgomery back at Micanopy, and he probably served as the best man at the wedding. Surgeon Moore was present on duty at Fort King when Capt. Rains is wounded in April 1840, at Micanopy when Lt. Montgomery's first wife was killed, and the skirmish at Orange Creek near Fort Russell in March 1841.

In 1844, Lt. Montgomery led scouting expeditions of 7th Infantry soldiers from Pensacola up the Choctawhatchee River to search for Indians said to be committing depredations. They burned a few camps but did not capture any Indians. [250]

Lt. Montgomery appears on the Post Returns of April 1845 at Fort Pickens, and then May to August 1845 for the military facility in Pensacola until he left for Texas in August 1845. In March 1846 to June or July 1846, he was part of the U.S. forces at Point Isabel, Texas (Fort Polk), preparing for entry into Mexico. He was promoted to Captain, 12 years after his graduation at West Point. He served in Mexico during the US-Mexican War, but there is little record of what he did. [251]

After the Mexican War, Montgomery spent the next few years in Arkansas. From Sept. 11, 1849, to May 24, 1854, at Fort Smith. There are no post returns between June 1850 and March 1851. February 1852, he is moving property up the Arkansas River. July 1853, he is away purchasing horses and returns the next month. In September 1853, he was scouting between Ft. Smith and Ft.

---

[250] Baton Rouge Gazette, Jun. 8, 1844. The Times Picayune, Feb. 29, 1844.
[251] The Daily Delta, May 22, 1846. The Times Picayune, Aug. 28, 1845.

Arbuckle in southern Oklahoma.

The 1850 census for Fort Smith, Arkansas lists 38-year-old Alexander Montgomery, his wife 25-year-old Matilda E.; their daughter, 7-year-old Elizabeth F.; 72-year-old Samuel K. Montgomery from Pennsylvania (his father?), and two other officers or clerks in the Quartermaster Department that are sharing the same residence.

Capt. Montgomery returns to Florida from June 1854 to March 1855 at Fort Brooke. He is at Fort Myers from April 1855 to February 10, 1856, during the Third Seminole War. There are missing months of post returns after that. From 1 June 1857 to Jan. 1861, he is back at Fort Smith, Arkansas, although some months are missing.

Montgomery raises the indignation of General Jesup when he is slow to close his property records and settle his accounts. Jesup wrote an angry letter to Montgomery to close his accounts in January 1857, and that he has not turned in his report for over $7,000 in property. Once the records are settled, Jesup sends Montgomery to Jefferson Barracks, St. Louis, Missouri.[252]

Montgomery requested an assignment in Washington at Jesup's office. Jesup showed a strong dislike for the idea and sent him out west instead. Jesup did not want anyone who didn't settle accounts in a timely fashion. And, Montgomery still owes money to the post sutler at Fort Brooke. [253]

Capt. Montgomery again raised the anger of Jesup at Fort

---

[252] "Letters Sent by the Office of the Quartermaster General, Jan. 21, 1857, Jesup to Montgomery
[253] "Letters Sent by the Office of the Quartermaster General, Jesup to Montgomery

Smith shortly after. Major Richard Gatlin (the former commanding captain at Micanopy 17 years earlier) proposed that quarters be built for the laundresses at Fort Smith. Montgomery figured out cost estimates and materials needed for boards that could be cut at a local mill and sent the proposal to General Jesup. The General was not pleased and chastised Montgomery by saying that the quartermaster has never spent money on billets constructed for laundresses. [254]

Montgomery is in the Indian Territory of Oklahoma and Arkansas at the outbreak of the Civil War. The post returns of Fort Arbuckle for April 1861 have written General Order #5, March 1st, of the dismissal of Brig. Gen. Twiggs from the Army of the United States. Twiggs is the only General officer in the Army who resigned and joined the confederacy, although he died next year at age 72.

In April 1861, Arkansas has not yet left the Union and joined the Confederacy, but already seized the state arsenal and supplies being sent to Fort Smith. 300 Arkansas Infantry soldiers with eight artillery pieces are sent to seize Fort Smith. U.S. Captain Samuel Sturgis is under orders to hold the fort with two under-strength cavalry companies but decides it is better to abandon the post and leave in haste on April 23rd. The small number of personnel who didn't have horses remain; the hospital steward, the laundresses, the bugler, and the quartermaster, Capt. Alexander Montgomery. Nothing was worse for your career than surrendering a fort without a courageous fight to the death, and Sturgis wanted none of that, so he left the job to Montgomery and Richard Gatlin. The move didn't hurt Sturgis' career since he is

---

[254] AG 1857 M549.

soon promoted to Major.

Major Richard Gatlin was not even assigned to Fort Smith, but unfortunately, is in the area taking care of personal business. Sturgis gave him the unenviable duty of surrendering the post to the state. Both Gatlin and Montgomery are taken prisoner, and only released when they promise not to take up arms against the state of Arkansas and the Confederacy. Gatlin soon resigned his commission and joined the Confederacy, and was a general in the Confederate Army. Montgomery stayed loyal to the Union and departed for Fort Washita in southeast Oklahoma. [255]

During the war, Montgomery is stricken from the roll of officers for charges of mismanagement, but accusations were eventually proven false. Near the end of the war, Montgomery is cleared and restored to his former rank and position. He was returned to the Army Register as if nothing happened. [256]

After the Civil War, Alexander Montgomery is still at the rank of Major after participating in four wars and 31 years in service. He is appointed the district Quartermaster in charge of Buffalo, Fort Niagara, and Plattsburg Barracks. [257]

The 1870 census shows Montgomery living in Buffalo, New York, with his wife Matilda, their 24-year-old daughter Elizabeth, and their 23-year-old son Robert.

I could find no other records of Robert Montgomery, and he only shows up on two census records. The family name is very

---

[255] Fort Smith Times, May 2, 1909.
https://encyclopediaofarkansas.net/entries/abandonment-of-fort-smith-6640/.
[256] Daily National Republican, June 24, 1864
[257] General Orders No. 46, Headquarters Dept. of the East, July 26, 1867.

common, and I even found several Matilda Eastin/Easton's.

Mrs. Matilda Montgomery kept close ties with friends in Fort Smith because the Daily Arkansas Gazette published a short notice of her death when she died on March 20, 1876, at Georgetown, D.C. [258]

The Washington Evening Star newspaper on December 4, 1883, reports that Col. Alexander Montgomery (now 72 years old) and his daughter return to the city after traveling several months in Canada. It does not give the reason for the travel. Maybe he settled the arrangements for his burial plot?

The 1892 state census from Warren, New York, shows the 81-year-old Alexander Montgomery with his daughter Elizabeth living in the same residence.

The elder Montgomery dies the next year at age 82, on October 13, 1893. He is buried at St. Peter's Anglican Church in Cobourg, Northumberland, Ontario, with his wife Matilda who was reinterred from where she was originally buried at the Congressional Cemetery in Washington, D.C. (Another similarity between both wives of Montgomery, is that they were reinterred elsewhere from where they were originally buried.) Daughter Elizabeth Frances Montgomery died of tuberculosis on September 17, 1914, and is buried with her parents. Elizabeth is listed on the cemetery records as "spinster." [259]

---

[258] Daily Arkansas Gazette, March 22, 1876.
[259] Cemsearch; Canadian grave search. cemsearch.ca; and Ancestry.com

# Chapter 17: Those Who Also Did Their Duty

Lt. Nevil Hopson, one of the few survivors of Martin's Point, was from Hopkinsville, Kentucky, in the southwest part of the state. His father (Nevil Sr.,) was considered one of the founders of Hopkinsville and died in 1835 while his son was at West Point. Coincidentally, Major Francis Dade also has Dade relatives who settled west of Hopkinsville. [260]

Nevil Hopson graduated from the US Military Academy in 1837, the same class as Lt. Walter Sherwood, and married Ellen Long on 24 April 1838. [261]

Lieut. Hopson seems to have had a drinking problem. He is diagnosed with an ailment related to his drinking. In the Surgeon's report of Lt. Hopson, 26 March 1839, Newport, Kentucky, Dr. Collins writes, "I have carefully examined this officer and find that he has been for some time labored under inflammation of the kidneys and bladder from which he has not entirely recovered. In case he can't be permitted a further leave of absence or to remain at some healthy post, and on light duty, he won't in all probability soon be entirely relieved from his present disability."[262]

When the 7th Infantry came to Florida, Hopson receives a wound to his hand in battle. (It doesn't say how or where.) He writes to the Army Adjutant General from his home in Hopkinsville, Kentucky.

(Lt. N. Hopson, to Genl. R. Jones, Adjutant General,

---

[260] Hopkinsville Kentuckian, May 4, 1905 & Nov. 19, 1908
[261] Kentucky County Marriage Records, Christian County, 1838; Ancestry.com.
[262] AG 1839 H80.

Washington.)

*Hopkinsville, KY*
*May 5th, 1840*

*You will perceive by the accompanying certificate that my
hand although improving is far from being well, and as I have
received your orders assigning me to duty in Florida, I have the
honor to request (as I am unable to duty with my Regiment) that I
may be excused from going South at this season of the year and
that I may be assigned to light duty elsewhere.* [263]

(Statement of F.G. Montgomery, Physician, Hopkinsville, May
1st, 1840.)

*Lieut. Nevil Hopson of the 7th Regt. Of Infantry, having applied
for a certificate, I do hereby certify, that I have frequently &
carefully examined this officer, & find that he is still laboring under
the effects of a very severe wound of the right hand, received as,
he states, sometime during last autumn, while at his station in
Florida. That although the wounded hand has slowly improved for
some time, yet on account of exfoliation of the bones of the
injured hand, which is still progressing, he is, in my opinion unfit
for any duty which may require the grasping or use of a sword.
And, that in all reasonable probability, several weeks will elapse
before he will be able to resume such duties.* [264]

Two months later, Hopson writes from Rodney, Mississippi,
near Natchez, with another physician report.

(Lt. N. Hopson, to Genl. R. Jones, Adjutant General,
Washington.)

---

[263] AG 1840 H127 and H197
[264] Ibid

*(Near) Rodney, Miss.*
*July 9th, 1840*

*Herewith I have the honor to forward the enclosed certificate of my ill state of health which prevented my joining my regiment. And to request an extenuation of my leave of absence until my health is sufficiently improved to do duty. So soon as my health will admit of my traveling on a steamboat I shall proceed to Hopkinsville, Kentucky where I shall await your answer.*

*[P.S.] Please address to Hopkinsville, Kentucky.* [265]

*Lieutenant N. Hopson, 7th Regt. U.S. Infantry. Having applied to me for a certificate I hereby certify that I have carefully examined and attended this officer—and he has been for the last six or seven weeks confined to his bed with the congestive fever and as he is yet confined to his bed and unable to leave it. I further declare my belief that he will not be able to resume his duties in a less period than two months. (signed) W.B. Keen, M.D., Near Rodney, Miss., July 8th, 1840, V.B. Johnston, MD, Attest, W. H. Anderson, J.P.* [266]

(Lt.Col. Wm. Whistler, 7th Infantry, to Gen. R. Jones, Adjutant General, Washington.)

*Fort Micanopy*
*July 29th, 1840*

*Permit me to draw your attention to the continued absence of Major Nelson and Lieut. Hopson. The first was ordered to join his Regiment the 1st May 1840 and the latter has been absent without leave since the 7th February.* [267]

---

[265] AG 1840 H197
[266] Ibid
[267] AG 1840 W280

Finally, on Dec. 7, 1840, Hopson reports for duty in Tampa Bay. If he knew what was going to happen a few weeks later, he probably would have wanted to stay in Kentucky. [268]

A Court of Inquiry is held after the Battle of Martin's Point to see if Hopson had deserted Lt. Sherwood or rode off under orders. He was cleared of charges of deserting his fellow officer, but a dark cloud hung over him for the rest of his career. Nevil Hopson was dismissed from the Army for drunkenness in August 1846 and died in Texas in 1847.

---

[268] AG 1840 H337

A flagpole is all that is left of Newport Barracks (above) in Newport, Kentucky, across the Ohio River from Cincinnati. It was the main recruitment, enlisted processing center, and basic training camp for many in the 7th Infantry Regiment.

Newport Barracks was an active military installation from 1803 to 1894. The biggest use of the facility was before the Civil War, and during the war as a hospital. In 1894 after many years of frequent flooding from the river, it was abandoned.

Interpretive signs tell the history of Newport Barracks.

(Photos of Newport Barracks/Gen. James Taylor Park by Chris Kimball.)

Today this location in the city of Newport is known as General James Taylor Park. There are several interpretive signs in the area that tell the history of the site.

General James Taylor (V), is known as the founder of Newport and established the barracks. He is not closely related to Griffin Taylor in Cincinnati. It is said that he is related to Zachary Taylor, but I have not been able to find the connection in his family tree. He was the cousin of President James Madison.

According to both Heitman and Cullum references, Walter Sherwood was born in New Jersey and appointed from New Jersey to West Point. He was born March 30, 1816, and graduated the academy in 1837 with a class ranking of 38 out of 50. He was killed at age 24, and his will and probate were in the state of New York (West Point), brother Stanley Sherwood as executor. His father, Salmon Sherwood, died in Pennsylvania in 1853 and is buried in Connecticut.[269]

The New York Military Magazine in 1841 had more insight into Sherwood, his past and character.

*Lieut. Sherwood, late of the United States Army.—We are indebted to a friend from Newark, we believe, for the following sketch in relation to this lamented officer, to whom we return our thanks. It appears to have been taken from the Newark Daily Advertiser; and was accompanied by several verses of excellent poetry. But our friend will perceive that our work is adapted to no other than strictly military subjects.*

*To most of your readers, the announcement that Lieutenant Walter Sherwood had fallen a victim to the treachery of the Indians, was but the adding of another to the long list of sacrifices in the ill-fated and disastrous war which has so long scourged our southern frontier. But to others, it came with a far deeper and more melancholy interest: it was the sudden crushing of fond hopes—the rude sundering of cherished friendships. Although not a native of our state, Lieutenant Sherwood passed several years of his earlier life in this city, and received his appointment to the United States Military academy at West Point as a Jerseyman.*

*Having enjoyed but few opportunities for education, except*

---

[269] Information found on Ancestry.com—Wills & Probate.

*those furnished by a common village school, he early commenced a system of self-instruction with all the ardor and resolution which strongly marked his character. His was not a disposition to falter or draw back; and he pursued the course upon which he had entered with the zeal which difficulties could not quench, and an industry which no obstacle could resist. Gifted by nature with no mean intellect, and prompted by a strong desire of improvement, he eagerly and successfully availed himself of the opportunities afforded him at West Point. He graduated in the summer of 1837 with great credit, and shortly after joined the regiment to which he was assigned at Fort Gibson. Here he remained about two years, during a considerable portion of which time he was employed in surveying and laying out a road to the western frontier; a service in which he acquired the high approbation of his official superiors. In the fall of 1839 he returned, on furlough, among his friends to recruit his health, which he suffered severely from the climate to which he was unaccustomed, and the fatigues and exposure to which he was subjected. Unwilling to hold a commission without discharging fully all its duties, as soon as his health would at all permit he reported himself for orders, and spent the last summer in the recruiting service.*

*When his regiment was ordered to Florida in the fall, an opportunity was offered him to remain in the vicinity of his friends, and at a distance from the hardships and perils which were but too well known to attend that service. But his was not a spirit that could brook even the appearance of shirking from any toil or any danger that lay in the path of duty. He had deliberately attached himself to the military service of his country, and was prepared and determined to fulfill all its requirements. Imbued with a high sense of 'the port and bearing which become a soldier,' nothing could deter or dissuade him from performing all that is demanded.*

*The same chivalrous spirit characterized him to the last. Had he consulted his own safety he might, in all human probability, have escaped the murderous rifle of the savages: but he disdained to abandon to their ruthless violence the lifeless corpse of his fair charge, who was killed at the first fire. He dismounted, and seizing a musket from a wounded soldier placed himself by her dead body, there to meet his own death. He lived just long enough to say to the agonized husband, who hurried to the spot, 'I have fought for your wife as long as I could stand,' and expired!*

*This perished at the early age of twenty-three one who was beloved and admired by all who knew him. Kind and amiable in his disposition and deportment; warm and sincere in his friendships; animated by a high sense of honor and a generous ambition; of unspotted morals and unbending integrity; firm in purpose and resolute in heart; he has passed away while 'the dew of his youth was yet upon him.' His friends will cherish with melancholy pleasure the memory of his many virtuous and amiable qualities, and mourn that his hopes and their anticipations have been thus suddenly blighted and buried in an untimely grave.* [270]

Sherwood's family requested that his remains be shipped north for burial.

(Quartermaster General Thomas S. Jesup, to Benjamin Sherwood.)

*January 27th, 1841*
*The Secretary of War has referred to this office your letter of the 21st Instant, in which you ask the aid of the Department to obtain from Florida the body of the late Lieutenant Sherwood,*

---

[270] *New York Military Magazine*, Vol. 1 (Labree & Stockton, New York, August 21, 1841) 172.

*killed in action with the Indians on the 29th of last month. Every*
*facility will be afforded by this Department to meet your wishes in*
*the matter. It will be necessary to procure a leaden coffin in which*
*to place the body when disinterred. If you will obtain one, and*
*have it delivered to Major Eneas Mackay, Quarter Master, New*
*York, he will forward it to Florida, and the necessary instructions*
*will immediately be given to the principal officer of the*
*Department in that Territory, to have the body taken up and sent*
*to you. The expense of transportation will be paid by the public.* [271]

(General Jesup, to Major Eneas Mackay, Quarter Master, New
York.)

*January 27th, 1841*
*Mr. B. Sherwood, of New York, has addressed a letter to the*
*Secretary of War, which has been referred to this Office, asking*
*the aid of the Department in obtaining from Florida the body of*
*the late Lieutenant W. Sherwood, who was killed a short time*
*since in action with the Indians. He has been informed, that if he*
*will procure a leaden coffin and have it delivered to you, it will be*
*sent to Florida, and instructions given to have the body disinterred*
*and sent to him. Should he do so, I will thank you to forward it to*
*Palatka, by the earliest opportunity, to Lieutenant Colonel Hunt, to*
*whom instructions on the subject will be immediately given.* [272]

(General Jesup, to Lt.Col. Thomas F. Hunt, Deputy
Quartermaster General, Palatka, Florida.)

*January 27th, 1841*
*"Mr. B. Sherwood, of New York, has addressed a letter to the*
*Secretary of War, which has been referred to this office, asking the*

---

[271] "Letters Sent by the Office of the Quartermaster General, 1841, 209-210.
[272] Ibid, 210

*aid of the Department to obtain from Florida the body of the late Lieutenant W. Sherwood, lately killed in action with the Indians near Micanopy. He has been informed, that if he will procure and deliver to Major Mackay, a leaden coffin, it will be forwarded to you, and his wishes in regard to the body complied with. On receiving the coffin, I will thank you to have it sent to the proper point, and cause the body to be disinterred and deposited in it, and, after having it properly secured, send it to New York, for delivery to Mr. Sherwood. [273]*

Finally, Sherwood's remains are shipped to New York, where they are placed at West Point Cemetery. This was before the establishment of Arlington and other national cemeteries, which would happen during the Civil War and shortly after.

(Gen. Jesup, to Major Eneas Mackay, Quartermaster, New York.)

*May 10th, 1841*

*You will pay the expense of transporting the body of the late Lieutenant Sherwood from Savannah to New York. I have received information that the body was shipped from Savannah, some three or four weeks since. [274]*

(Gen. Jesup, to Benjamin Sherwood, New York.)

*May 11th, 1841*

*The Secretary of War has referred to this office, your letter to him of the 25th ultimo. Instructions have been given to Major Eneas Mackay, Quarter Master, New York, to pay for the transportation of the remains of the late Lieutenant Sherwood from Savannah to New York. In reply to your request for*

---

[273] Ibid, 210-211
[274] Ibid, 439

*information as to the state of Lieutenant Sherwood's accounts with the Government, I have to say that his accounts are still open on the books of the Treasury. If you are the executor or administrator of his estate, I would suggest to you to address yourself to William B. Lewis, Esquire, 2nd Auditor of the Treasury, from who all information necessary to the adjustment of his accounts can be obtained.* [275]

Being killed in action doesn't take away the responsibility for Sherwood to settle his quartermaster accounts. Gen. Jesup doesn't take death as an excuse!

Walter Sherwood's brother Burrill was a doctor in New York City. It's possible Benjamin and Burrill are the same person. No one had written a biography of Sherwood since his obituary in 1841, and it is difficult to verify records.

The remains of Walter Sherwood are buried at the cemetery in West Point. The following year in 1842, the Army Adjutant records say that his remains were dug up at Micanopy and moved to St. Augustine. This is impossible because he can't still be there after being removed the previous year. Apparently, the Adjutant Corp and the Quartermaster Corp did not communicate with each other that he was dug up in 1841. So, if Sherwood was first buried at West Point, whose remains were sent to St. Augustine?

One of the failures of Lt. Sherwood and the disastrous battle at Martin's Point, was infantry soldiers riding horses. When attacked, ground troops are not prepared to fight on horseback. It is very difficult to load a muzzleloader on a horse.

(General Jesup, to Lt.Col. Thomas Hunt, Deputy Quartermaster

---

[275] Ibid, 439

General, Palatka.)

*January 28th, 1841*

*Enclosed you will receive a copy of a letter of the 10th instant, addressed to General Armistead by the Secretary of War, directing that "the horses stationed at the different posts to mount Infantry soldiers for the purpose of escorting trains from post to post, be immediately withdrawn." It has been referred to this office by the Secretary, that the necessary arrangements may be made for the disposal of the supernumerary horses.*

*You will communicate with General Armistead on the subject, and will be governed by his directions in carrying out the views of the Secretary. Such horses as may be withdrawn from the posts referred to, will be disposed of in such manner as you deem most advantageous to the service. If General Armistead consider them necessary to be retained as at present, they will of course, on his order, be retained.* [276]

Due to all the ambushes at Martin's Point, the road from Micanopy to Wacahoota is widened and cleared. It should have been done a year before!

(General Jesup, to Lt.Col. Henry Whiting, Deputy Quartermaster General, Palatka.)

*May 12, 1841*

*I have received your letter of the 3rd instant, covering a muster roll of extra duty men employed in repairing the road from Fort Micanopy to Fort Wacahoota. If the repairs are of a permanent nature and even made on your requisition or under your direction, the men, if employed ten consecutive days, are entitled to the per*

---

[276] Ibid, 214

*diem authorized by law.* [277]

Sergeant Major Francis Carroll was born about 1810, and his enlistment record says that he has hazel eyes, brown hair, ruddy appearance, and was from Armagh, Northern Ireland. His profession is listed as a weaver. In 1831 at age 21, he enlisted in New York; reenlisted for three years at Ft. Gibson in 1836, and again at Ft. Gibson in 1839. He died at age 30 at Martin's Point with Lt. Sherwood. He survived the ambush on Lt. Sanderson's command in May 1840, but not with Lt. Sherwood the following December. He was most likely the Sergeant Major who replaced James Sanderson as regimental Sergeant Major, and tragically witnessed Sanderson's death. [278]

The casualty report says of his character: *"...eliciting by his good conduct and soldierly bearing, the respect, and esteem of his officers."* [279]

The month after his death, Fort Carroll is established on Jan. 22, 1841, by Capt. Thomas P. Gwynne, 8th Infantry, located about three miles north or Bartow, and subordinate of Fort Cummings at Lake Alfred, Polk County. The post is mentioned again in 1842 as a camp for one of the bands of Indians being removed to the west. [280]

Private Lansing Burlingham was born in 1816 (the same age as Lt. Sherwood) at Otsego, New York; his profession is listed as a laborer. He died at age 24, defending Mrs. Montgomery's body, in

---

[277] Ibid, 444
[278] 7th Infantry Enlistment records, Ancestry.com
[279] Sprague, *The Origin, Progress, and Conclusion of the Florida War*. Brown, *Ponce de Leon Land and Florida War Record*.
[280] Bloomington Herald, Apr. 8, 1842. New York Herald, March 23, 1842. Sprague, *The Origin, Progress, and Conclusion of the Florida War*, 257.

a rare description of events in the casualty records. His original enlistment in 1837 has blue eyes, light hair, and light complexion. But when he reenlisted at Fort Russell by Capt. Holmes in 1840, has a different description of grey eyes, brown hair, and a dark complexion. That's what happens when you are working out in the sun all the time. [281]

Army life was very harsh, and it was rare for a soldier to reenlist. His death defending Mrs. Montgomery took the attention of the country, in a war that had almost no acts of honor. The casualty list said of him:

*Killed under command of Lieutenant Sherwood. He sacrificed his own, in attempting to save the life of a lady. His last words were, 'I did my duty.'* [282]

---

[281] 7th Infantry Enlistment Records, Ancestry.com.

[282] Sprague, *The Origin, Progress, and Conclusion of the Florida War*. Brown, *Ponce de Leon Land and Florida War Record*.

# Chapter 18: "I Found the Cypress Bottom Overflowed"

Despite the attack near Micanopy, Lt.Col. Loomis reports that a large group of Indians surrendered at Fort Clinch. (This fort was near the mouth of the Withlacoochee River; not the brick fort at Fernandina Beach which was built later.) Most are Creeks and not the Miccosukees who are responsible for the attacks near Micanopy.

(Lt.Col. G. Loomis, 6th Infantry, Capt. W.W.S. Bliss, Asst. Adjutant Gen. at Fort Brooke.)

*Fort Clinch*
*10th Jan. 1841*

*I have the honor to report for the information of the General that Co-chuck-me- hadjo, the Arkansas Indian, and Cosa, a Sub-Chief of the Tallahassees, with some 7 or 8 Warriors, and their women and children, amounting in all to Thirty-Three came into my Camp on the 8th Inst., and are awaiting the arrival of Echo-E-Mathla from [Fort] "No. 4". I am looking for him daily. I am obliged to send my Mackinac boat to Cedar Keys express for a supply of medicines and avail myself of the opportunity to make this report.*

*I shall use all proper exertions to get the Indians to go to Tampa to see the General as soon as possible. Those in here seem very contented and disposed to emigrate; to judge from their conversation.* [283]

---

[283] AG 1841 A6 and A10

At Fort Micanopy, Capt. Bonneville is having continual problems with grog shops. When on shop owner is evicted from the post, he sues Capt. Bonneville.

(Lt.Col. Wm. Whistler, 7th Infantry, to the Hon. Joel R. Poinsett, Secretary of War, Washington.)

*Fort Micanopy, E.Fla.*
*January 20, 1841*
*Sir, this post has long been annoyed by a great number of grog shops and tipping houses. In September last, Capt. Bonneville was in command, one of the worst of these, kept by Francis Bray, a discharged soldier, had his liquor destroyed, and his family removed from the post. This act has met my approbation as one indispensably necessary to the discipline and efficiency of the garrison. For this, suits have been instituted against the Captain. Deeming it proper that this officer should receive every legal support in his efforts to preserve good order; I have the honor to solicit in his behalf that, the U.S. Attorney for Florida, Mr. Thomas Douglas, may be directed to associate with Mr. D[avid] Levy who has been employed by Capt. B. as his attorney in the case. Also, I have the honor to enclose the copy of a letter from the Commanding General, which is merely a repetition of what he strongly urged upon the Commanding Officer, during his visit to this post in the Month of August preceding.* [284]

And attached with the following enclosure of a similar situation a few months earlier.

(Asst. Adjt. General W.W.S. Bliss, to Adjutant R.C. Gatlin, 7th Infantry.)

---

[284] AG 1841 W57

*Tampa, Fla.*
*Oct. 2, 1840*

*It having been represented to the Commanding General that the presence at Micanopy of a resident citizen named Horace Merry, is prejudicial to the public interest. You are authorized by him, to order the said Merry from the post, if in your judgment the interest of the service requires such a measure.*

*The Commanding General expects that you will exercise the same authority in all cases which seems to demand it.* [285]

On February 18, 1841, the Secretary of War approved the services of David Levy to represent Capt. Bonneville in his defense against the owner of the grog shop.

(Sec. of War Roger Jones, to Lt.Col. Wm. Whistler.)

*The Secretary of War has been pleased to grant the request contained in your communication to him of the 20th of January, that the District Attorney of Florida may be associated with D. Levy, Esq., in the defense of Captain Bonneville, 7th Infantry, in the suit brought against him by F. Bray.* [286]

David Levy Yulee is the congressional delegate, and later Senator. He is one of the best lawyers that Bonneville can have. David Levy Yulee is the son of Moses Levy, so most likely very familiar with Micanopy from his father's plantation.

Soldiers are actively scouting for the warriors who attacked Lt. Sherwood. They find hidden villages in what is today the northern Ocala Forest.

---

[285] Ibid
[286] "Letters Sent by the Headquarters of the Army 1828-1903"; Records of Headquarters of the Army, Record Group 108, 32.

Capt. John MacKay, *Topographical map of the northern portion of the country between the Oklawaha and St. John's Rivers*, 1841. A detailed map that you may recognize as the northern Ocala Forest. Noted are Silver Springs, and Silver Glen Springs is marked as Silver Spring. Lake Churchill is called Lake Kerr today. Also, Salt Springs and Grassy Pond. It does not have Fort MacKay but does have a military camp marked in that area. [287]

---

[287] MacKay, John (Capt.); *Topographical map of the northern portion of the country between the Oklawaha and St. John's Rivers* (2nd Seminole War); National Archives, 1841. Copy in the State Library of Florida.

(Capt. E.K. Barnum, to Lieut. J.W. Anderson, Adjutant, 2d Infantry.)

*Fort Russell, E.F.*
*18th of Jan. 1841*

*I have the honor to make the following report of my operations for the last week in on the 11th Inst. I left this post with three officers and seventy-five men and took a Northwest course until I struck Lake Lochlosa. I skirted the shores of that lake to the north end of it where I encamped for the night.-- The 12th I resumed my march in a northerly direction, crossed the Micanopy road, and after a march of about three hours, varied the course to East and continued that course until evening when I encamped near a pond on the Palatka and Micanopy road, passing near what I supposed to be Big Fish water.*

*On the 13th Inst., I took a S.W. course until I struck the trail leading from Fort Russell to Micanopy when (having seen no signs of Indians in my route and being quite lame myself) I concluded to return to my post, and did so. One-day sooner than I intended when I started on the scout.*

*On the 15th Inst., I proceeded to Paynes Landing to ascertain if it were possible to cross the Ocklawaha at that point, which I found to be impracticable.*

*On the 16th I proceeded with Company K, 2d Infantry (Lieut. Alburtis) to Fort Brooks and commenced building a bridge across the river there. I left Lt. Alburtis in charge of the work, and returned. I visited Fort Brooks again yesterday and found Lieut. Alburtis had made good progress in building the bridge and hope it will be passable this afternoon. I shall therefore leave this post in an hour from this for a scout south of the Ocklawaha, to be absent*

*12 or 13 days. The aggregate of the command I take with me is 109, with six wagons. Lieut. Lovell, Asst. Surgeon Conrad, and sixty men are left at this post.* — [288]

Fort Brooks, sometimes written as Brook or Brooke, is a small fort near the confluence of Orange Creek and the Ocklawaha River, five miles east of Fort Russell. It is a sub-fort of Fort Russell in the post returns. Not to be confused with the more famous Fort Brooke at Tampa Bay. (There are three different Fort Brooks/Brooke in the Florida Seminole Wars.)

(Capt. J. R. Smith, to Lieut.Col. B. Riley, 2d Infantry.)

*Fort Holmes, E.F.*
*23rd Jan. 1841*

*I have the honor to report that on Monday, the 11th inst., I examined the country extending between the Palatka road, and the Ocklawaha, and as far east as the 9-mile hammock, and up on the Micanopy road—finding no traces of the Indians. The hammock bordering the river, is a cypress bottom; and, at this stage of the water—it is overflowed, back from the river, half a mile, in some places farther; and two or three feet in depth.*

*On Thursday following, I detached Lieut. Woodruff, with 30 men, north to the Micanopy road, with instructions to examine the portion of country, lying between that road and the one leading to Fort King. This, he executed without discovering any recent signs of Indians.*

*Having understood that Capt. Barnum intended crossing the Ocklawaha, at Paynes Landing, I made my arrangements to cross at Fort Brooks; and on Monday, the 18th, I left my post—taking*

---

[288] AG 1841 A37

Lieut. McKinstry,--and sixty men with me—and such tools as we should require, in constructing a raft. On my arrival, however, at that crossing place, I found Lieut. Alburtis, with a portion of the command and from Fort Russell, employed in making a bridge.

I had learned, two or three days previous to this, that Capt. Barnum had changed his original intention, of crossing at Paynes Landing, and would cross at Fort Brooks; but I did not deem it necessary, on that account, to alter my plan. Accordingly, after giving some assistance with my command, in placing the strong pieces of the bridge, and having nothing to cross, but the men with six days' rations in our haversacks, I availed myself of that means of crossing, and encamped in the dry hammock, on the south side of the Ocklawaha. I scoured the country, between that and the St. John's river, and as high up as Fort Gates. In returning, I commenced crossing, and examining the islands of the Ocklawaha. Soon again, I found the cypress bottom overflowed back, from a quarter to half a mile, and in some places, taking us up to our middle, in mud and water. I crossed the first channel (of 25 or 28 yards in width,) by felling a tall cypress across;—and found on crossing--only a continuation of that wet, cypress bottom. In about a quarter of a mile farther, we came to another channel, near 50 yards in width, and which I considered the principal channel of the river.

Here, we commenced making a raft, to cross. But, from the high, and rapid stage of the water, and consequent difficulty of effecting a landing, I reluctantly abandoned the idea of crossing as impracticable at present; and retraced my steps entering the river hammock, at several places, and invariably finding the same overflowed cypress bottom, Extending back, far from the river. I returned to my post, about noon of Saturday, the sixth day out;

having seen but two tracks of a single person, made probably, within a week, previous to my scout. I recrossed the river at Fort Brooks. In one cabbage hammock, probably within four or five miles of the mouth of the river, we discovered cabbage trees cut, but probably some months previously. I doubt whether there can be any dry islands in the river, as low down as this; but, a boat expedition from Palatka would easily settle the point.

I would mention here, that we prepared and used on the scout, parched corn, ground, and mixed with sugar; as an experiment which I think, succeeded. The men can easily carry ten or twelve days of this ration, and have no more weight than five or six days of the ordinary ration. [289]

(Capt. E.K. Barnum, to Lieut. J.W. Anderson, Adjutant, 2d Infantry, Fort King.)

*Fort Russell, E.F.*
*Jan. 28th, 1841*

I have the honor to report that agreeably to my arrangement as communicated to you on the 18th Inst. I left this post on that day with 102 men for a scout south of the Ocklawaha. On the 19th inst. I crossed the river with the wagons and encamped on the south side, sent out a small party under command of Lt. Hayden to examine if there was any trail of Indians leading up the river; the party returned in the evening and reported they could find no signs of Indians in that direction. On the 20th the command marched at daybreak taking the road leading to Lake Churchill, at a distance of about six miles, a large trail was discovered running east and west crossing the road.

Lieuts Alburtis and Hayden with 40 men were ordered to take

---

[289] Ibid

*the trail to the east & follow as long as they should judge there was any probability of finding Indians, and afterward join me at Lake Churchill. I proceeded with the remainder of the command and at half past 11 o'clock a.m., came in sight of the Lake, being some mile or so in advance with a few mounted men. I discovered some Indians on the pine barren. They were immediately taken and proved to be three squaws and one child who had been in the hammock cutting cabbage trees, one of them having in her possession, a very good public axe. As soon as the footmen came up I examined the hammock & found where many cabbage trees had been recently cut and signs of many ponies having grazed there, but could discover no more Indians after a search of two or three hours. I returned to my wagons where I found Lieut's. Alburtis and Hayden who reported they had followed the trail as directed by me as far as they judged necessary without discovering any fresh signs. I then took one of the squaws and directed her to conduct me to her camp; she either did not or would not understand me, as she merely took me round the Lake and showed me where she had cut cabbage. Upon my threatening to keep her marching all night unless she would do as I wished her, she promised that in the morning she would conduct me to Alleck Tuskenugge's camp where there were a great number of Indians with their families.-- Accordingly at daybreak on the 21st Inst, I took Lieut. Alburtis and Hayden with 60 men and guided by two of the squaws we returned on our road, to where the trail crossed it, when we turned to the West and after a march of about two hours, came in sight of the swamp on the Ocklawaha. The squaws here described to me the situation of the camp, and were left with a guard, while the command took the trail leading into the camp, which we found situated on the river bank surrounded by a thick scrub, but the Indians had left, the squaws were then brought in and we took the trail up the river, which we followed until our guides assured me it was useless to think of finding the Indians in less than four days as they had nearly two days the start of us and had gone to the Panee-Soffkee. I then returned to the deserted camp, killed about twenty hogs found there and remained the night. On the 22d Inst, I returned to the wagons on Lake Churchill, and sent a party under the command of Brevet 2d Lieut. [John] Bacon to examine the south shore of the Lake. The party returned in the evening having found three ponies hobbled and feeding near a cabbage hammock. On the 23d I divided the command into two parties (leaving a sufficient guard for the wagons) taking one party with me round the south side of the lakes and sending Lieut. Alburtis with the other to the north side with orders to examine the hammocks closely. We met in the east side, neither party having discovered anything of consequence. On the 24th I left Lake Churchill at daybreak and took the road to Silver [Glen] Spring, where I arrived in the evening without meeting with anything worthy of note. The 25th I remained at Silver [Glen] Spring examining the Country around it and the shore of Lake George without making any discovery of Indians. On the 26th, I took the road leading north from Silver [Glen] Spring and arrived in the evening at our old camp on Lake Churchill.* [290]

The place names can be confusing. Lake Churchill is today called Lake Kerr in the middle northern Ocala Forest. It is not named after Captain Croghan Ker of the 2d Dragoons, but from a later settler who established Kerr City. Silver Glen Springs that runs into Lake George, was known as Silver Springs at the time. The "Glen" was later added so it wouldn't be confused with Silver Springs near Ocala, which was originally called Glassell Springs, named after Capt. James M. Glassell, 4th Infantry, who built Fort

---

[290] AG 1841 A37

King and commanded there from 1827 to 1829. [291]

*On the 27th started at daybreak, on my return to this post. Crossed the Ocklawaha by Lieut. Alburtis' bridge at Fort Brooks and arrived here at 3 O'clock P.M.*

*In the deserted camp on the Ocklawaha was found two saddles (Dragoons). Two new pattern Forage Caps, some pieces of blue cloth (one of which was part of the front of an officer's pantaloons) and part of a Jacket marked "John Walsh 7th Infantry".* [292]

Capt. Barnum found a well-established camp with livestock, hogs, horses, an ax that the woman was using to cut palms, and Dragoon soldier equipment and uniforms taken from ambushed soldiers.

Pvt. John Walsh was a 7th Infantry soldier who disappeared on express rider duty a year prior and presumed dead. Since Walsh's clothing was found in a camp near his disappearance, it is assumed that the Indian camp has been in the area for at least a year. [293]

---

[291] Heitman. Post Returns of Fort King

[292] AG 1841 A37

[293] Sprague, *The Origin, Progress, and Conclusion of the Florida War*. Brown, *Ponce de Leon Land and Florida War Record*.

# Chapter 19: "I Anticipate a Favorable Result"

General Armistead writes the Secretary of War about the effective use of mounted infantry versus foot soldiers.

(Brig. Gen. W.K. Armistead, to the Honorable Sec. of War, Washington.)

*Tampa*

*Feb. 1ˢᵗ, 1841*

*I have the honor to acknowledge the receipt of your communication of the 10ᵗʰ ult., relative to the proper strength and composition of escorts.*

*In relation to the use of mounted Infantry, I would respectfully state that I deem such an escort more efficient than mere Infantry. The moral effect of mounted troops upon the Indians is great, and with them alone can we hope to pursue and overtake the enemy in the pine barrens. I trust, therefore, that the department will not insist upon the order, directing the withdrawal of the horses from the various stations, as independently of escort duty, many emergencies require their use.* [294]

General Armistead also approves the appointment of Lt. John W. Martin as clothing officer since Martin is still not able to do field duty.

(Gen. Armistead's Adjutant W.W.S. Bliss, to Lt. J. Martin, Tampa.)

*Tampa*

*Feb. 12ᵗʰ, 1841*

*In answer to your communication of this date, requesting to be*

---

[294] AG 1841 A42

*placed on duty at this post, as Clothing Officer, I am directed by*
*the Commanding Officer to say that although it is not deemed*
*advisable by the Medical Officer whose certificate you enclose that*
*you should for some time perform duty in the field, it is believed*
*you are quite competent to discharge duty with your company at*
*the post. You will accordingly proceed as early as practicable to*
*join your company.* [295]

Lt. Alexander Montgomery is given assignment at Fort Fanning
as Assistant Commissary of Subsistence. This includes buying and
issuing food rations and was a separate bureau under the
Quartermaster.

(Gen. Armistead's Adjutant W.W.S. Bliss, to Major H. Wilson,
3d Infantry, Fort Fanning.)

*Tampa*
*Feb. 4th, 1841*

*It is understood that Capt. Terrett has resigned his situation as*
*Assistant Quartermaster and awaits the arrival of a successor to*
*be relieved in his duties at Fort Fanning.*

*As an Assistant Quartermaster cannot at once be ordered*
*there, the Commanding General directs that a suitable officer of*
*your command be designated to relieve the Captain in his duties,*
*unless the latter should choose to remain until the arrival of an*
*Asst. Quartermaster.*

*It is contemplated to place Lieut. Montgomery on duty as Asst.*
*Com of Subsistence at Fort Fanning.* [296]

General Armistead writes to Lt.Col. T. Hunt, Deputy

---

[295] AG 1841 A52, 17-18
[296] Ibid, 8-9

Quartermaster General at the Quartermaster Depot at Palatka, about major reorganizations in Florida.

(Gen. Armistead's Adjutant W.W.S. Bliss, to Lt.Col. T.F. Hunt, Deputy Quarter Master General, Palatka.)

*Tampa*
*Feb. 14<sup>th</sup>, 1841*

*In relation to the depot at Garey's Ferry, you will see by the order herewith enclosed, that it has been determined by the General to reoccupy that station. He does not wish therefore that any of the public buildings should be given up to Citizens.*

*You are respectfully informed that it is contemplated to place Lt. Montgomery, 7<sup>th</sup> Infantry, on duty as A.C.S. at Fort Fanning; it having been represented to the Commanding General, that the duties of both departments at that station, were too onerous for one officer.*

*With regard to the withdrawal of horses from the various posts, it is the direction of the Commanding General that they be retained until further instructions from the Secretary of War, with whom he has corresponded on the subject.*

*For considerations of health, Col. Twiggs has been authorized, if he deems advisable, to abandon Fort Reid and remove the garrison to any point within his district which he may think proper.*

*Should it become necessary to evacuate Fort Reid, the General directs that steps be taken to secure the public property &c at that place.* [297]

Fort Reid is abandoned soon after, and the garrison moved to

---

[297] Ibid, 20-21

Fort Shannon/Palatka by the end of the month. [298]

(Gen. Armistead's Adjutant W.W.S. Bliss, to Lt.Col. Whistler, 7th Infantry, Micanopy.)

*Tampa*
*Feb. 28th, 1841*
*In reply to your communication of the 17th inst., relative to the detail of Lt. Montgomery on detached service, you are respectfully informed that Lt. Montgomery was represented to the Commanding General, as physically unfit for company duty at present, & was accordingly directed in Special Order No. 15 / which you have doubtless received / to relieve Lt. Britton at St. Marks. The General being equally anxious with yourself that no officer should be detached from your Regiment, who is competent to perform duty with it. [299]*

The surrender of Coosa Tustenuggee is considered an important concession since he is an important Miccosukee leader.

(Brig. Gen. W.K. Armistead, to the Adjutant General, Washington.)

*Tampa*
*February 28th, 1841*
*Since my last report to the War Department, two Miccosukee Indians came into this place. They belong to a party of sixteen— four of whom are warriors, who are on the coast north of this and about two and a half days' journey distant. Upon the return of the runners, the whole party is to come in.*

*Yesterday, Coosa Tustenuggee, principal chief of the*

---

[298] Post Returns Fort Reid.
[299] AG 1841 A52, 37.

*Miccosukees, came in with a small party. He says that he will bring in his immediate band 80 in number, and that Halick Tustenuggee, who has 130 people, will follow his example. From the tenor of his conversation and conduct, I anticipate a favorable result.*

*A talk has been sent to the Seminoles proper in the neighborhood of Pease Creek and Charlotte Harbor, who have sent in runners to inform me that they are now collecting to hold a council. No means have been spared to produce a favorable impression upon these people, and I entertain sanguine hopes that all or greater part of them will consent to emigrate.*

*I would respectfully ask the instructions of the War Department, relative to the Indian negroes who are now here or those who may come in.-- Whether they are to be shipped with the Indians to Arkansas? It is important to know the views of the department, as citizens will be continually claiming the negroes, and indeed have already commenced doing so, as expressed in my communication of this date, relative to [Mr.] Brown & his party.* [300]

Certain plantation owners and slave catchers are after the Black Seminoles and seek to collect the bounty as escaped slaves. They were prevented by both General Taylor and General Jesup because the only way to get the Indians to agree to removal was to allow their Black allies to go with them. The slave catchers are a problem in New Orleans to Indian Territory.

---

[300] AG 1841 A50

# Chapter 20: "I Immediately Extended and Charged"

Fort Russell is along Orange Creek, halfway between Orange Lake and the Ocklawaha River. Five miles away is Fort Brooks on the mouth of Orange Creek and the Ocklawaha River. Fort Brooks sits on the road that goes from Fort Micanopy to Palatka and is a satellite of Fort Russell on the same post returns. [301]

(Capt. E.K. Barnum, 2d Infantry, to Brig. Gen. R. Jones, Adjutant General, Washington.)

*Fort Russell, E.F.*
*2 March 1841.*
*I have been out all day in pursuit of the enemy who made their appearance between this post and Fort Brooks, and shall leave again at daylight tomorrow, to be absent 3 or 4 days; consequently, shall not be able to forward the muster rolls of the four companies under my command before the 10th Inst.* [302]

(Capt. E.K. Barnum, to Lt. J.W. Anderson, Adjutant, 2d Infantry, Fort King.)

*Fort Russell, E.F.*
*2 March 1841.*
*I have to report that Lieut. Alburtis, commanding Company "K" 2d Infantry, was attacked by a large party of Indians at Orange Creek hammock this day between 11 and 12 O'clock.*

*Lieut. Alburtis had 18 or 20 men with him and was obliged to retreat to this post.*

---

[301] Post Returns Fort Russell-Fort Brooks.
[302] AG 1841 B108

I immediately repaired to Orange Creek and Fort Brooks, but the enemy had fled.-- The heavy showers during the day had obliterated all signs of their trail and it continued to rain in the evening, I considered it useless to remain out all night; accordingly, returned to my post.-- I shall leave at daylight tomorrow morning to scour the hammocks of the Ocklawaha.

I brought up from Fort Brooks (or rather the scenes of action) two men who were killed & six wounded, two more of "K" Company are missing. [303]

(Col. D.E. Twiggs, 2d Dragoons, to the Adjutant General, Washington.)

*Fort Shannon, Palatka*
*8 March 1841.*
Enclosed herewith, I have the honor to send for your information copies of Lieut. Alburtis's and Lieut. Patten's communications in reference to the recent attack made by the Indians near Forts Brooks and MacKay. They contain all the information I am as yet in possession of on this subject. Captain Ker and Lieut. Sibley are still absent with their commands. Additional supplies of forage have been thrown into Fort Holmes and orders sent to Captain Ker not to return while the slightest probability of coming up with the Indians exists.-- The reports made by the express rider as you were informed of in my letter of the 5th Inst., appear to be without any foundation; none of Captain Barnum's command having been killed.

The late scene of action being without the limits of my command. I have issued no orders whatever to the Infantry, my instructions to Capt. Ker and Lt. Sibley to cooperate with, and obey

---

[303] AG 1841 B111

*implicitly all orders they might receive from Infantry officers, their
seniors, and remain as long as their supplies would hold out.* [304]

(1st Lt. W. Alburtis, 2d Infantry, Commanding K Compy., to
Capt. E.K. Barnum, 2d Infantry, Fort Russell.)

*Fort Brooks, E.F.*
*March 3, 1841*
*I have the honor to make you the following report. Yesterday,
about 11 o'clock, A.M., I heard a singular and unusual noise, in the
direction of Orange Creek bridge, and believing that the Indians
had attacked the escort and team which I had sent to Fort Russell
for supplies early in the morning, I immediately divided my
company, taking the Orderly Sergeant, two Corporals and
nineteen privates, and leaving an equal force in charge of a
confidential Sergeant; Lieut. Martin being absent at Fort Russell,
attending to receiving and sending some supplies to the company
at Fort Brooks, to guard and defend the Post, & proceeded in
pursuit of the enemy.*

*I soon found him in and near the Orange Creek Hammock, not
far below the bridge, numbering in strength at least sixty or
seventy warriors. I gave him the first fire, which was returned with
promptness, by the enemy, he at the same time making the most
demonic yell imaginable, which were answered in a taunting and
deciding manner by my men. After this, the firing became general
on both sides. The Indians several times made very adroit and
sagacious efforts to out-flank my command, but were severely
repulsed and driven back to take shelter in the hammock. They
again returned from the hammock, on my left, in apparently
larger force, and after a great deal of firing, were a second time*

---

[304] AG 1841 T69

*repulsed.*

*I am confident with much loss, as several of their warriors were seen to fall at the discharge of our muskets. But, for the consummate coolness, firmness and gallant conduct exhibited by my men throughout, I must have been the greatest sufferer, as the enemy was three or four times my superior in point of number. As it was, they evidently sustained the greatest injury and loss, my ammunition being almost entirely expended, besides having my Orderly Sergeant, one Corporal, and three privates, severely wounded.*

*I returned with my Command to the post, bringing off all the wounded without pursuit. Immediately after returning to the Post, I dispatched an express to Fort Russell, for the purpose of informing the Commanding Officer what had happened in order that he might reinforce me. I gave the express rider (a Private of Company K) positive instructions to cross Orange Creek, on the upper road, to prevent if possible being cut off by the enemy. He did not reach Fort Russell.*

*Not having accomplished the ostensible object which I went in pursuit of, I again divided my Company to the best advantage, leaving that part at the Post in the same charge as before. My command amounted to seventeen men; and I proceeded with it by the road to Orange Creek near which I discovered the dead body of Corporal Laing of "I" Company* ["G" Company in post returns and Eaton's casualty list], *which accounted to me satisfactory for the alarm in the first instance. Still having fear for the safety of the escort and train, I determined to continue on the road until I should find them, and in passing out of the hammock in the direction of Fort Russell, I was fired upon by the Indians from either side of the road.* [305]

The fire of the enemy was instantly returned, with the most marked effect. I distinctly saw three or four warriors fall and carried off. The Indians had now acquired more strength than they had at the first and extended themselves on both sides of the road as high up as the old fort, and so formidable were they as to appear to be almost an impossibility for me to break through their ranks. But the indomitable firmness, perseverance, and true courage displayed by my little command, soon overcame the superiority of their numbers, and I was enabled to gain the high pine barren near Old Fort Russell. The firing of the Indians continued to be very severe and heavy, and was kept up and constantly returned by my command. The enemy showed himself an adept at "treeing" and I frequently cautioned my men to do the same and keep properly extended—to fight them in their own way—and not to expose their persons more than could be avoided.

At the point stated above, I felt confident of my ability to maintain my ground against the enemy, and keep him in check, until I could get assistance from the Commanding Officer of Fort Russell, and therefore dispatched a man for the purpose of informing him of my situation, but he was discovered by the Indians in making his way by them, and driven to the hammock on the Ocklawaha for safety without being able to accomplish so desirable an object to us. I however, continued the fight as long as the enemy made a show, advancing upon him until the command had got half a mile or more beyond and to the left of the junction of the upper and lower road, when the enemy retreated in the

---

[305] Eaton, "Returns of Killed and Wounded in Battles or Engagements with Indians, British, and Mexican Troops, compiled 1850-1851".

*direction of the Orange Creek and Ocklawaha hammock.*

*Immediately after I met the escort and team, and took them back to Fort Russell. Thus, saving them from the inevitable destruction which awaited them, and communicated the information to the Commanding Officer of my encounter with the enemy.*

*I lost one man killed, and had but one wounded in the last affair. My total loss in killed and missing, is two privates; and in wounded, one Sergeant, one Corporal, and four privates, making a total of six. The loss &c., sustained by the enemy, I have no accurate means of judging, as they are always known to carry off and conceal their dead and wounded; but I feel confidently assured that it is much greater than mine.*

*P.S.—Since the above report was written, the body of an Indian warrior was found in the camp on the Ocklawaha, discovered by Captain Barnum. His death had evidently been caused by a musket ball, received in battle but the day before.* [306]

Once again, as at Fort King in April and Fort Wacahoota in September, Lt. Alburtis survives being overwhelmed by a force five times his size. Using sound infantry tactics and holding his ground prevents him from being wiped out like Lt. Sanderson or Lt. Sherwood.

---

[306] AG 1841 T69 Enclosure, and A69.

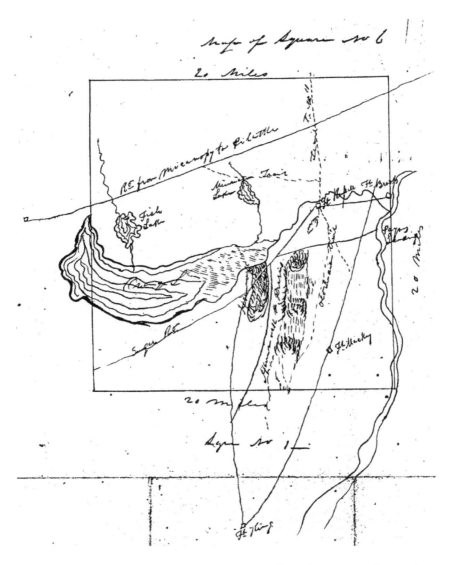

Map of Square No. 6. (1839?). Fort Russell and Fort Brooks are in the center with connecting roads down to Fort Mackay and Fort King. Orange Lake, Orange Creek, and the Ocklawaha River with Paynes Landing are shown. [307]

---

[307] Map of Square No. 6. (2nd Seminole War); National Archives, 1839(?). Copy in the State Library of Florida.

(Capt. E.K. Barnum, 2d Infantry, to Lieut. J.W. Anderson, Adjutant, 2d Infantry, Fort King.)

Fort Russell, E.F.
11$^{th}$ March 1841

I left my post on the morning of 3d Inst., with three officers and 99 men in pursuit of the Indians who attacked Lieut. Alburtis at Orange Creek. And having reason to believe they had gone up the Ocklawaha on this side, I examined the hammocks from Orange Creek up as far as Paynes landing, from whence I went to Fort MacKay.

On the morning of the 4$^{th}$, I took a south course to strike the river, as I had been informed by the squaws I took at Lake Churchill in January last, there was a trail leading up the Ocklawaha from some point near there. After marching three or four hours, a single pony track was discovered leading into a hammock & crossing a branch. I followed this track through the hammock when I struck a large trail leading in the direction of the river & followed it, until it came to an opening of high land of Oak Scrub descending to a thick hardwood & cabbage tree hammock. When we were within about ¼ of a mile of the hammock, two Indians were discovered entering it upon the run.

I immediately extended and charged; the center of my line fell upon two Indian Camps of 20 lodges, each from which the Indians had fled. Company 'G' on the right under command of Lieut. Hayden struck a camp of 22 lodges from which the Indians were retreating; they were fired upon and returned a few shots, wounding one man (Private Bower of G Company) badly. They then scattered and fled in every direction; immediate pursuit was made and continued until near sundown by Companies I & F, commanded by Lieut's. Patrick & Lovell, but without success, in consequence of the enemy having separated & fled in such small and numerous parties.

Four of the mounted men who became separated from the command were fired upon by a large party of Indians who had fled around the right of the line and gained the oak scrub in the rear. The non-commissioned officer Sergeant Pierson of Company 'G' was severely wounded by this fire, and fearing he would not be able to join that command again, he returned with the three men to this post.

From all reports made to me, I judge there must have been at least 60 or 70 Warriors in the hammock, but most probably they had but little ammunition as they made so small a return of our fire. They had a full view of us in the oak scrub, sufficient time to have prepared themselves had they been disposed to fight us, as they also had the advantage of being in the hammock while we were advancing through the scrub. I am inclined to think that two or three Indians were killed, badly wounded, as men assert they are certain that some shots took effect, and Lieut. Patrick reports having seen considerable blood on the trail he followed.

I remained at the Indian camp on the night of the 4th -- and in the morning of the 5th I destroyed it with all the plunder found there which could not be transported. The pony saddle & bridle on which the express left Lieut. Alburtis for Fort Russell during the fight on the 2d Inst. was recovered as also the clothing of the other men killed at Orange Creek that day. I destroyed or brought away a large quantity of Coonty, dried meat, corn, Garden seeds, 14 Hoes, three axes, Iron Pots, Bake Kettles, frying pans, Baskets, Bear Skins, Deerskins dressed, two undressed sides—a frock coat supposed to have belonged to Lieut. Sherwood, and a piece of a green riding habit of Mrs. Montgomery, were also found in the camp.

*Having only one days' provisions left in our haversacks, I concluded to return to my post, & near Fort MacKay I met with Capt. J.R. Smith 2d Infantry with 54 men from Fort Holmes, and Lieut. Sibley with a detachment of 2d Dragoons; the latter sent out by Col. Twiggs to reinforce me on the application of Lieut. G.W. Patten 2d Infantry, whom I had left in command of Fort Russell. Lieut. Sibley supplied me with one day's provisions, and it was proposed to return and follow the trail, but the heavy rain on the night of the 5th and morning of the 6th rendered it impracticable. We therefore marched to Fort King on the 6th with the intention of crossing at Fort Fowle and scouring the hammocks down on the south side of the rivers. But, meeting with Capt. Ker 2d Dragoons at Fort Fowle on the 7th who had come upon that side, I concluded to examine the hammocks down as far as the camp I attacked on this side. And with Capt. Smith's command did so without discovering any Indians.*

*I arrived at my post on the evening of the 9th, having parted with Capt. Smith near the Ocklawaha south of Fort MacKay; he keeping the river down in the direction of Fort Brooks.* [308]

(Capt. J.R. Smith, 2d Infantry, to Lt. R.C. Asheton, Adjutant, 2d Dragoons, Fort Shannon. March 2, 1841.)

*Fort Holmes, E.F.
Tuesday 2nd, 3 O'clock P.M.*
*An express has just come in—bringing the intelligence that a large party (about 180) of Indians attacked the command at Fort Brooks, about 11 or 12 this day, and that Lt. Alburtis after fighting them about an hour, and losing some of his men, retreated before them to Fort Russell. I hasten to inform you of the fact for the*

---

[308] AG 1841 B130 and A67.

222

*information of Colonel Twiggs.*

*P.S. Captain Barnum is out with his command in pursuit.* [309]

(Col. D.E. Twiggs, 2d Dragoons, to the Adjutant General, Washington.)

*Headquarters St. Johns District*
*Fort Shannon, Palatka, E.F.*
*5th March 1841*

*For your information I have the honor to enclose the copy of a letter received at 11 O'clock last night from Lt. Patten 2nd Infantry. At 12, I dispatched Lieut. Sibley and fifty men to Capt. Barnum's aid. Fearful that an attack might be made on the Wagon Train returning from Ft. King to this post, guarded by twenty-five Dragoons under Lt. Lawton, I have by a special express this morning ordered Capt. Ker to add a reinforcement of twenty-five from his command. The three Detachments now out from this post leave but thirty men for duty, and ten of these leave today for St. Augustine to attend the trial of Captain Howe by the civil power. From the express man, I learn that Captain Barnum was attacked in front where his foot men were marching and that his rear consisting of thirty mounted men (Infantry) on coming up; were with three exceptions, shot from their horses. These three men made good their retreat to Fort Russell. This I do not of course rely on as yet.*

*From the pacific measures for some weeks pursued, I have been obliged by the present urgency of circumstances to set aside all existing orders and send a force out of my command. Should the Commanding General be of opinion any other than mine, I must rest alone satisfied with the consciousness of having acted*

---

[309] AG 1841 T65 Enclosure.

*for the best.* [310]

(Lieut. G.W. Patten, 2d Infantry, to Col. D.E. Twiggs, 2d Dragoons.)

*Fort Russell, East Florida*
*7 O'clock P.M., 4 March 1841,*
*I have to report that Captain Barnum with Ninety-nine men of this command left yesterday morning in pursuit of a large body of Indians near the Ocklawaha. I heard he has met with them near Fort MacKay and is now fighting. As I learn from three of his wounded mounted men, who have this moment arrived at this post—one of them, the sergeant of the escort, severely wounded.*

*They represent the Indian force as very large, and the result doubtful. I have guides at this post who will take your Dragoons to the spot and I earnestly wish you will send a reinforcement as soon as possible. Capt. Ker left here this morning, but has gone around Orange Lake and of course is off the trail.* [311]

---

[310] AG 1841 T72
[311] AG 1841 T72 Enclosure.

# Chapter 21: "There is Bad Management Somewhere"

(Brig. Gen. W.K. Armistead, to the Honorable Secretary of War.)

*Tampa*
*March 5th, 1841*

*I have the honor to inform the department that the principal sub-chief of the Miccosukees, Coosa Tustenuggee, left my Headquarters yesterday to collect his people for emigration. They are to be in by the 20th Inst., and it is not doubted that Halick Tustenuggee's band will follow their example. As their leaders have during the war proven themselves among the most implacable of the hostiles, I consider the appearance of Coosa-Tustenuggee and his avowed determination to join the emigrating party as a decided indication of the approaching close of this long & expensive war.*

*I am now anxiously waiting the funds that have been appropriated to enable me to fulfill my promises with the chiefs and people who have come in. Until they arrive I cannot think of shipping any of the Indians, as all the promises I have made, I expect punctually to fulfill, & this cannot be done until the means are placed at my disposal. This want of the necessary funds has alone prevented an immediate shipment of those now here. I therefore most respectfully request that the funds should be sent with all possible dispatch. The Indians are becoming restless, and expecting what I have promised, they must not be deceived.*

*A party of fifty Seminoles will be at Fort Armistead in a few days. They broke from their camp, leaving a large party behind, who declined coming with them. After the peace party had traveled some distance, runners were sent after them to say that* the others would join them. The united party with those now in will comprise the entire band of Hospitakee.

Col. Worth has opened a communication with Wild-Cat who is expected at his camp tomorrow. Should he be induced to bring in his people, of which there is little doubt, Sam Jones will follow, and then there will remain only the scattered Creeks in Middle Florida, & some Seminoles & Spanish Indians in East Florida. [312]

(W.W.S. Bliss, Adjutant, to Lt.Col. B. Riley, 2d Infantry.)

*Tampa*
*March 9th, 1841*
Should you on your return to Fort King, find the Indians in that vicinity still in a hostile attitude, you are directed by the Commanding General to take such measures for their destruction and capture as you may deem expedient. Should they on the contrary evince pacific intentions, and a desire to come in and emigrate, you will adopt such measures as circumstances may call forth, remembering the desire of the General to affect their removal, if possible, in a peaceable manner.

The interpreter Charles will accompany you to Fort King. [313]

(W.W.S. Bliss, Adjutant, to Capt. S. Casey, Fort King.)

*Tampa*
*March 10th, 1841*
Your communication of the 7th inst. is just received. The commanding General regrets that Capt. Barnum should have thought it necessary to confine the Indians at Fort King and directs that they be at once released and all means taken to restore and

---

[312] AG 1841 A74
[313] AG 1841 A141, 6.

*preserve their confidence.* [314]

(W.W.S. Bliss, Adjutant, to Col. W. Worth, Commanding Tampa District.)

*Tampa*
*March 13th, 1841*
*A report has been received from Capt. Casey commanding at Fort King to the effect that Captain Ker, 2nd Dragoons, had surprised the camp of Coosa Tustenuggee & made prisoners of that chief and a considerable number of his people—thus breaking up an amicable negotiation which promised the most favorable results.*

*The General accordingly directs that you proceed with all possible expedition to join that part of your command under Capt. Wright, taking such reinforcements as you may deem necessary. Upon meeting the captured party, now on their way here, you will immediately release them, inform them that the Commanding General had nothing to do with breaking up their camp, and that they must forget it. That all his promises shall be made good &c, and endeavor to resume negotiations.*

*The General expects that you will remain as long as you may seem necessary and take such measures as the public interest may demand.* [315]

(W.W.S. Bliss, Asst. Adjutant Gen., to Lt.Col. B. Riley, 2d Infantry.)

*Tampa*
*March 14th, 1841*

---

[314] Ibid, 7.
[315] Ibid, 9-10.

*The Commanding General directs that you make a full investigation of the circumstances attending the late imprisonment at Fort King of certain Indians who were at, or about that post, at the time of the skirmishes near Fort Russell, and report the result for his information.* [316]

(W.W.S. Bliss, Adjutant, to Col. W. Worth, Commanding Tampa District.)

*Tampa*
*March 16ᵗʰ, 1841*

*Your report of this date has been received and laid before the Commanding General who directs me to express his high gratification at the success which has attended your efforts to reestablish a friendly understanding with Coosa and his people. Agreeably to your request, Catsa will proceed to you tomorrow, the other members of the delegation mentioned by you, left for Camp Cummings yesterday.* [317]

(Brig. Gen. W.K. Armistead, to the Adjutant General, Washington.)

*Tampa*
*March 14, 1841*

*I have the honor to inform you that a party of 57 Indians arrived here today from Fort Fanning. A report from the Commanding officer of which post, I herewith enclose. They are Tallahassees and Miccosukees from Middle Florida and report that a small party still remains out. I shall dispatch some of their connections to bring them in and entertain little doubt of their success. Little apprehension need now be entertained of depredations in Middle Florida, as the runaway Creeks have left*

---

[316] Ibid, 14.
[317] Ibid, 18.

*that section of country in considerable numbers and have lately been in the vicinity of Fort King.*

*I sent a command from this place on the 11th inst. to aid Coosa Tustenuggee in bringing in his people, but unfortunately, his party was surrounded by a detachment of Dragoons from Fort King and twenty captured, himself one of the number. I shall use every means to reassure these people and convince them that the capture was made without my knowledge or sanction. The matter will be fully investigated, and of the fault be with the Officers commanding the Detachment, I shall bring him before a Court Martial.*

*The intelligence from Fort Armistead is most cheering. Hospitakee, a principal chief of the Seminoles is expected there daily with 60 or 80 of his people.*

*Wild Cat or Coacoochee is to be at Fort Cummings in a few days with his party.*

*No intelligence has yet reached me respecting Sam Jones, but it is expected that he will see the necessity of joining the peace party, as well as Halick Tustenuggee.*

*These Chiefs once in, the war may be considered at an end, which I hope will take place early in the summer.* [318]

(Capt. H. Bainbridge, 3d Infantry, to Capt. W.W.S. Bliss, Asst. Adjutant General.)

*Fort Fanning*
*March 11th, 1841*
*I have the honor to report, for the information of the*

---

[318] AG 1841 A79

Commanding General, that between the 9th and 10th Inst., there came into this post, from Middle Florida; 57 men, women and children, of the Tallahassee & Miccosukee tribes. They have been dispatched in a steamer to Cedar Keys under charge of Lieut. J. L. Folsom, who is ordered to conduct them to Tampa by the first conveyance.

It affords me great pleasure to speak in the highest terms of Pas-sac-a-hola – Tus-te-nue-mico, Charles, and Interpreter Primus, for their great exertions in overcoming the aversions of the hostiles to emigrate.

By their statements of the intention of the hostiles to come in, if time was allowed them, I have been guided, and found myself not deceived in a single instance. [319]

(Capt. H. Bainbridge, 3d Infantry, to Brig. Gen. R. Jones, Adjutant General, Washington.)

*Fort Fanning*
*March 12th, 1841*

I have the honor to communicate for the information of the Commander-in-Chief, that a party of hostiles, of the Miccosukee & Tallahassee Tribes, came in to my post between the 9th & 10th inst.— Amounting to fifty-seven, men, women, & children; nearly one-half warriors. Yesterday morning I embarked them on board the Steamer Izzard destined for Tampa Bay via Cedar Keys. Lt. Folsom is ordered to accompany them to their destination.

P.S. The commanding officer of the Wacasassa District, Maj. Wilson, 3d Infantry, is at present absent at Tampa Bay—otherwise this information would have been communicated from his office.

---

[319] AG 1841 A79 Enclosure.

(Capt. Croghan Ker, 2d Dragoons, to Lt. R.C. Asheton, Adjutant, 2d Dragoons, Ft. Shannon, E.F.)

*Fort Shannon, Palatka, E.F.*
*13th March 1841.*

*I have the honor herewith to state for information of the Colonel Commanding, that leaving this on the 3d Inst., at 8 P.M. with four subalterns and one hundred men, I proceeded to Fort Brooks where I arrived at 3 A.M. the following morning, when I crossed the Ocklawaha and examined the surrounding country. But finding no recent signs of the enemy, I returned towards Fort Russell and shaped my course for Orange Creek, up which I proceeded 8 or 10 miles, still unsuccessful in coming on any fresh trails. My march up to this time has been thro' torrents of rain. So that all hopes of meeting with any success were at an end, and I was induced to turn towards this post. When near Ft. Shannon, I was met by your Special express informing me of the attack on Captain Barnum near Fort MacKay, and directing me to detach one Subaltern and twenty-five men to reinforce the Wagon Train escort. On arriving at Ft. Brooks and learning from Lt. Alburtis that his command was small and a renewal of hostilities on part of the Indians expected, I left a Sergeant and twelve Privates. Returning to Ft. Russell I learned from Lt. Patten that the reported attack on Capt. Barnum was an exaggerated one, and the capture in the meantime. Lt. Sibley was in pursuit of the Indians on the left bank of the Ocklawaha, marching up the right bank of the river and examining all suspected places. I reached Fort Fowle on the 8th and meeting Captain Barnum, was furnished by his order, with Isaac a negro guide, then in confinement at Fort King. I was here*

---

[320] AG 1841 B112

joined by Lieut. Sibley and his command with whom I left for the Ouith-la-coo-chee, where Isaac led me to believe the late war party would be come up with. Reaching Pe-lack-li-ka-ha on the 10th, I dismounted my command and had nearly surrounded a large Indian Camp when my approach was discovered by the dogs and several rifles discharged at us, but happily without effect. Four Warriors, one Indian Squaw, and one Negro Woman escaped. Among the first were three who had just returned from the attack on Capt. Barnum and Lt. Alburtis. The Indian Tom in confinement last May at Fort King was among these. Among those captured is Cosa Tustenugga, a Miccosukee chief and all his family, Three Warriors, one Negro Man and three Negro Women belonging to a citizen in St. Augustine, making in all twenty-one Indians and four Negros. Nearly ten pounds of powder was found in the camp which Cosa Tustenugga told me he had received from Genl. Armistead to shoot him some White-birds. [General Armistead denied that he gave him any powder.]

On securing my prisoners I detached Lt. Rogers and ten men to collect the Indian ponies and cattle. He soon succeeded in capturing a Euchee Indian and one Negro Woman and six ponies. I made particular inquiries before securing the Indians, respecting their having papers, but did not gain any information on that Scout.

I returned to Fort King on the 11th where I received orders from Captain Casey to leave my prisoners and all their property, when I set out for this Post where I arrived this day at 2 P.M. [321]

(Capt. John Page, to T. Hartley Crawford, Commissioner of Indian Affairs, Washington City.)

---

[321] AG 1841 A82 and T73 Enclosure.

*Tampa Bay*
*March 14, 1841.*
*Since last report, negotiations have been going on successfully. Notwithstanding efforts of a war party to prevent Cosa Tustenuggee, the most important chief in the nation left, with the intention of bringing in his people, 80 in number, and of convincing Helick Tustenuggee to come in also. Cosa on his return, was captured with all his people by Capt. Ker, and though they had papers from Genl. Armistead, were confined at Fort King &c &c. There is bad management somewhere.*

*A Steam Boat has just arrived from Fort Fanning with 60 Indians.* [322]

(Capt. John Page, 4th Infantry, to T. Hartley Crawford, Commissioner of Indian Affairs, Washington City.)

*Tampa Bay, East Florida*
*14th March 1841.*
*I have the honor to report since my last communication, negotiation has been going on with great success. Cosa Tustenuggy left here a short time since; while here a war party had a skirmish with a small detachment of soldiers for the purpose of breaking up the negotiation. Cosa disregarded that, and said he would bring in his people, 81 in number. And at the same time send runners up to Fort King, there to hold a talk with Helick Tustenuggy and bring his people here also. Cosa appointed a place 35 miles from this on the road, to meet the Wagons and escort, to bring in his people. Captain Wright started with seven wagons and eighty soldiers and two Indians. When he arrived at the place*

---

[322] "Letters Received by the Office of Indians Affairs, 1824-1881 Florida Superintendency, 1824-1853"; Record Group 75, Roll 291, (1841) March 14, 951.

appointed by Cosa to come to him, he did not find him. The two Indians went out to Cosa's camp and found the mounted companies under Capt. Ker had been there and captured him and his people, and carried them to Fort King; also the runners he sent to Fort King with a talk to Helick; notwithstanding they all had passes from General Armistead, expressing the object of their mission. They were confined, also this Cosa, who was the most important chief in the Nation. I was sure if he came, the whole must follow, and he said we must not mind a little party that was trying to break up the Treaty. He would make all come in after he had got his own people in.

I do not know what effect this unfortunate occurrence will have with this chief, it is possible he may be reconciled upon explaining &c. I hope Captain Ker will not claim it as a victory in surprising a party of Indians on their way here. Cosa had a passport with him and told Capt. Ker, as he says, he was on his way to meet Captain Wright who was waiting for him but; Capt. Ker took them to Fort King instead of bringing them here. And from that point, wanted to take them to Pilatka about sixty miles farther off. If this Officer had come ten miles this side of where he captured the Indians, he would have found Capt. Wright waiting for them, as Cosa the chief told him. This is the way the business goes on, and has ever since I arrived at this place: with this kind of management, it will take twelve months to do what might be done in two.

A Steamboat has just arrived from Fort Fanning with sixty Indians, most of them Miccosukees. Par-Buck-E-ohola (one of the delegation, and two other Indians have been out collecting them for three weeks in Middle Florida, and others are still coming in at this place.)

*I shall hope that my reports will continue to be favorable, I shall persevere so long as there is any hope, and by the end of this month, be able to tell you if we can conquer them by negotiation. I do not say these officers are wrong in capturing these people; but, there is bad management somewhere, that these occurrences should happen so often as this is not the first or second time it has happened.*

*I find it hard work to go against wind & tide.* [323]

(Capt. John Page, 4th Infantry, to T. Hartley Crawford, Commissioner of Indian Affairs, Washington City.)

*Tampa Bay, East Florida*
*22nd March 1841.*

*I have the honor to report that about 220 Indians were shipped yesterday for New Orleans, on their way to Arkansas. There are remaining in camp, eighty-five. I did not intend to leave any, but, while I was rallying them to go on board, the General was constantly giving some permission to stay. He was not aware, if he gave one man permission to remain, all his brothers and sisters and their children remain with him. I told him if he did not stop giving permissions, and leave it to me to judge, I could not get off Fifty Indians, without forcing them with the aid of troops. The General stopped his permissions, and I started them off at once without any difficulty. They were all unwilling to start, but I gave but <u>one talk;</u> that was, you have to go. This settled the point; but when they found they could get leave to remain by going to the General, it destroyed my influence and authority over them. And for a short time, some considerable excitement was produced until the General left the business with me altogether. Too many people*

---

[323] Ibid

*acting and directing in a case of this kind is very injurious. There should be but one talk and one action in the business, and they will know what to depend on.*

*I leave tomorrow for Sarasota, where I expect to meet 90 or 100 that have come in there. There are about sixty with Capt. Wright at Toa-choat-Kee and others coming in. Coacoochee is expected here in two or three days with Colonel Worth. Everything is prospering at this time, and I hope it will continue so without a breach. By the first of April, I shall be back here, and will report to you the particulars and the prospects of our success. But; at this time it is impossible.* [324]

After several failed talks with Coacoochee, who comes in to parlay, and loads up on supplies to leave until the next time. The chief is taken prisoner in May 1841 and held hostage until the rest of his band surrenders. He is reunited with his daughter and relatives who were captured a few months earlier.

Halleck Tustenuggee does a similar tactic of taking supplies at various posts and then departing. He is imprisoned during a talk in a similar manner as Coacoochee in May 1842. [325]

---

[324] "Letters Received by the Office of Indians Affairs, 1824-1881 Florida Superintendency, 1824-1853"; Record Group 75, Roll 291, (1841) March 22, 955
[325] AG 1842 W205

# Chapter 22: "Have the Post Broken Up Immediately"

(Capt. E.K. Barnum, 2d Infantry, to Brig. Gen. R. Jones, Adjutant General, Washington.)

*Fort Russell, E.F.*
*8th May 1841*

*I have most respectfully to inquire if the 2d paragraph of a Regulation of the War Department promulgated in General Order No. 100 of 1832 prohibiting the introduction of Ardent Spirits into any fort, camp or garrison of the United States does not apply to all, <u>commissioned officers</u> as well as the enlisted men of the Army.*

*I am induced to make this inquiry from a knowledge that many officers are of the opinion the Regulation does <u>not</u> apply to them; and the fact that an officer of this Post made use of such argument this morning, when checked by me for keeping liquor publicly in his quarters.*

*I therefore request the question may be settled from General Headquarters.*

*I have, and am daily using my utmost endeavors to prevent the introduction of liquors of any description into this garrison, and I believe to my partial success, may be attributed the better state of health of the troops here compared with other posts where facilities for obtaining it are greater. But, if the enlisted men see that officers pay no respect to the regulation, or are allowed to keep and use ardent spirits openly, they will take every means in their power to evade the regulation and obtain it themselves.*

General Jones responds, "The answer: "Order No. 100 of 1832

never having been Countermanded is still in force." [326]

The following inspection report by Lt. Col. Bennett Riley shows how bad conditions have become at Fort Micanopy.

(Lt.Col. B. Riley at Fort King, to Col. W. Worth, Commanding.)

*Fort King, E.F.*
*August 5th, 1841*

*I have the honor to inform you that I have been to Micanopy in obedience to your order and examined everything as respects Whiskey selling and inspected the troops, and found them in a horrible state both as respects health and discipline. I have never seen men in such a state since I have been in the Army; there were ninety-nine on the sick report and about 50 or 60 in the guardhouse. Some of the companies had only eight on parade and others had fifteen, but none more than that; some of which were drunk at the time, and others had all the appearance of having very recently been drunk. In fact, I saw very few sober men during my inspection. I told the Officers what I was sent to do, and they said that nothing in their opinion, could stop the liquor trade, but breaking up the Post. There being no Magistrate at the place, I went with Capt. Seawell to some of the most respectable inhabitants and told them that if the whiskey trade could not be broken up, that you were determined to break up the Post. They said they were very sorry – that they could not blame you, and that they could not stop it, in as much as the whiskey sellers were too strong for them, numbering more than two to one, and it became impossible for them to do anything. The Officers also say that nothing under the sun can remedy the evil, but a total break up [of the post]. You can have no idea of the extent it is carried*

---

[326] AG 1841 B214

*too, drinking and shouting all night, almost under the walls of the Commanding Officer, and he at the same time guarded by a chain of sentinels to keep off the improperly named, civil authority. I considered it dangerous to go out after night, one hundred yards from the Post. I hope for the sake of the Army and humanity, that you will have the Post broken up immediately, or as soon as practicable.* [327]

(S. Cooper, Asst. Adjutant General, to Lt.Col. Whistler, Commanding, New Orleans Barracks.)

*Headquarters of the Army of Florida*
*Cedar Keys, June 28th, 1842.*
*Major Staniford reports in a letter dated Micanopy June 23rd, "that some of the men belonging to the two companies, that left this post with Lt.Col. Whistler, just before leaving, went into the post gardens with their knives and destroyed nearly all the vegetables. Conduct such as this cannot be too strongly reprehended, and in order that it may be duly brought to the notice of the proper authority, the Col. Commanding requests you will ascertain and report the facts and circumstances of the case, believing it is only necessary to call the subject to your notice to ensure the most rigid scrutiny. He would be pleased to hear from you on the subject as early as practicable.* [328]

The war was declared over by Commanding General William J. Worth on August 14, 1842. The next day, a memorial and interment service is held in St. Augustine.

An estimated 300 Seminole & Miccosukee Indians remained in Florida.

---

[327] AG 1841 R146
[328] AG 1842 W326, 4.

# Appendix: Who's Who

It is helpful to give a short explanation of many of the characters involved in these pages. Most have been lost in time with very little information outside of the Cullum or Heitman references.

**Alburtis, William A.** (1st Lt.) 1815-1847. 2d Infantry. A former newspaper publisher from Virginia, he was breveted for the skirmish at Fort Russell in March 1841. He was killed at Vera Cruz in the Mexican War.

**Anderson, James Willoughby** (1st Lt.) 1812-1847. 2d Infantry. Served as regiment adjutant during the Seminole War. Breveted to Captain late in the Seminole War. Died of wounds from the Battle of Churubusco in the Mexican War.

**Armistead, Walker K.** (Brig. Gen.) 1780?-1845. The third graduate of West Point Military Academy. Former Chief Engineer of the Army and Colonel in the 3d Artillery. Commanded the Army in Florida, 1840-1841. His brother George Armistead defended Fort McHenry during the War of 1812, and his son Lewis Armistead was killed at Pickett's Charge during the Battle of Gettysburg.

**Asheton, Robert C.** (Lt.) Promoted from Sergeant Major to Lieutenant in the 2d Dragoons. Served as 2d Dragoons Adjutant. Dismissed from the Army in 1841.

**Barnum, Ephraim K.** (Capt.) 1797-1847. 2d Infantry. Not much is known of his background. He joined the Army in 1817 and died in 1847. He was acquainted with Creek Indians and the first Native American who graduated West Point, David Moniac.

**Beall, Benjamin Lloyd** (Capt.) 1801-1863, was appointed to West Point but dismissed from the academy for going AWOL. He became Captain in the Washington City Volunteers who went to Florida in 1836 and was appointed Captain in the newly created 2d Dragoon Regiment the same year. He served a distinguished career with the 2d and 1$^{st}$ Dragoon Regiments. Brother of 2d Dragoon Capt. Lloyd Beall.

**Bliss, William Wallace Smith** (Capt.) 1815-1853. He was a professor of mathematics at West Point. Served in the 4$^{th}$ Infantry Regiment and appointed as Assistant Adjutant General under Gen. Armistead. He distinguished himself in the War with Mexico. Personal Secretary to President Zachary Taylor. Died of Yellow Fever in New Orleans in 1853. Fort Bliss, Texas, is named after him.

**Bonneville, Benjamin L.E.** (Capt.) 1796?-1878. 7$^{th}$ Infantry and commanded at several forts in Florida. Served 51 years in the Army.

**Burlingham, Lansing** (Pvt.) 1816-1840. Killed at the Battle of Martin's Point, Dec. 28, 1840.

**Call, Richard K.** 1792-1862. Territorial Governor of Florida twice, 1836-1839, and 1841-1844. He was a protégé of Andrew Jackson, served as an Infantry Officer in the Creek War, at the Battle of New Orleans, and in the First Seminole War. He was General of the Florida Militia at the Battle of the Withlacoochee before becoming Governor. He briefly commanded the armed forces in Florida but came under much criticism for not ending the war. His mansion "The Grove" can be toured in Tallahassee, Florida.

**Carroll, Francis** (Sgt. Maj.) 1810-1840. Sergeant Major in the 7$^{th}$ Infantry. Survived the battle with Lt. Sanderson in May 1840, but killed at the Battle of Martin's Point in December 1840.

**Casey, Silas** (Capt.) 1807-1882. 2d Infantry. Wounded at the Battle of Chapultepec in the Mexican War and breveted to Lt.Col. In the Civil War as Major General, he was President of the Board of Examination of Candidates for Officers of Colored Troops.

**Churchill, Sylvester** (Maj.) 1783-1862, 3d Artillery. Former journalist and newspaper publisher from Vermont. Served as Inspector General in Florida who was responsible for mustering in the Florida Volunteers.

**Coacoochee** (also Wildcat) 1807?-1857. The son of Chief Emathla (King Philip) and nephew of Chief Micanope. One of the most famous Miccosukee War Chiefs. He fought most of his battles in the area south of St. Augustine and along the St. Johns River. He was captured and escaped from the Spanish Castillo/Fort Marion in St. Augustine. When he was taken prisoner near the end of the war, his family was used as hostages to force his band to surrender. Out west in Indian Territory (Oklahoma), he led a large party of Seminoles, Black Seminoles, and Kickapoo into Mexico to escape slave hunters. He was given a commission as a Colonel by the Mexican government. He died of Smallpox in Mexico in 1857.

**Crawford, T. Hartley**, 1786-1863. Appointed by the President as Commissioners of Indian Affairs from 1838 to 1845. He was a staunch Jacksonian and strongly supported Indian removal.

**Eastin, Matilda**, 1825-1876. Daughter of Thomas Eastin in Mount Vernon, Alabama. Second wife of Lt. Alexander Montgomery. Her father was a personal friend of Andrew Jackson, and her uncle married Jackson's niece, Rachael Donalson.

**Gatlin, Richard C.** (1st Lt.) 1809-1896. 7th Infantry. Appointed to West Point from North Carolina, his brother, Dr. John S. Gatlin, was killed with Major Dade's command in 1835. He commanded at Fort Micanopy, but much of his military career was out west at Fort Smith, Arkansas. After being captured by Arkansas troops in 1861, he joined the Confederacy and was a General in the Confederate Army.

**Greene, William Batchelder** (2nd Lt.) 1819-1878. He resigned from West Point but was still commissioned in the 7th Infantry. He resigned from the Army in 1841 and became part of the Utopian community of Brook Farm in Massachusetts. He lived many years in England, but returned and was a U.S. Colonel during the Civil War.

**Halleck-Tustenugge** (also Alleck, Haleck) One of the main Miccosukee war leaders, said to be second only to Sam Jones/Abiaka. He may have been wounded in the battle with Captain Rains near Fort King. He committed some of the most vicious raids in Florida. After being captured and sent to Oklahoma, he became a strong leader for his people out west. He returned to Florida to negotiate with Billy Bowlegs in 1849. During the Civil War, he fought on the side of the Union and may have died of exposure in Kansas.

**Hanson, John M.** (Lt.Col./Col.) A longtime resident of St. Augustine. He handled business affairs for Moses Levy but became a political opponent to his son David Levy Yulee. Hanson was a customs collector and one of the wealthiest plantation owners in St. Augustine.

**Hanson, Weightman K.** (2nd Lt.) 1816-1844. 7th Infantry. He fought in many battles in Florida but died in 1844 from illness contracted during the war. His brother Charles Hanson was also in the 7th Infantry and was killed in the Mexican War.

**Harney, William S.** (Lt.Col.) 1800-1889. 2d Dragoons. One of the most controversial officers in the Army. He went from Army Paymaster to second in command of the 2d Dragoon regiment. He is known for his brutality, from beating to death a female slave in St. Louis, to wiping out a Sioux village in Nebraska, known as the Harney Massacre (1855). He was recalled to Washington after nearly starting a war with the British in the San Juan Islands on Washington/Oregon Territory, known as the "Pig War." During the Civil War, he retired after he was refused field duty, probably because President Lincoln distrusted him. Harney spent his last days in a retirement home by Lake Eola in Orlando, Florida.

**Hopson, Nevil** (2nd Lt.) 1816-1847. His father was one of the founders of Hopkinsville, Kentucky. Nevil graduated West Point in the same class as Lt. Sherwood. He was sent by Lt. Sherwood back to get help at Fort Micanopy at the Battle of Martin's Point, which unfairly caused a cloud of suspicion of cowardice over him.

**Hunt, Thomas F.** (Lt.Col.) Deputy Quartermaster General, headquartered at the Quartermaster Depot in Palatka.

**Jenckes, Edwin T.** (Mr.) 1797-1847. One of the wealthiest merchants and plantation owners in St. Augustine. He had business interests in Rhode Island and St. Thomas. He weighed between 450 and 500 lbs. and was known as "the greatest man" at the state constitutional convention in 1838.

**Jesup, Thomas Sidney** (Maj.Gen.) The Army Quartermaster General, which position he held from 1818 to 1861. Originally from Tennessee, he also served as Commander of the Army in Florida from 1836-1838. He successfully led the Creek Removal in 1836 before arriving in Florida but had a lot more trouble with the Seminoles. He resorted to capturing under a flag of truce, which his capture of Osceola is what he is most famous, or infamous, for.

**Jones, Roger** (Brig.Gen.) 1789-1852. The U.S. Army Adjutant General from 1825-1852. He served in the Marines, then resigned and became Captain of Artillery in the U.S. Army. His family has a long history of serving in the military.

**Ker, Croghan** (Capt.) 1817-1858. He was another officer who was with the Louisiana volunteers in Florida in 1836 and became an officer with the newly formed 2d Dragoon Regiment. He caused trouble in the Seminole War when he detained Chief Coosa Tustenuggee, who had a pass by Gen. Armistead to bring his people in.

**Kingsbury, Julius** (Capt.) 1797-1856. 2d Infantry. He received a brevet promotion during the War with Mexico. He was dismissed from the Army in 1853 after he disappeared for four years in California to look for gold.

**Lawson, Thomas** (Surgeon General) 1789-1861. He started his career as a surgeon in the Navy and then went to serve as a surgeon in the 6th and 7th Infantry Regiments. He was in the First Seminole War, the Creek War of 1836, and the first part of the Second Seminole War. President

Jackson appointed him Surgeon General in 1836, a post he held until his death.

**Levy, David** (see David Levy Yulee)

**Levy, Moses**, 1782-1854. He attempted to establish a Jewish utopian community near Micanopy in the 1820s. His plantation was destroyed in 1835 by Seminoles. He was an abolitionist, but his son David Levy Yulee was pro-slavery.

**Loomis, Gustavus** (Maj.) 1789-1872. He graduated from West Point and served over 50 years in the Army until after the Civil War. He commanded in the 2d Infantry and was promoted to Lt.Col. and commanded 6$^{th}$ Infantry in Florida from 1842 – 1844.

**MacKay, John** (Capt.). He graduated from West Point in 1829. In the U.S. Army Topographical Engineers, he created the 1839 MacKay-Blake map of Florida. He died in 1848.

**Macomb, Alexander** (Maj.Gen.) 1782-1841. Commanding General of the Army from 1828 until his death in 1841. His son Alexander Jr. served in the Seminole War in Florida. He attempted to negotiate an agreement or unsigned treaty with the Florida Indians in 1839 that if they were peaceful, they would be allowed to remain in South Florida, which brought condemnation from Florida citizens.

**Martin, John W.** (Lt.) Served in the 2d Infantry Regiment in Florida, where he was wounded in May 1840. During the Mexican War, he resigned and joined the 3d Dragoon Regiment. He died in 1848.

**Mason, James B.** (Capt.) A Captain of the Florida Volunteers who was very popular, but accidentally killed by one of his men.

**McDougall, Charles** (Dr.) 1804-1885. He had a long career as an Army doctor and surgeon.

**McKinstry, Justus** (2$^{nd}$ Lt.) 1814-1897. 2d Infantry. He served with distinction in the Mexican War. As quartermaster in the Civil War, he was brought up on charges of dishonesty, but the charges were dropped with his resignation. He afterward became a stockbroker in New York City.

**McRae (Rev.),** also McCray. A Methodist Circuit rider in Alachua County who was killed by Indians.

**Montgomery, Alexander** (1st Lt.) 1811-1893. 7th Infantry. Served as quartermaster for most of his career. His first wife was killed by Indians in Florida shortly after their marriage.

**Montgomery, Elizabeth Francis (Fanny) Taylor** (Mrs.) 1821-1840. The first wife of 1st Lt. Alexander Montgomery. Her father was Griffin Taylor, one of the wealthiest businessmen in Cincinnati.

**Moore, Samuel P.** (Dr.)1813-1889. He became an Army surgeon in 1835. He joined the Confederacy in 1861 and became the Surgeon General of the Confederate States. He was a long-time friend of Jefferson Davis. (And he has the largest sideburns of anyone I've seen in the Civil War.)

**Nelson, Joseph S.** (Maj.) 7th Infantry. He had distinguished service during the War of 1812. He suddenly died at Fort Brooke in 1843 just after he was appointed to command the 7th Infantry in Florida.

**Newton, Washington Irving** (2nd Lt.) 1810-1876. 2d Dragoons. Another Dragoons officer who was appointed into the regiment and did not attend West Point. His father was a Virginia congressman.

**Page, John** (Capt.) 1795-1846. 4th Infantry. He participated in the Creek and Seminole removal and is known to have treated the Indians with kindness and empathy. At the Battle of Palo Alto during the Mexican War, his lower jaw was shot off by a cannon shot, where he lingered for a month until he died.

**Poinsett, Joel R.** (Sec. of War) 1779-1851. He was a member of the House of Representatives and Minister to Mexico. He was a Unionist despite being a slave owner. He was Secretary of War during the Van Buren Administration and in charge of Indian Removal of the Five Civilized Tribes.

**Rains, Gabriel J.** (Capt.) 1803-1881. 7th Infantry. With his younger brother George Washington Rains, they are known as the father of land mines or torpedos. He tested out his first explosive devices in Florida.

**Read, Leigh** (Gen.) 1809-1841. He became General of the Florida Militia when Richard K. Call became Governor. He was wounded at the Battle of Withlacoochee. He became the Speaker of the House in the Florida legislature and was assassinated in the streets of Tallahassee by the brother of a man that he had killed in a duel.

**Reid, Robert Raymond** (Gov.) 1789-1841. The fifth Territorial Governor between Gov. Call's two terms. He vigorously promoted Indian Removal and the Seminole War. He died of yellow fever at home a few months after his term of Governor ended.

**Riley, Bennett** (Lt.Col.) 1787-1853. He served in the 2d Infantry in Florida but had a distinguished military career from the War of 1812 to the Mexican War. He was the last military governor of California. Fort Riley, Kansas, is named after him.

**Sam Jones (Abiaka)**, Chief & Medicine man as one of the most powerful Miccosukee leaders during the war. So resolved was he, that he would not let any of his people discuss removal. Sam Jones is not his real name, but a name the soldiers gave him from a popular song at the time.

**Sanderson, James S.** (2nd Lt.) 1799-1840. 7th Infantry. A promising officer who was commissioned after serving as the sergeant major in the regiment with the recommendation signed by every regiment officer present in the region.

**Sherwood, Walter** (2nd Lt.) 1816-1840. 7th Infantry. Killed in Florida a few weeks after his arrival. The death of his command is blamed on his inexperience and carelessness.

**Sloan, William J.** (Dr.) Became an Army surgeon in 1837, which he remained until his death in 1880.

**Smith, Joseph R.** (Capt.) 1801-1868. 2d Infantry. He graduated from West Point in 1823 and later served in both the 2d and 7$^{th}$ Infantry. He distinguished himself in the Mexican War where he was wounded, which would plague him for the rest of his life.

**Taylor, Griffin** (Mr.) 1797-1866. One of the wealthiest businessmen in Cincinnati, Ohio. He started a mercantile business, was a bank president, and president of the Board of Trustees of Spring Grove Cemetery.

**Taylor, Zachary** (Brig. Gen.) 1784-1850. Died in office as President of the United States. Commanding General of the Army in Florida, 1838-1840. He was one of the few officers who had his reputation enhanced by the war due to the Battle of Okeechobee in 1837.

**Thomas, George C.** (1$^{st}$ Lt.) 1812-1882. 4$^{th}$ Artillery. He resigned from the Army in 1842 and had a successful career as a surveyor and engineer.

**Twiggs, David E.** (Col.) 1790-1862. He was made the commander of the 2d Dragoon Regiment when the regiment was created in 1836. He was the only General Officer in the Army to resign and join the Confederacy, although he died the following year.

**Whiting, Daniel P.** (1$^{st}$ Lt.) 1808-1892. A Company Officer with the 7$^{th}$ Infantry. He had an extensive military history out west and illustrated several lithographs of the Mexican War, where he was also promoted for meritorious conduct.

**Whistler, William** (Lt.Col.) 1780-1863. 7$^{th}$ Infantry, which he commanded in Florida. He served an incredible 60 years in the Army. He was the uncle of the famous American painter, James A. McNeil

Whistler.

**Wood, Robert Crooke** (Dr.) 1799-1869. An Army surgeon who married Zachary Taylor's daughter. He served a distinguished career and was acting Surgeon General in 1861.

**Worth, William Jenkins** (Col.) 1794-1849. Made Commander of the 8th Infantry at the creation of the regiment, he served a distinguished career from the War of 1812 to the Mexican War. He was able to end the Second Seminole War and remained as Commander of the Army in Florida until 1845.

**Yulee, David Levy** (also Levy, David) 1810-1886. Was territorial delegate to congress and one of the first state senators. His father was Jewish, but David became an Episcopalian. He adopted the last name Yulee from his mother's family after his marriage. He was pro-slavery and pro-confederacy. He built one of the first railroads in Florida and acquired a large amount of land for the railroad and his plantations.

# Bibliography

## Books
Brackett, Albert G.; *General Lane's Brigade in Central Mexico*; H.W. Derby & Company, Cincinnati; 1854. The Mexican War record of Lt. John W. Martin.

Brown, George M. (Ord. Sergt.); *Ponce de Leon Land and Florida War Record*, The Record Co., St. Augustine, Fla., 1902. Sgt. Brown reprints the casualty list from Sprague & Eaton. Many of the colorful antecedents in this book are from Ellen Call Long, who wrote a newspaper column of greatly embellished tales from her father's papers, Governor Richard K. Call, which she changed many of the details.

Carter, Clarence Edwin; *The Territorial Papers of the United States, Volume XXVI, The Territory of Florida, 1839-1845,* The National Archives, Washington D. C., 1962.

Crane, Ichabod; *The Adventures of Captain Bonneville: or Scenes, Incidents, and Adventures in the Far West*, 1837 https://www.jstor.org/stable/24453053.

Cullum, George Washington; *Biographical Register of the Officers and Graduates of the U.S. Military Academy at West Point, New York, since its establishment in 1802*; Seeman & Peters, Saginaw, Michigan, 1920. An important source for biographies of West Point officers, but he doesn't include any history of Confederate service of them.

Denham, James M, and Keith L. Huneycutt (Edited by); *Echoes from a Distant Frontier, The Brown Sister's Correspondence from Antebellum Florida*; University of South Carolina Press, Columbia, SC, 2004.

Drake, Samuel G.; *The Aboriginal Races of North America; Comprising Biographical Sketches of Eminent Individuals, and An Historical Account of the Different Tribes, from the First Discovery of the Continent to the Present Period with a Dissertation of their Origin, Antiquities, Manners and Customs, Illustrative Narratives and Anecdotes, and a copious Analytical Index*. Philadelphia: Charles DeSilver & Sons; Claxton, Resen & Haffelfinger; J.B. Lippincott & Co. Boston: Nichols & Hall; 1859. This book was in print from at least 1840 until after Drake's death forty years later. It includes much information on the Seminole War. Drake was one of the founding members of the New England Historical and Genealogical Society.

Evans, Clement A.; *Confederate Military History: A Library of Confederate States History*, Vol. IV, 339-341; Atlanta, GA., 1987 reprint, Wilmington, N.C., 1899. For information on Gabriel Rains.

Givens, Murphy (Editor), Daniel Powers Whiting; *A Soldier's Life: Memoirs of a Veteran of 30 Years of Soldiering*, Nueces Press, Corpus Christi, Texas, 2011. An invaluable eyewitness account that gives a different description of the death of Lt. Sherwood & Mrs. Montgomery, from Daniel Whiting in the 7th Infantry.

Heitman, Francis B.; *Historical Register and Dictionary of the United States Army, From Its Organization, September 29, 1789, to March 2, 1903*. Volume 2, 1903. Washington: Government Printing Office. University of Illinois Press, Urbana, 1965. A valuable resource because it includes background information of the officers and a short bio of their promotions and career.

Kimball, Christopher; *Army and Navy Chronicle: Seminole War Guide, 1835-1844*; CreateSpace; 2018. A guide to the Seminole War references in the journal of the Army and Navy Chronicle.

Kimball, Christopher; *Seminole and Creek War Battles and Events*; Ingramspark; 2018. My third version of the timeline book.

Knetsch, Joe; *Fear and Anxiety on the Florida Frontier; Articles on the Second Seminole War, 1835-1842*. Seminole War Foundation, 2008. Much good information from journals of the era.

Mahon, John K.; *History of the Second Seminole War, 1835-1842*; University Presses of Florida, Gainesville, 1968. The primary source for the war since it was first published. Still an excellent reference and a great bibliography.

Missall, John and Mary Lou; *The Seminole Wars, America's Longest Indian Conflict*, University Press of Florida, 2004. An updated version is in the works.

Smith, Jr., George G.; *The History of Methodism in Georgia and Florida, From 1785 to 1865*; Jno. W. Burke & Co., Macon, Georgia, 1877. The best information I have found on Rev. McRae/McCray, and it still doesn't say what his first name was!

Smith, Isaac; *Reminiscences of a Campaign in Mexico: An Account of the Operations of the Indiana Brigade on the Line of the Rio Grande and Sierra Madre, and a Vindication of the Volunteers, Against the Aspersions of Officials and Unofficials*; Chapmans and Spann, Indianapolis, 1848. Information on Lt. John W. Martin in the Mexican War.

Sprague, John T.; *The Origin, Progress, and Conclusion of the Florida War*; 1848, Seminole Wars Historic Foundation Reproduction, University of Tampa Press, Tampa, Florida, 2000. As adjutant under Colonel Worth, Sprague reprinted a lot of letters and reports. He also married Worth's daughter, and their daughter married a close relative of Major Dade!

Stuart, Allan R.; *The History of Methodism in Alachua; The Alachua Methodist Church*, Alachua, Florida, 1962. For information on Rev. McRae/McCray.

Welch, Andrew; *"A Narrative of the Early Days and Remembrances of Oceola Nikkannochee, Prince of Econchatti, Written by his Guardian"*; Facsimile Reproductions of the 1841 edition, and the pamphlets of 1837 and 1847, 203; the University Presses of Florida, Gainesville, 1977.

Wickman, Patricia Riles; *Osceola's Legacy*, The University of Alabama Press, Tuscaloosa, 1991. Genealogy information on Osceola, and possible clue of the identity of Old Betsy.

## Journals and Papers

Boyd, Mark F.; "The Seminole War: Its Background and Onset"; *Florida Historical Quarterly*, Vol. XXX, Num. 1 (July 1951): 57. Also reprinted as "Florida Aflame; the Background and Onset of the Seminole War, 1835", the Florida Board of Parks and Historic Memorials, 1951.

Cunningham, Denyse; "Edward Fredrick Leitner (1812-1838) Physician Botanist", *Broward Legacy*, Vol. 27, Number 1 (2007). Information on Dr. Leitner.

Denham, James M.; and Keith L. Huneycutt; "Everything is Hubbub Here": Lt. James Willoughby Anderson's Second Seminole War, 1837-1842. *The Florida Historical Quarterly*, Vol. 82, No. 3 (Winter 2004): 313-359.

Gulf Archaeology Research Institute (GARI); "Fort King Road: Battlefields and

Baggage Trains (A report prepared for the American Battlefield Protection Program.)", Crystal River, Florida, 2017. An important study on Fort King.

"Jacksonville and the Seminole War, 1835-1836, Part II"; *Florida Historical Quarterly*, Vol. III, Num. 4 (April 1925): 15-16. Reprints of the letters from the beginning of the war. Then entire Quarterly collection can be viewed online through the University of Florida library catalog.

Knetsch, Joe; "Fort Micanopy and the Second Seminole War"; paper for the Micanopy Historical Society, 1994. A great paper on Fort Micanopy.

McGaughy, Felix P.; "The Squaw Kissing War" Master Thesis, Florida State University, 1965. An important eyewitness account of a soldier's life in Florida, from the diary of Private Bartholomew Lynch. I wish there could be an updated reprint of it.

New York Military Magazine, Vol. 1, Labree & Stockton, New York (August 21, 1841): 172. This publication filled in the gaps when the Army and Navy Chronicle suspended publication in 1841 and gives background information on Lt. Sherwood.

United States Quarter-Master's and Ordnance Departments, "Report on India Rubber Air Pontoons, and Bridges, from the United States Quarter-Master's and Ordnance Departments"; New York, printed by Daniel Fanshaw, 1849.

Waters, W. Davis; "Deception is the Art of War: Gabriel J. Rains, Torpedo Specialist of the Confederacy," *The North Carolina Historical Review*, Vol. 66, No. 1 (January 1989) 29-60. A good biography on Rains, although it does not cover his time in the Seminole War.

## Army and Navy Chronicle

The Army and Navy Chronicle (ANC) is an important journal from the time of the 2nd Seminole War because it reprints letters and reports from the field. It can be found on microfilm in libraries and universities, on hathitrust.org, and Google Books. Below are some of the sources that I used from the Chronicle.

Homans, Benjamin; *The Army and Navy Chronicle,* (ANC) Washington, D.C., 1835-1842.

Force, William Q; *The Army and Navy Chronicle and Scientific Repository*, Washington, D.C, 1843-1844.

Pages quoted from the Army and Navy Chronicle:

ANC Vol. 6, 108
ANC Vol. 10, 269
ANC Vol. 10, 297
ANC Vol. 10, 348
ANC Vol. 11, 12-13
ANC Vol. 11, 13-14
ANC Vol. 11, 175
ANC Vol. 11, 214-215
ANC Vol. 11, 220
ANC Vol. 11, 250
ANC Vol. 11, 268
ANC Vol. 11, 384

## Maps

All these maps are originally from the National Archives, but copies can also be viewed in the state library in Tallahassee.

1.  MacKay, John (Capt.); *Topographical map of the northern portion of the country between the Oklawaha and St. John's Rivers* (2nd Seminole War); by [Capt.] John MacKay, Topographical Engineers Corp (formerly 2nd Artillery.) National Archives, 1841. Copy in the State Library of Florida, Tallahassee.
2.  MacKay, John (Capt.), and J.E. Blake (Lt.); *Map of the Seat of War in Florida, Compiled by Order of Brevet Brig. Genl. Z[achary] Taylor*, 1839. By Capt. John MacKay and 1st Lt. Jacob Edmund Blake, Topographical Engineers (formerly 6th Infantry). Copy in the State Library of Florida, Tallahassee.
3.  Map of Square No. 1. (2nd Seminole War); National Archives, 1839(?). Copy in the State Library of Florida, Tallahassee. Map of the military Square with Fort King in the middle.
4.  Map of Square No. 6. (2nd Seminole War); National Archives, 1839(?). Copy in the State Library of Florida, Tallahassee. No surveyor is listed.
5.  Thomas, George C. (Lt.); *A Topographical Survey of Military Section No. 7* (2nd Seminole War); National Archives. Copy in the State Library of Florida, Tallahassee.
6.  Tompkins, C. (Lt.); *Map of the Ocklawaha River &c &c*; National Archives, January 1839. Copy in the State Library of Florida, Tallahassee. Drawn by

[1st]Lieut. C[hristopher Quarles] Tompkins, 3d Artillery and transmitted by Maj. S. Churchill to Adjt. Genl. Of the Army, Feb. 11, 1839.

## Newspapers

I went through hundreds of newspapers. Many were repeated copies of articles, so I included the ones below that I ended up using. Often, newspapers reprinted letters and reports from the field are contemporary to the times.

Alexandria Gazette, May 18, 1840
American Citizen (New York, N.Y.), Jun. 20, 1840
Arkansas Democrat (Little Rock, AR), Feb. 16, 1892
Arkansas Gazette, May 20, 1823
Baltimore Pilot & Transcript, Jan. 11, 1841
Baton Rouge Gazette, Feb. 6, 1841
Baton Rouge Gazette, Jun. 8, 1844
Bloomington Herald (Bloomington, Iowa), Apr. 8, 1842
Boston Post, April 11, 1840
Cahaba Gazette (AL), Oct. 21, 1859
Camden Journal (SC), Jan. 20, 1841
Cheraw Advertiser (SC), Sept. 16, 1840
Cheraw Advertiser, Sept. 30, 1840
Daily Arkansas Gazette, March 22, 1876
Daily Delta (New Orleans), May 22, 1846
Daily Green Mountain Freeman (Montpelier, VT), April 24, 1861
Daily National Republican (Washington, D.C.), June 24, 1864
Evening Post (New York, N.Y.), Sept. 9, 1840
Fort Smith Times, May 2, 1909.
Hopkinsville Kentuckian, May 4, 1905, & Nov. 19, 1908
Mississippi Free Trader (Natchez, MS), April 13, 1840.
Mississippi Free Trader, Jun. 10, 1840
Mississippi Free Trader, Sept. 18, 1841
National Gazette (Philadelphia, PA), August 31, 1840
National Gazette (Philadelphia, PA), Sept. 17, 1840
New York Herald, March 23, 1842
Newbern Spectator (North Carolina), 19 August 1836, page 1
Niles National Register (Niles, Mich.), June 22, 1839
North Alabamian (Tuscumbia, AL), April 17, 1841
Pilot and Transcript (Baltimore, MD), Nov. 18, 1840
Richmond Enquirer, May 26, 1840
Richmond Enquirer, May 12, 1840
Richmond Enquirer, June 2, 1840

Richmond Enquirer, Jun. 5, 1840
Richmond Enquirer, Jun. 19, 1840
Richmond Enquirer, June 26, 1840
Richmond Enquirer, Nov. 13, 1840
Richmond Enquirer, Jan. 9, 1841
Richmond Enquirer, Sept. 17, 1841
Richmond Enquirer, Jan. 9, 1841
Richmond Enquirer, Jan. 16, 1841
Savannah Daily Republican, Apr. 2, 1840
Southern Banner (Holly Springs, MS), June 26, 1840
Times-Picayune (New Orleans), Jun. 6, 1840
Times-Picayune, Sept. 15, 1841
Times-Picayune, Jan. 21, 1841
Times-Picayune, Feb. 29, 1844
Times-Picayune, Aug. 28, 1845
Weekly Arkansas Gazette (Little Rock, AR), July 1, 1840
Wetumpka Argus (Wetumpka, AL), Dec. 16, 1840

## National Archive & Adjutant General letters

The following are the letters and reports researched from the microfilm of the National Archives. Recently many of these resources are now available online through Ancestry.com and Fold3, although most all that I researched was on microfilm.

AG is the acronym for Adjutant General, of the letters received at the office of the US Army Adjutant General. Then it is filed by year, then by the first letter of the last name of the person who sent the letter, filed in the order it was received at the war department. So, AG 1841 A5 is a letter sent to the Adjutant General in 1841; by a person whose last name begins with "A," like General Armistead, and it is the 5th letter received in 1841. This takes research because Armistead letters are also filed under "B" because his adjutant/aide was Capt. Bliss. Capt. Rains have letters filed under R, and also "W" because his commander was Lt.Col. Whistler. And they have even further filed under "T" for Col. Twiggs since he was the commander of the eastern district. So you often have to follow the chain of command. Letters mailed from Philadelphia to Washington would get there quicker than letters sent from Fort Brooke, Florida, which arrived before letters from Arkansas. So the numbering does not always indicate the order that the letters were written.

The Indian Affairs letters are filed the same way: year and the first letter of the last name of the person who wrote the letter, in the order received. But it is not marked as clearly as the Adjutant letters. The microfilm rolls of Indian Affairs are separated by agency or state.

"Letters Received by the Office of Indian Affairs, 1824-1881 Florida Superintendency, 1824-1853"; Record Group 75, Bureau of Indian Affairs. National Archives Microfilm M234.

INDIAN AFFAIRS PAPERS, ROLL 291, 1841, PAGE 951 (MARCH 14)
INDIAN AFFAIRS PAPERS, ROLL 291, 1841, PAGE 955 (MARCH 22)

"Letters Sent by the Office of the Quartermaster General (Main Series) 1818-1870"; Record Group 92. National Archives Microfilm M745. The QM office copied the letters it sent out in a ledger book. There might be two or three letters to a page, and in the order they were sent out.

US ARMY QUARTERMASTER LETTERS SENT 1840, PAGE 102-103 (OCT. 13)
US ARMY QUARTERMASTER LETTERS SENT 1841, PAGE 209-210
US ARMY QUARTERMASTER LETTERS SENT 1841, PAGE 210
US ARMY QUARTERMASTER LETTERS SENT 1841, PAGE 210-211
US ARMY QUARTERMASTER LETTERS SENT 1841, PAGE 214
US ARMY QUARTERMASTER LETTERS SENT 1841, PAGE 439
US ARMY QUARTERMASTER LETTERS SENT 1841, PAGE 444
US ARMY QUARTERMASTER LETTERS SENT, JAN. 21, 1857
US ARMY QUARTERMASTER LETTERS SENT, JUNE 1, 1857

"Letters Received by the Office of the Adjutant General (Main Series) 1822-1860"; Records of the Adjutant General's Office, Record Group 94. National Archives Microfilm M567. The Army Adjutant is the scribe or administrator who handles all the correspondence from the commander. For the time covered in this book, the Army Adjutant General is Roger Jones.

AG 1827 R24, ROLL 30
AG 1836 G238, ROLL 142
AG 1837 R9, ROLL 151
AG 1838 S160, S170, S208, ROLL 175
AG 1839 D46, ROLL 185
AG 1839 H80, ROLL 188
AG 1839 M224, ROLL 192
AG 1839 R141, ROLL 194
AG 1839 R149, ROLL 194
AG 1839 R203, ROLL 194

AG 1839 W130, ROLL 199
AG 1839 W194, ROLL 199
AG 1839 W325, ROLL 200
AG 1840 A124, ROLL 201
AG 1840 A130 & A130 ENCLOSURE, ROLL 201
AG 1840 A132, ROLL 201
AG 1840 A133, ROLL 201
AG 1840 A136, ROLL 201
AG 1840 A146, ROLL 201
AG 1840 A155 & A155 ENCLOSURE (FROM A139) , ROLL 201
AG 1840 A159 ENCLOSURE, ROLL 201
AG 1840 A161, ROLL 201
AG 1840 A175 PAGE 1, 2-4, 13, 13-16, 20, 28, ROLL 201
AG 1840 A176, ROLL 201
AG 1840 A192 ENCLOSURE, ROLL 201
AG 1840 A204 PAGE 13, 18-20, 22, 29-30, 36, 39, ROLL 201
AG 1840 A233, ROLL 201
AG 1840 A234 PAGE 11, 12, 23, 24, ROLL 201
AG 1840 A261 ENCLOSURE, ROLL 202
AG 1840 A273 PAGE 32-33, ROLL 202
AG 1840 A287, ROLL 202
AG 1840 A295, ROLL 202
AG 1840 A306 PAGE 13-14, 25, 31, ROLL 202
AG 1840 A312, ROLL 202
AG 1840 A315, ROLL 202
AG 1840 A331, ROLL 202
AG 1840 A342 PAGE 28, 29 , ROLL 202
AG 1840 A349 ENCLOSURE, ROLL 202
AG 1840 A357 PAGE 4, 11-13, 13-14, 29-30, 30, ROLL 202
AG 1840 B391, ROLL 204
AG 1840 B408, ROLL 204
AG 1840 D127, ROLL 206
AG 1840 G265, ROLL 209
AG 1840 H127, ROLL 209
AG 1840 H197, ROLL 209
AG 1840 H337, ROLL 210
AG 1840 L88 & L88 ENCLOSURE, ROLL 211
AG 1840 M81, ROLL 212
AG 1840 M353, ROLL 213
AG 1840 R229, ROLL 215
AG 1840 S7, ROLL 216
AG 1840 S59, ROLL 216
AG 1840 S182, ROLL 216
AG 1840 S193, ROLL 216

AG 1840 T140, PAGE 12-14, 13, ROLL 218
AG 1840 T149, ROLL 218
AG 1840 T160, ENCLOSURE, ENCLOSURE 5, ROLL 218
AG 1840 T178, ENCLOSURE, ROLL 218
AG 1840 T179, ROLL 218
AG 1840 T183, PAGE 9, ROLL 218
AG 1840 T185, ROLL 218
AG 1840 T199, ROLL 218
AG 1840 T328, PAGE 13-14, ROLL 218
AG 1840 W77, ROLL 220
AG 1840 W176, W176 ENCLOSURE, (1876 7329), ROLL 220
AG 1840 W280, ROLL 221
AG 1841 A5, ENCLOSURE, ROLL 222
AG 1841 A6, ROLL 222
AG 1841 A10, ROLL 222
AG 1841 A11, ENCLOSURE, ROLL 222
AG 1841 A33, ROLL 222
AG 1841 A37, ROLL 222
AG 1841 A42, ROLL 222
AG 1841 A50, ROLL 222
AG 1841 A52, PAGE 8-9, 17-18, 20-21, 37, ROLL 222
AG 1841 A66, ROLL 222
AG 1841 A67, ROLL 222
AG 1841 A69, ROLL 222
AG 1841 A74, ROLL 222
AG 1841 A79, ENCLOSURE, ROLL 222
AG 1841 A82, ROLL 222
AG 1841 A141, PAGE 6, 7, 9-10, 14, 15, 18, ROLL 222
AG 1841 B108, ROLL 223
AG 1841 B111, ROLL 223
AG 1841 B112, ROLL 223
AG 1841 B130, ROLL 223
AG 1841 B214, ROLL 224
AG 1841 G46, ROLL 229
AG 1841 G226, ROLL 230
AG 1841 R90, ROLL 236
AG 1841 R146, ROLL 236
AG 1841 R175, ROLL 236
AG 1841 T65 ENCLOSURE, ROLL 238
AG 1841 T69, ENCLOSURE, ROLL 238
AG 1841 T72, ENCLOSURE, ROLL 238
AG 1841 T73 ENCLOSURE, ROLL 238
AG 1841 W27, ENCLOSURE, ROLL 240
AG 1841 W57, ROLL 241

AG 1842 W205, ROLL 262
AG 1842 W326, PAGE 4, ROLL 262
AG 1857 M549, ROLL 563

"Letters Sent by the Office of the Adjutant General (Main Series) 1800-1890";
Records of the Adjutant General's Office, Record Group 94. National
Archives Microfilm, M565.

Eaton, Joseph Horace, Lt.Col.; "Returns of Killed and Wounded in Battles or
Engagements with Indians, British, and Mexican Troops, compiled 1850-
1851, documenting the period 1790-1848. (Eaton's Compilation); Record
Group 94, Microfilm M1832, Records of the Adjutant General's Office.
About 1848, the Army decided that it needed a list of all battles or
skirmishes to determine pension or benefit eligibility. Lt.Col. Eaton was
given the task of compiling a list. The information is invaluable because it
was done when veterans of the war were still alive and could verify the
accuracy.

"Letters Sent by the Secretary of War Relating to Military Affairs, 1800-1889,
Records of the Office of the Secretary of War, Record Group 107. National
Archives Microfilm M6.

LETTERS SENT BY THE SEC OF WAR, 1840, PAGE 51 (NOV. 2)
LETTERS SENT BY THE SEC OF WAR, 1840, PAGE 60 (NOV. 10)
LETTERS SENT BY THE SEC OF WAR, 1841 PAGE 327
LETTERS SENT BY THE SEC OF WAR, 1841 PAGE 419

"Letters Sent by the Headquarters of the Army 1828-1903"; Records of
Headquarters of the Army, Record Group 108. National Archives Microfilm
M857.

LETTERS SENT FROM THE WAR DEPARTMENT, 1841 PAGE 32
LETTERS SENT FROM THE WAR DEPT., 1841 PAGE 41
LETTERS SENT FROM THE WAR DEPT., 1841 PAGE 132

## Post Returns

The fort post returns & commissioned officers present are invaluable for
researching individual officers and movement of companies or troops. Pay
attention to the notes written in the remarks because the information can be
valuable for research.

"Returns From U.S. Military Posts, 1800-1916"; M617; Records of the Adjutant
General's Office, Record Group 94. (National Archives Microfilm).

Post Returns Fort Barrancas, Fort Pickens, Pensacola Harbor
Post Returns Fort Defiance, Fort Micanopy
Post Returns Fort King
Post Returns, Fort Kanapaha
Post Returns Fort Russell & Fort Brooks
Post Returns Fort Sanderson
Post Returns Fort Wacasassa
Post Returns Forts Fulton, Fort Peyton, St. Augustine
Post Returns Fort Reid
Post Returns Fort Arbuckle, Fort Smith, and Fort Washita in Indian Territory

## Websites & On-Line Records
Some websites that proved very useful for research for this book. Through Ancestry, I found some valuable documentation of many of the officers in this book.

Ancestry.com; Appleton's Cyclopedia of American Biography, 1600-1889.
Ancestry; National Cemetery record cards, St. Augustine National Cemetery
Ancestry; US Civil War Soldier Records and Profiles, 1861-1865
Ancestry; family trees for Griffin Taylor
Ancestry; Deaths, Ontario, Canada
Ancestry; Kentucky County Marriage Records, Christian County, 1838
Ancestry; 7th Infantry Enlistment Records
Ancestry; Mobile County book of Marriages, Alabama, 1843
Cemsearch; Canadian grave search. cemsearch.ca website
Cincinnati History Library; Christ Church Records, 1821-1996, MSS 1034 & 1052,
     Hamilton County, Cincinnati Library; http://library.cincymuseum.org
ChroniclingAmerica.loc.gov; a newspaper archive.
Dvidshub; Master Sgt. Thomas Kielbasa, "Seminole War battlefield visit caps
     Florida National Guard soil collection project"; **Florida National Guard
     Public Affairs Office**; https://www.dvidshub.net/news/printable/113465
Findagrave.com
Fort Smith, Arkansas, "Abandonment of Fort Smith," 2018.
     https://encyclopediaofarkansas.net/entries/abandonment-of-fort-smith-
     6640/
FortWiki; Fort Sanderson; FortWiki.com; sometimes has good fort information.
Newspapers.com; a newspaper archive.
Spring Grove Cemetery, Cincinnati, Ohio. Cemetery card for Spring Grove
     Cemetery, SpringGrove.org

# Index

Fort Tarver (see also Tarver's) 5, 21, 125, 127, 128, 169
Fort # 3, East Florida 151
Fort # 2, East Florida 60
Fort Wacahoota 5, 21, 24, 25, 72, 78, 79, 82, 128-130, 132-135, 154, 156, 158, 162, 163, 166, 167, 194, 218
Fort Wacasassa 5, 16, 72, 82, 135
Fort Walker 5, 6, 21, 81, 128, 130, 133, 167
Fort Washita (OK) 180
Fort Wheelock 21, 126, 132, 165-167
Fort Wood (also Fort Macomb) (LA) 63-65
Foss, William (Pvt.) 79
Foster, William (Lt.Col.) 35
Fowltown 8
Fulton, William (Capt.) 6
Gainesville 3
Gannett, Lt. 12
Garey's Ferry. See also Fort Heileman. 93, 101, 107, 123, 210.
Gaston (steamboat) 59
Gates, Lemuel 3
Gates, William 88
Gatlin, John S. (Dr.) 242
Gatlin, Richard C. 47, 81, 100, 130, 162, 165, 167-169, 179, 180, 198, 242
Gayle, John 176
Geiger, Mr. 132, 133
Geisse, Paul (Lt.) 131
General James Taylor Park 187
George (slave) 116-118, 121
Georgetown (WDC) 181
Georgia 1, 8, 86, 124, 134, 136
Georgia Militia 124
Gettysburg (Battle of) 73, 240
Gilchrist County (Fla.) 8
Glassell, James (Capt.) 206
Glassell Springs. See also Silver Springs. 61, 206
Glynn County (GA) 86
Gopher John (also John Horse) 107
Grace, Richard (Pvt.) 55
Graham, Lt. 121
Grassy Pond 200

CPSIA information can be obtained
at www.ICGtesting.com
Printed in the USA
BVHW041252100222
628586BV00011B/776

9 781087 808208